THE OTHER
GLORIA

ARC
Thank you and Best Wishes!

L. A. Villaf

L.A. Villafane

Printed in the United States of America

ISBN: 978-0-9989496-7-3

10 9 8 7 6 5 4 3 2

Empire Publishing and Literary Service Bureau

www.empirebookpublishing.com

This is a work of fiction. Names, characters, businesses, events, and incidents are the product of the author's imagination. Any resemblance to actual persons, living or dead, or actual events is purely coincidental.

Published by: L.A. Villafane
P. O. Box 5853
Granbury, TX 76049
lorivillafane@lavillafane.com

Cover design by: Bespoke Book Covers

Website: www.theothergloria.com/book

Library of Congress number. 2019913230

Acknowledgements:

Peter and Caroline with Bespoke Book Covers, thank you for such a wonderful cover. I would also like to thank the following for editorial input: Kevin Anderson (with Kevin Anderson and Associates), Brunella Costagliola, Paula Munier, Michael Neff, Jennifer Banash, and Erin McKnight.

I don't want to forget my husband, Larry. Thank you for putting up with me during the two year process of writing this book. Also, my Mother, Ann, and Father, Roy, along with my daughters, Misty and Michelle, and my granddaughters, Kaitlyn and Cheyenne. I couldn't have done it without you.

Chapter 1

January 2019

It's happening again. There's a missing memory. This time, Gloria realizes with frightening certainty, it's a serious lapse. She comes to full consciousness, finding herself behind the wheel of a car, speeding down a dark highway. She must remember what happened to bring her here. Something about the road seems familiar, but there is only a vague recognition. She has no idea where she is driving from - or for that matter, driving to.

There are few passing cars to light up the night. The blackness seems to swallow her whole, sending her careening into the dark and utterly blind as to what lies ahead. Only able to see where her headlights direct, she has no idea of her destination.

Finally, she spots a road sign. As it quickly comes into focus, she can see she is heading down Highway 58. And then another sign, indicating she is 21 miles from Bakersfield. It makes sense that she would be driving to Bakersfield - after all, she lives there. But Highway 58? This means she has driven through the Tehachapi Mountains. She has absolutely no memory of it.

A car begins to pass as she looks slightly downward. The quick flash of lights reveals what looks like a massive amount of blood on her hands, which are currently perched at ten and two on the steering wheel. Her eyes widen as she flinches, jerking the wheel.

She almost sideswipes the rear of the passing car. Her car crosses farther into the left lane and then farther, almost hitting the concrete barrier as she tries frantically to correct. Fighting for control, she is finally going in a straight line once more. The red taillights of the car that has just passed are nearly out of sight, and the leaden darkness envelops her once more.

There is a trembling that seems to originate in the pit of her stomach and emanates out through her hands. A nagging voice from deep inside pushes her forward, but, try as she might, she can't remember a thing up until a few minutes ago.

She glances at the speedometer and realizes she is slowing. Somehow she musters the courage to bring her full attention to the task at hand. Her hands still shaking violently, she fights to keep control as she continues to slow. Pulling onto the shoulder, she pushes the shift lever to park.

With her head now on the steering wheel between her hands and her breathing coming in long hard gasps, she waits a moment to try the impossible: Compose herself. *There's a simple explanation for all of this*, she thinks. At least, she is trying to think. She is mostly reacting at this point. With her hands trembling on either side of her aching head and her chest heaving, she attempts to bring her breath under control.

For a moment, she focuses on her aching head. It's beginning to feel like a bass drum resounding in rhythmic beats off every inch of her skull. She doesn't know how long she will be able to keep on like this, but something urges her forward.

Remembering her hands, she is unable to comprehend the blood she has just seen. She can't understand, with all that blood, why she hasn't passed out by now. Another car is coming up behind her, and she lifts her head, praying what she saw was just an illusion, a trick of the lights, or her out-of-control imagination.

Her eyes widen in shock as the car passes, and she realizes what she has seen is real.

She fumbles around the dashboard, frantically turning every switch and knob until she finds the interior lights. She winces and closes her eyes tightly once she has switched them on. Slowly opening her eyes, she begins to inspect her hands. They are still shaking. There is a lot of blood, so much blood, but she can see no cuts of any significance. Still, she turns her hands over and over again.

Pull yourself together, she demands of her muddled brain. She's running on adrenaline now. *Slow down and think, Gloria*, she chides herself, as she looks out into the utter blackness beyond her headlights. It's no use. Her mind is spinning in a hundred different directions.

She turns her head slightly to look down at her right arm. What she sees makes her stomach churn. She thinks, for one terrible moment, she might throw up. Her entire sleeve is covered in blood, drenched in it. Looking further, she sees her white shirt is now almost completely stained red. Her mouth gapes in horror as her brain attempts to take it in. She can't comprehend this as reality.

Her mind finally takes in the gruesome fact - what used to be a white, long-sleeved shirt is now mostly red with blood, only a few white patches remaining. She attempts to calm her wildly beating heart. After a moment, she begins to unbutton her sleeve, gently pulling it up as high as it will go. Try as she might, she can find no cuts deep enough to cause such heavy bleeding. All the while, she is thinking she might pass out from her ever-growing headache.

As she reaches to pull down the visor and look into the mirror, she thinks the blood might be coming from her head. She gasps at her reflection. Blood smeared on her face and in her hair. Makeup

3

smeared all over her face. She looks like a clown from a horror movie, dark tear stains of mascara running down to her chin. Her red lipstick, intermingled with blood, is gobbed in streaks around her mouth.

As she scrutinizes her own reflection, she finds a knot about the size of a golf ball forming on the left side of her scalp. It went nearly unnoticed under her matted hair. Pulling her long blond hair aside to examine further, the lump is blue and ugly, but there's no blood to speak of.

She decides to examine the rest of her body. Every movement is painful. It's not only her head that aches; her entire body seems to be aching. Gently pulling up the sleeve of her left arm, she finds no cuts. Next, she unbuttons her shirt to inspect her stomach and chest. It's hard to tell with so much blood covering her, but the bleeding, wherever it's coming from, seems to have stopped.

Think! What happened tonight?

It's no use. She lowers her head to the steering wheel again, hoping to find some clarity. She feels she could sleep, but she knows, with a head injury, sleeping could be dangerous.

Snapping out of her mind and back into her gruesome reality, she raises her head to inspect the interior of the car. There are streaks of blood on the steering wheel, the shift lever, the dash, and the seat around her, but nowhere else that she can see. The interior is light gray. This reignites the confusion. She has never owned a car with a gray interior.

A sickening dread comes over her; the feeling of someone watching. It's overpowering. *Is there someone in the car?* She can't bring herself to turn and look into the back seat. Then she feels it. She's had this feeling before . . . the feeling . . . of nothingness.

4

Chapter 2

March 2003

<u>After</u>

Gloria wakes trembling. *It must have been a nightmare*, she thinks. After a few moments of deep breathing, she begins to feel herself relax. Rolling onto her side, she lets out a sigh and closes her eyes. She snuggles into the blankets, the warmth and comfort thankfully overriding her ragged nerves.

Opening her eyes once more, she begins to register what she is seeing. A sensation creeps into her entire body, a thousand tiny hands seeming to grip every muscle until she is completely rigid with fear. The morning sun is beginning to shine through a slit in the drapes. With the small amount of light coming in, she is just able to make out the man lying beside her. She knows something is terribly wrong, even though his back is facing her. Bile begins to rise in her throat, as her mind seems unable to make sense of what she is seeing.

She blinks. As she tentatively reaches out a trembling hand, she can only hope the vision will disappear. Slowly, she reaches toward the man, praying she will feel nothing. What her fingers feel is the warm flesh of the man's naked shoulder. She jerks back reflexively. Gasping, she quickly slaps a hand over her mouth, staring wide-eyed at the man's back. She holds in a breath until she can see that, thankfully, she has not disturbed him.

5

Gloria wills herself to lie as still as possible. Attempting to slow her breathing, she knows she must force her brain to work. She cannot make sense of this man lying beside her, no matter how she turns it over in her head.

The man in bed beside her should be her fiancé, Rick, but this is definitely not him. Rick is six feet tall, with broad, muscular shoulders and thick dark hair. The man lying beside her is definitely smaller framed, with lighter hair. She is still unable to see him clearly with only a sliver of light, but this is surely not Rick.

Glancing around, she realizes she is not in her own bed. Her breathing quickens. The only explanation is, she must be in his bed, whoever he is. She closes her eyes as her stomach begins to turn. Everything in her body wants to get up and run from this place, but all she can do is lie still and try to calm down and think.

Her thoughts are churning wildly in an effort to come up with a sensible explanation for what she is experiencing. Did she get drunk last night and go home with a stranger? No, that couldn't be it. Alcohol gives her migraines. She never drinks, and she doesn't currently have a migraine. Someone must have slipped something into her Diet Coke, but she doesn't remember drinking anything with anyone last night.

She glances around once more, looking for something familiar to use to ground herself. As she peers down at the blanket covering her, she recognizes it. *Impossible*, she thinks, as she looks at the familiar cover and runs her hand over its velvety surface. She remembers this spread. She won it in a drawing at a bridal show. That was before her marriage to her ex, Charles. It's a black, tan, and brown checked pattern. It's not the prettiest bedspread, but it is about the softest thing she has ever felt. She has never seen another like it, before or since. Not many things in life were ever truly hers,

6

but this had been hers and she always kept it. Why would her bedspread be on his bed?

As more light streams into the room, she gathers herself and continues gazing at the other objects surrounding her. The dresser on the wall past the foot of the bed is the same massive dark walnut dresser she shared with Charles.

It slowly begins to register. The entire room is filled with things that seem familiar. As she looks over the man's sleeping form, she can see the matching walnut chest on the far wall next to the draped sliding glass doors. The king-sized, four-poster bed is also familiar. She looks up at the vaulted ceiling. She knows this room. It's the same bedroom she and Charles shared so many years ago. Everything is duplicated in amazing detail.

Reminiscing for a few moments, she has almost forgotten about the man lying beside her. She slowly turns her head to look over again, praying he isn't there. With more light streaming into the room now, the urge to run becomes almost unbearable. She could swear this is Charles, even though his back is facing her. The bedspread covers halfway up his shoulders, but she doesn't need to see more. His light brown hair is cut just above the familiar heart-shaped mole which stands out against the pale skin at the nape of his neck.

None of this makes sense. She left Charles in 2017 when she was about to turn forty. There is no reason she would be in bed with him now. There is no way on earth she would have returned. She has just recently become engaged to Rick, and they are very happy. There's just no way.

Something unbelievable begins to dawn on her. Did she just wake up next to her ex-husband . . . in the past? That is the only explanation that makes sense; not that it makes any sense at all. Her body seems to become weighted down with the incredible thought. Staring up at the vaulted ceiling again, the fan spinning slowly above her, she is not sure of the last thing she can remember before waking up. Her mind is unable to put together the pieces of a very strange puzzle.

But it was 2019. She is sure of that.

She pinches her arm; sure she must be in a dream and will not feel the pain. But she does feel it, and she has to quell the need to cry out. She decides she must pull herself out of bed and at least find a place to hide. She needs to figure things out. She cannot face her ex, even if this is a dream. She has been away from him for two years now, and her skin still crawls at the thought of feeling his hands on her body - the crushing grip of his fingers around her neck.

Slowly, she pushes back the covers. Trying not to disturb the bed, she gently pulls herself up to a sitting position. She moves inch by inch, glancing over her shoulder to see that she is not disturbing him. Her heart feels as if it might beat out of her chest as she pulls herself to standing. She is sure he will wake.

Looking around, she considers where to hide. She takes in the large master suite. Staring at the wall to her right, she knows on the other side is the master bathroom. She peeks around the corner and sees herself in the long mirror above a double sink vanity. She jumps slightly when she spots her reflection. She seems to be staring into the wide blue eyes of a younger version of herself. Her straight blond hair, wild from sleep, hangs just past her shoulders. She reflexively reaches up her hands to smooth it before quickly looking away.

Thankfully, the closet next to the vanity is a large walk-in, and she makes the quick decision to head in that direction. She softly tiptoes on the thick carpet and creeps through the open closet door. She soundlessly shuts the door and turns on the light. Settling, curled up in a ball behind some clothes hanging on the lower rail, she feels somewhat protected. She must sit here for a moment and force her brain to work.

She begins to remember how Charles would constantly set her up for failure, and how she had to endure his temper when, at every turn, he claimed she had inevitably failed. She was so naive when she met Charles.

She had been raised in a loving home. She had tried to emulate her patient and steadfast mother. She had hoped she would be the kind of wife who always supported and stood by her husband, but Charles used that against her. She sees now how calculating he was. It was hard to see when she was in the middle of it, though. Her shoulders slump, and her head drops to her knees as she thinks of how he convinced her she was nothing but a failure as a wife. He always seemed to know how to keep her at all times, slightly off balance.

Reigning in her thoughts, she realizes she hadn't planned too far ahead when she hid in the closet. She can't draw herself in enough to completely disappear behind the clothes. Surely, he will come in and find her when he wakes up. She would have no way of explaining herself.

She looks down at her bare legs and decides she should take off the silky peach nightgown barely covering the tops of her thighs. The thought of meeting him this way causes her to shiver. It's not like a flimsy piece of cloth is going to actually form a protective barrier between them, but in her mind, it does.

Pushing her way from behind the clothes, she straightens up and takes a look around. Riffling through the rail above, she quietly pulls tops apart and scans them with disturbing recognition. They bring back memories from a very long time ago. These aren't pleasant memories. They are memories of survival. Memories of

9

trying to pull together from the minuscule pieces she had to choose from a decent outfit for yet another charity or political function. The embarrassment of wearing the same outfit too many times, while he was always turned out immaculately. His thought processes had boggled her mind. She would have expected he would have wanted to dress up the woman on his arm.

Snapping to attention once more, she scans the rail below. Pulling out a pair of women's jeans in a size 6, she shakes her head when she realizes the pants she's holding are mom jeans. She can't believe she actually used to wear them. But they definitely seem to be hers.

Turning back to the task at hand, she slips the jeans under her gown; they zip up loosely. They're too big, but she is in a hurry and decides to wear them anyway. Turning back to the top rail again, she grabs the first blouse she sees after letting her gown drop to the floor. The top she holds is a cropped red and white cotton blouse, gathered at the waist.

As she peers around the closet, she is again reminded of how little clothing she used to have. Men's clothing is surely the majority in this closet. Nice men's clothing to boot: Expensive suits and perfectly pressed dress shirts, sorted by color; designer jeans and slacks. Her clothing, on the other hand, covers less than one-quarter of the closet space and was purchased from sales racks.

Peeking out into the room, she sees he is still asleep. She decides to make a break for the bedroom door. As she glances out, she spies a brush on the vanity. The bedroom door is in the opposite direction, but she takes a second to look into the mirror. She sees her blond hair is still sticking out here and there. Instinctively, she picks up the brush and makes a couple of passes through her hair.

Looking more closely at her face, not quite believing what she sees, she puts a hand to her cheek. It's definitely her wide blue eyes staring back at her. Her heart-shaped face is dewy, and her lips seem to be fuller. Even with no makeup, her cheeks are rosy.

Reeling in her thoughts, she pads softly across the room, her heart thumping wildly in her chest. She reaches the bedroom door and carefully opens it. Grimacing, she waits for the door to creak, but to her relief, it opens silently. Stepping out into the hall, she pulls the door shut behind her. Turning, she sees an open door to the bedroom on her right.

She walks through the door, taking in the Cinderella-patterned wallpaper running partway up the pink walls, meeting a white chair rail about three feet high. Turning the corner, she spots a small blond head barely visible under a colorful Cinderella comforter. Powerful memories and feelings begin flooding back. Memories of a cherub's face and sweet smile looking up at her. Her daughter's tousled blond hair and gleaming blue eyes, when she would look up at her and say, "I love you, Mommy." She knows at once this is Chrissy. She is so small, and all Gloria wants to do is wake her and hold her tight.

As a rush of warmth runs through her, she closes her eyes and brings her hands to her flushed cheeks. She decides against disturbing Chrissy. She wouldn't want to make noise right now. She needs to figure out how to face Charles when he wakes. This thing she's in feels so real, and she can hardly stand the thought of coming face-to-face with him. It takes enormous effort to break herself away from the sight in front of her, but she knows she must.

Softly padding out of the room, she turns the corner to head back down the hall. In the room straight in front of her, she spies a little red-headed angel standing and holding onto the side of her crib. Gloria's hand flies to her mouth in wonder. The baby is

11

gurgling and cooing happily, a huge smile on her face. With fine wisps of red hair and porcelain skin, she reminds Gloria of a baby doll. Dressed in a pink onesie, her diaper sagging out the sides, it's clear she needs to be changed. She begins jumping up and down when she spots her mommy. This would be Sarah, and Gloria thinks she looks to be seven or eight months old.

Unable to contain her excitement, she sprints into the room and picks up her happy baby. She squeezes her close and takes in the sweet smell of baby powder as she nuzzles her hair. Gloria wishes time, or whatever is happening, would just stand still. She could enjoy this moment forever. She thinks of the joy she felt while raising her two beautiful girls. She shakes her head as she remembers how her sweet little ones had grown so fast in front of her eyes.

After changing Sarah's diaper and pulling on a pretty lavender dress, Gloria picks up her little one from the changing table and heads to the kitchen to feed her. She knows her way because she knows this house. After all, she lived here for years.

Pushing through the bar-style swinging doors leading to the kitchen, she walks across the cool tile floor to open the refrigerator. She pushes aside what appears to be meant for the evening's dinner. After pulling out some formula, she turns and grabs baby cereal from the cupboard. She pulls a pink, plastic baby bowl from the upper cabinet and places it on the mocha-colored tile counter. She mixes it up like it was yesterday when she used to do this, not years ago.

Instead of placing Sarah in her high chair, after heating the cereal in the microwave, Gloria decides to hold her on her lap. She takes a seat at the kitchen table and begins to spoon the mushy cereal into Sarah's mouth.

Once she's finished and the bowl has been rinsed, they head around the corner to the den where she takes a seat in one of two plush beige rockers. Gloria has never experienced a dream so vivid. She can feel the comfortable rocking chair and the weight of Sarah's warm little body cuddled against her chest. She can't help but think it all feels and smells too real.

"Mommy," Gloria hears, softly behind her shoulder. She turns, and standing there in her little blue bunny nightgown is Chrissy. *She looks to be about four and a half years old*, she thinks, *judging by the age of Sarah*.

"Hi Chrissy," Gloria says with a huge smile on her face. "I'm *so* glad to see you this morning. Jump up here and give me a big hug."

In a split second, Chrissy is with her sister on Gloria's lap. "Is Daddy still asleep?" Gloria whispers in Chrissy's ear.

"I think so, Mommy."

"Well," says Gloria, softly, "let's not wake him up then. Let's be very quiet, okay?"

"Okay," Chrissy whispers, smiling up at her mommy with big blue eyes.

Checking the mantel clock above the red brick fireplace, Gloria can see it's 7:45. *It must be the weekend*, she guesses, since Charles obviously hasn't left for work. Fortunately, she remembers he used to sleep until late in the morning on weekends. She lets out a sigh. It looks like she has a couple more hours to spend alone with her little ones.

Sarah, now standing on her mother's lap, has her little fingers caught in the long, tangled strands of her sister's blond hair. Chrissy struggles to extricate herself from her sister's grasp.

"Ow, Mommy, it hurts," Chrissy cries, wincing as Sarah giggles and tugs.

13

"Wait just a second, and I'll get you loose." Gloria works nimbly to free Chrissy from Sarah's grip. "There we go," she says. "All better?"

"Yeah." Chrissy rubs her head, frowning, while letting out the slightest whimper.

Settling the girls on her lap again, one at a time she nuzzles their hair, squeezing them to her. Feeling the warmth of Sarah's chubby little body and Chrissy's thin form against her chest, her heart feels as if it might burst. In this moment, she thinks she might never let go.

She hopes the little ruckus hasn't disturbed their father. She always worked hard to keep the children quiet on weekend mornings. Heaven help any one of them, had they woken him. Gloria usually took the brunt of it, but the shouting that resulted from disturbing him would upset the girls.

"Are you hungry, Chrissy?" she asks.

"Yes, Mommy." A bright smile replaces Chrissy's frown.

Remembering Chrissy's preference for Cheerios and bacon, Gloria returns to the kitchen with Sarah on her hip and Chrissy at her heels. Placing the baby in her high chair, Cheerios spread around the tray, she pulls out some bacon from the refrigerator. On second thought, she puts the bacon back. The smell might wake Charles, and that would not be good right now.

"How about just Cheerios for now, Chrissy, and we will make some bacon later?"

"Promise?" Chrissy looks up with pleading eyes.

"Promise," Gloria whispers, close to her ear, and gives her a little peck on the cheek.

At this moment, Gloria knows she should have been more appreciative of what happy, sweet-tempered girls she had. She spent too much of her time and energy trying to keep Charles in a decent mood, which she now sees was an impossible task.

What they say about hindsight is so true, she thinks. She should have been a better mother to these two girls.

With her newfound confidence and freedom, she realizes how she allowed Charles to monopolize her thoughts and her life. She has no idea how she will react when she comes face-to-face with him, but she is certainly not the same girl she used to be. In the two years since she left him, she has grown quite a backbone. She had to, or she would've ended up right back with him.

She has lost so many memories due to her condition. Dissociative Disorder was the diagnosis from her psychologist so many years ago. A condition supposed to protect her mind from the truth of what was happening to her, but that in the end left her confused and frightened. As a result, there are huge blocks of time that are just a blank.

It's not only the bad memories she has lost, but so many good memories as well. So many moments with her girls growing up are lost memories she can never get back. Could this actually be a do-over? Is God giving her another chance? She can't believe it, but a part of her hopes this is true . . . until the fear of Charles creeps in.

Chrissy climbs up onto a chair at the table which sits by the bay window in the kitchen nook. Snapping out of her thoughts, Gloria pours cereal into a bowl and sets it down in front of Chrissy.

"Here you go, honey," she says, as she pours the milk.

"Thank you, Mommy." Chrissy grabs up her spoon.

Gloria smiles as she turns to put the milk away in the fridge and pull out what looks like the makings for stew. She places the contents into the Crock-pot sitting out on the counter and turns it on low. Heaven help her if it turns out badly, or is not ready in time. Charles never failed to remind her how things had been on

15

schedule before the kids. They had thrown his world into "turmoil," as he put it. He also never failed to remind her that, "Everything was so much better when it was just the two of us."

Gloria worked frantically after the girls were born to keep his schedule. She didn't want to bring his wrath on all of them, so she would do everything she could to take on his anger herself, hopefully saving the girls from his outbursts. Thinking about it now, maybe it wasn't weakness. Maybe she had been strong all along. She was just protecting her girls in the only way she knew how.

Back in the den, Gloria settles the girls in front of the TV. She changes channels, finally landing on *Looney Tunes* cartoons.

"Yay." Chrissy claps her hands.

She turns and smiles at Chrissy, who is sitting cross-legged behind her on the floor, cuddling her tattered yellow teddy bear, Pookie. Sarah, sitting in her playpen, grabs up a rubber mouse and starts chewing on its ear, causing it to squeak. Gloria's first instinct is to take the toy away, but she decides, beginning with this one, she is going to change her nervous habits.

As long as Charles doesn't wake, this is much-needed time for Gloria to try and come up with a game plan for when he does turn up. *Will he wake up in a foul mood, berating me for who knows what? Worse, will he take me to the bedroom and lock us in?* She shivers at the thought. Looking at the clock on the mantle again, she sees her time dwindling.

Deciding to busy herself, she heads to Chrissy's room to grab her hairbrush. She brings it back and sits cross-legged behind Chrissy before beginning to run it through her hair. Chrissy sits wrapped up in cartoons while Gloria works to gently brush the tangles out of her thick locks. As she is brushing, her mind begins to drift to Charles once again.

16

There were so many conflicting feelings when it came to Charles. She felt so much fear, but she also felt pity for him. She had often wondered why Charles was the way he was with her. She always assumed it was because he had had so little control over his life when he was a child. Maybe that's why he had to be in control of every aspect of his life as an adult.

Charles was an only child for the first eight years of his life. That's when his parents began to have child after child, giving him six siblings by the time he graduated high school. It always seemed that whatever was wrong with their marriage, it could be solved by another baby. Gloria thought he must have felt displaced, being left to his own devices at a very young age. He usually tried to avoid his father who, over the years, had become a very angry man. His mother always seemed to suffer from depression. All the children suffered from neglect and abuse.

Often she would ask him about his childhood, trying to gain some insight, but he would deny any feelings toward the matter. He never gave her a glimpse into his obviously troubled mind. So she tried to give him the benefit of the doubt, but his true feelings stayed locked behind an impenetrable fortress and were replaced with anger, control, and intimidation.

There were times when he was there for her. She remembers when he helped her canvas the neighborhood tacking up fliers when her beloved gray tabby cat, Sassy, had gone missing. She had been inconsolable. Gloria hoped she would have a few more years with her beloved cat. Sassy's disappearance had just about broken her into pieces.

Charles gently stood there by her side as she cried. He was good to her, inconsolable as she was, over the next few weeks. He was her shoulder to cry on. Sassy had been her best friend. They had moved from Texas to Bakersfield together. Charles always knew they were a package deal, and he seemed to warm to her quickly when she first introduced them. He proved himself to be compassionate after her disappearance, patiently waiting for her to navigate the grieving process. During that time, she began to wonder if her misgivings about their relationship were all in her head.

Bringing her mind back to the present, she knows it's time to think of what to do today. Settled now in the rocker behind the girls, she tries to come up with a strategy to please Charles without having to, heaven forbid, kiss him. At the thought, her stomach roils. He would want a morning kiss and not just a peck. He always held her tighter and longer than she felt she could stand. Looking back, she knows it was all to show the control he had over her. Now that she has grown a backbone, will she be able to do it - or will she try to fight him off?

Knowing she has little time left, she straightens up, pulls back her shoulders, and lifts her chin with determination. After all, it's not going to kill her to act weak and pliable. Knowing she has changed is all that matters right now. Her brow furrows as she realizes she had no identity with him, other than being his dutiful wife. Lowering her eyes, she shakes her head as she thinks of how she completely lost herself.

With the girls settled, she returns to the kitchen. Thinking she will feel less nervous if she is doing something, she runs her fingers across the cool tiles on the countertop. Seeing milk droplets, she grabs cleaner and paper towels to wipe. She makes large sweeping circles, cleaning the entire countertop and then moving on to the electric stovetop.

After everything has been wiped down, she stands leaning against the counter by the cooktop and stares out the window over the sink as she ponders. This thing she is in is becoming more like reality; the further she drifts into it. She wonders if she will eventually lose herself to it entirely. In any case, she will not let things happen as they did before. She will extricate herself and the girls from him, at all costs. And if that means playing along for a while so as not to raise suspicion, so be it.

Her ear pricks at a faint noise coming from the master bedroom. Thinking quickly, she rushes to the refrigerator, pulling out the bacon again, and a carton of eggs. Heating up the frying pan, she places four slices of bacon in for Charles, and two for Chrissy. She covers it with a splatter screen and moves to quickly start the coffee. With her back to him as he slowly enters the kitchen, she plasters a smile on her face. She hopes it doesn't look more like a grimace.

Still fumbling with the coffee pot, not wanting to turn around, she greets him with as much enthusiasm as she can muster. "Good morning," she says, hoping her smile will radiate through her voice. She can't quite get the word "honey" out of her mouth. She hopes "good morning" will be good enough, but as he enters the kitchen, he begins complaining immediately.

She turns to see he is fully dressed in jeans and a peach-colored button-down shirt, sleeves rolled to his elbows. She can't help but think he looks so young with his light hair parted to the side, the way he always wore it. But then, he always looked young, and she only guesses his age by the age of the girls. That would put him at around thirty. As always, there is not a hair out of place.

She hadn't quite remembered how thin he used to be so long ago. Standing only a few inches taller than her, it doesn't seem he should be such a menacing presence - but he is. She knows he has strength that belies his size, and she is no match for him when he becomes enraged.

19

"Does this cheery mood mean you're apologizing for last night?" he asks tersely, green eyes squinting with suspicion.

"Of course. I'm sorry," she says nervously after a slight pause, for what, she's not quite sure.

As he comes closer, though, she can guess. The minty smell of his toothpaste has not managed to completely cover the odor of booze on his breath.

His drinking was usually the topic they fought over. A memory flashes through her mind, and it causes her to flinch. It was a December evening after they had attended her office Christmas party. She had just entered the bedroom after returning home as he rushed in behind her, slamming the door.

Gloria's shoulders shot to her ears, and her stomach did a flip, as she stood frozen in place. She knew there was about to be a fight, and she was glad the girls were with their grandparents for the night and would not witness what was about to happen.

"I saw you and your boss talking in the corner," he shouted. She could sense him closing the space between them.

Slowly turning to look at him, she cringed when she saw the look on his face. His eyes were black, his face contorted into a look of disgust, his upper lip curled in a snarl.

"He was just asking about the girls," she tried to explain, doing her best to look him in the eye.

"Yeah. Right." He glowered. "For half an hour?"

"It was only a few minutes, Charles. I was talking to everyone. You were talking to Samantha," she countered, immediately wishing she could take it back.

"Not the same. I don't want to sleep with Bradford's receptionist," he said, in a guttural tone, as he moved closer. "You, on the other hand, would rather be with Don Bradford than with me."

20

Reaching out his hand, he grabbed her right arm and yanked her toward him. "I know what you two do at the office, sneaking around in the back room," he said, his mouth on her ear.

As she backed away, he held his grip firm, his fingernails digging into the skin just above her elbow. "I hardly even see Don at the office. We work in different departments," Gloria tried to explain feebly.

He grabbed her left arm as she tried to back away, abruptly shoving her and then releasing his grip, causing her to fall violently backward onto the bed. He bent over, his knee pressing into her stomach. The smell of alcohol heavy on his breath, his hand raised, he seemed to be preparing to backhand her in the face, but he must have thought better of it. She knew he never wanted to leave obvious marks.

She flinched and raised her hands, ready for the blow if one were to come. When she saw it wasn't, she tried to think of how she might reason with him. Who was she kidding? There was no reasoning with him, so she tried apologizing. "I'm sorry if you felt like I was too friendly with Don. Really, Charles, we were just talking about our kids."

He bent down and breathed in her ear, "Not buying it, babe. Try again."

After that, her mind is blank. She has no memory of what happened next. She has no memory of what happened the entire next week. Noticing fading green bruise marks on her body a week later, she knew she had blacked out again and lost any memory of the event that had caused them. The Other Gloria holds all these memories now, along with hundreds more. That's actually what frightens her most: What she can't remember - all the times she can't remember.

She brings herself back to the moment as he leans in to kiss her. She jumps, dropping the spatula she's holding. Bending over quickly to pick it up, she apologizes. Straitening up, she pecks him on the lips and immediately rushes to the sink to rinse off the utensil before he can grab her. Soaping and scrubbing it like it's filthy, she hopes he will be satisfied and let her finish making his breakfast.

Sneaking up behind her, he wraps his arms around her waist and holds on tight, whispering in her ear, "You know how much I love you, don't you?"

His breath on the back of her neck causes her to automatically stiffen. She feels the need to take her mind somewhere else. She is suddenly looking out from deep inside. The kitchen and Charles are far away and fuzzy. The sound of his voice is muffled. Her own replies are foreign to her ears.

She catches herself and somehow forces herself to return. She doesn't know how she has done it, but she's back. This is the first time she has been able to force herself back. Once she starts to slip away, the need to go is too strong, and she has always given into it. She must stay focused now. She is determined to remain present.

"Yes, of course," she says, the familiar panic beginning to rise inside her again. She must quickly talk herself out of this and try to calm down. She attempts to take a few deep breaths, but he's holding her too tight, and it's difficult to breathe. While he is still holding on, she chokes out, "I better check the bacon. I don't want it to burn."

Of course, he has to hold her longer just to show who's in charge. Finally, he lightens up a bit. She turns around and smiles as sweetly as she can until he releases her. She sees an opening when he lets go and ducks past him to the stove.

After serving Charles a breakfast of bacon, scrambled eggs, and toast, she sits across the kitchen table from him, trying to keep a smile on her face. As she knew would happen, he pats the chair beside him with one hand, and with no emotion directs her to sit there. Smiling nervously, she obediently moves to the chair he indicates.

"What are you sitting way over there for?" he asks.

How was she able to stand it for so many years?" Even as she asks herself the question, she knows the answer: *Dissociation.*

Her psychologist had diagnosed her with dissociative disorder after a long stint in therapy. It had been a couple of years before she had unknowingly allowed the Other Gloria take over in front of Dr. Dyson. He recognized it immediately. A few minutes later, she came back and finally had an answer for all of her years of memory loss.

She had tried to describe the sensations she felt to Dr. Dyson. In one way, it felt like leaving her body, her consciousness moving a thousand miles away. On the other hand, at times, it felt as if she were the smallest person deep inside herself, while someone else took over. The Other Gloria. Everything around her seemed unreal and very far away. And then, when she would return, there was just nothing, her brain a complete blank.

She stares at the table in front of her and thinks of how the Other Gloria's memories are not available to her, which she finds very disconcerting. She may lose the bad memories, but the good ones are lost as well. She shakes her head in regret at the memories she doesn't have because of being in this state so often. She should have been able to handle being present for the girls' sakes. She flushes with shame at all the time she has missed.

She looks up at Charles and remembers quite vividly the day she left him. It was in January 2017, and, even though he was miles

23

away, she felt he would turn up at any moment to stop her and drag her back into his dark abyss.

Chapter 3

<u>Before</u>

Gloria found herself with the perfect opportunity to leave Charles as the gavel fell heavily, wielded by Judge Hendricks in court that January day in 2017. She flinched, sitting in the row behind the defendant's table where Charles stood in his best suit alongside his attorney. The Judge had just handed down Charles's sentence for a drunk driving charge. He had been ordered to enter a twenty-eight-day rehab program by the end of the month.

Gloria could hear the tap, tap, tap of Charles's keyboard behind her as he sat at the kitchen table that evening. While she stood at the sink washing dinner dishes, he grabbed her attention. She turned glancing over her left shoulder through the sliding glass doors looking over the deck to the back yard, before finally turning around to face him.

"Come look at this rehab facility I found. I think it will be perfect." Charles pointed at his laptop screen.

She stepped over to the table. Standing beside Charles, she leaned over to see what he was so animatedly pointing at.

"Look," he said.

What she saw was the image of a lush oceanside facility, along with information and a phone number. There was a picture of a three-story white stucco building surrounded by palm trees, along with bungalows with the sandy ocean beach just outside their front doors. It looked to Gloria more like a resort than a rehab facility. But, it made sense. It always had to be the best for Charles. She could see it was located in Long Beach, California, which wasn't too far from Bakersfield.

"It looks really nice, Charles. Are you going to call?" She waited hopefully for his answer.

"Yeah, I'll call tomorrow," he promised. Not that Gloria could ever count on his promises, but she hoped he would keep this one.

She tried to contain her excitement over him leaving, but it was difficult. At times she would find herself smiling widely, and would have to reel herself in and regain her composure before Charles noticed and wondered what she was up to.

"So are you going to have a job to go back to, when you finish the program?" Gloria asked.

"Yeah. Ed said it's no problem. I'm just taking sick time." He closed his laptop.

Gloria couldn't believe Charles was taking the situation so lightly. But then she thought of Reform, the nonprofit agency he worked for. It was a local agency formed to lobby for the rights of small independent oil companies. Charles was not alone in his drinking at the agency. Having drinks with potential donors and political allies was just a part of the job. His supervisor, Ed, was usually hefting a glass right alongside Charles. But there was a difference with Ed. He was not an angry drunk. He tended to be the life of the party when tipsy, not like Charles, who could fly into a drunken rage at the drop of a hat.

Gloria had plenty of time to think after dropping Charles off in Long Beach two days later. It would be a two-and-a-half hour drive back to Bakersfield. On the way back, she tried to forget about Charles. Instead, she began to think of her argument with Chrissy, who had just turned eighteen a few months before.

26

Gloria loved Alex, Chrissy's high-school sweetheart. He came from a large, boisterous Italian family. With a mop of wavy brown hair, he was a typical computer nerd. There was always mischief in his light brown eyes, and when Chrissy and Alex put their heads together, mischievous genius would ignite, and Gloria would be left flustered, red-faced and trying to recover, while they'd be laughing hysterically at her expense.

She was worried, though, and had begged them to wait before getting married. "Please don't follow in my footsteps, Chrissy," she pleaded with her daughter. "Eighteen is way too young to make such a life-changing decision. You can always get married later."

"Mom, I'm grown now, and I need to get out of this house." Chrissy gave her mom a knowing look.

"It would be so much easier on you and Alex if you both finished college first," Gloria tried to reason.

"I know it's going to be difficult with college and jobs and all, but I believe we're up to it, Mom. We have it all planned out."

"I know I'm not going to change your mind, but, please, will you try and think about it?" Gloria shrugged, looking into her daughter's eyes.

After a long pause and Chrissy's resolute smile, Gloria could see her pleadings were not going to get her anywhere and resigned herself to accept the inevitable. And, so they had been married in October, and Chrissy had moved to his apartment in Rosedale, thankfully, only about ten minutes away.

She found herself thinking of how different her daughters were. They had definitely not inherited her shyness. Although Sarah could be quite headstrong at times, she was a young lady who knew what she wanted and was ready and willing to put in the hard work to get there. Gloria would ask her occasionally about boys, and always got the same answer: "Mom, boys are a waste of time." Sarah would then give an incredulous look, as if to say, "What a dumb question, Mom."

"Good," Gloria always said, thankful for her daughter's answer. "At least I won't have to worry about you marrying young."

"No way, Mom. I happen to have goals that don't center around a guy," Sarah said with a tone of finality.

Gloria's thoughts seemed to be all over the place. She abruptly turned to thinking about her parents. She missed them since they had long ago returned to Dallas from Bakersfield. It had been many years since they had moved, but that's not what put the most distance between them. Charles had done that. Even when they were living in the same town, Gloria had missed them. She would have given anything to be able to run over to their house at the spur of the moment for a visit. No, the distance between them was not geographic. No matter how close they were physically, her parents might as well have been on the other side of the globe. Charles had separated them with a simple piece of paper: Their marriage license.

Gloria had called her parents the day before. "Hi, Mom." She tried to curb her excitement when she heard Dena's voice on the other end of the line.

"You're in a good mood. What's up?" She could hear the surprise in her mom's voice.

"Charles is going to rehab tomorrow, and I'm going to be moving out. It's really happening. I was wondering if your rental house is still available," Gloria sat, hopeful, thinking of the house her parents had lived in for so many years.

"Wow, Gloria. You're actually leaving him?" Dena sounded shocked, before pausing and saying, "Of course, of course, you can move into the house. It's empty right now. I just can't believe it. What happened?"

After filling her in on a few of the details that left Dena in a bewildered silence, Gloria turned the conversation back to the house. "I'm not sure if I can afford it, but I would sure like to try." She crossed her fingers.

"You know we wouldn't charge you any more than you can afford," Dena said. "You know that."

"I know, but I want to pay a fair price."

"We'll figure something out that works for all of us. Don't worry about it, Gloria."

"Thanks, Mom. It would really mean a lot, to be able to live there."

"I'll talk to your dad tonight, but everything will work out. I promise," Dena said encouragingly.

As Gloria came upon the Grapevine, she realized she would have to reel in her thoughts and concentrate on the road ahead. After leaving Valencia, she was always nervous coming down the steep grade which leads to the valley floor, 2,600 feet below. Trucks were directed to take the grade slowly. But there were times when one would lose its brakes and come barreling down from behind. The hope was that the truck would be able to make it safely to one of the runaway truck ramps, which were huge pits of gravel built into the sides of the hills. Hopefully, the truck would make it to the ramp without mowing over a car on its way down.

As she drove into the driveway of their tri-level home, her shoulders drooped with exhaustion. It had been a stressful drive to Long Beach and back. But she was home now and Charles was a couple of hours away. She would need to rest up for tomorrow.

She pressed the button on the garage door opener which was hooked to her visor. As the garage door rolled up, she slowly pulled in. Pressing the button again, the door closed behind her. She stepped out of the car and entered through the door into the house on the ground floor The stairs in front of her lead to a landing by the front door. Another set of stairs made a turn and lead up to the top floor where the living room, kitchen, and master suite were located. She turned to her right, through the den, and down the hall to Sarah's room. Knocking on the bedroom door, she called, "are you in there?"

"Yes, Mom," came the reply.

Gloria opened the door to find Sarah lounging on her bed reading a book. "I just dropped your dad off at rehab," she reported.

"Oh, how did it go?" Sarah looked up from her book.

"It went as well as could be expected, but I'm exhausted. I'm going to go up to my room. Do you need anything?" she asked.

"No. I'm fine," Sarah said, looking back down at her book.

"Okay. I'll be in my room," Gloria smiled before shutting the door.

Everything seemed to be in place bright and early Saturday morning as she began to pack with help from Chrissy and Sarah. There would be plenty of furniture since the current house they were living in boasted a den as well as a living room.

Their tri-level home was nestled in the midst of one of the many upper-middle-class planned neighborhoods throughout northwest Bakersfield. Each subdivision hidden behind massive block walls and most included schools, large green parks, and walking paths. Their subdivision happened to have a horse trail encircling just beyond the wall.

Except for the smog that frequently rolled down from the San Francisco area and lay trapped at the foot of the Tehachapi Mountains, Gloria saw the city as ideal. Her heart, though, would

30

always be in Texas, where she had spent a happy childhood. Even so, she had to admit Bakersfield was a great place to raise kids.

She looked over the living room on the top level of their home. The furniture, in almost new condition, was used mostly for show. The brown leather sofa and love seat were Charles's pride and joy, and she knew she would be lighting a match under him by taking them, but she was determined. She began to wonder if she was just a glutton for punishment. In the end, she said, "To hell with it," and made the decision.

It's so unlike her, but she was hoping to become a new person. She would make good use of the furniture now. She would also be making use of the furniture in their spare bedroom, along with Sarah's furniture. All she would have left to purchase would be a dinette since the kitchen would come fully equipped with all the appliances.

Gloria began in the kitchen, wrapping the colorful, mismatched dishes Charles hated so much, in white wrapping paper. She would leave the cream-colored, gold-rimmed set he liked. The set that had to be hand washed and were only used for the holidays.

Sarah and Chrissy by her side, she resolved to put her fear, lying just beneath her excitement, aside, and take things one moment at a time. Not that she was always able to keep up her resolve. She would catch herself in the middle of packing with the hairs standing up on the back of her neck, looking around, waiting to be caught in the act by Charles.

"What's wrong, mom?" Chrissy asked as Gloria shivered.

Shaking her head, Gloria said, "Nothing. It's nothing," dismissively, as she continued to pack.

Every time she turned around, she seemed to be thinking about Charles again. She was just glad he had never found out about her secret savings account. She had been planning for several years for when this day would finally come. She had been frugal over the years, buying things they needed at thrift stores and using coupons. She was able to put away $2,400. Although she was always forced to hand over her paychecks to Charles, she had been quite the penny pincher with her allowance and the small amounts here and there that her parents had pitched in. She knew it wasn't much and would not go far, but she was proud of her small accomplishment, nonetheless.

Saturday evening found three exhausted women sitting amid packed boxes and loose packing paper. They were all laughing and enjoying delivery pizza, sitting cross-legged in the middle of the living room floor. To Gloria, it felt like a sleepover. Actually, Chrissy was staying the night, so it technically was a sleepover. She felt nostalgic and giddy, giggling and gossiping with her two teenage daughters.

Gloria stared at her daughters as they sat munching on pizza, each so different. Sarah's long auburn hair hung halfway down her back. She had such a small frame, barely five feet tall, and petite, with pale features. She was a small package but loaded to the brim with an outgoing personality, not at all like her shy mother. Her thin oval face was usually made up immaculately. Even at her young age, she seemed to instinctively know how to use eyeshadow to brighten her striking blue eyes.

Chrissy, with her thick shoulder-length blond hair, was built just like Gloria; medium height, with more curves than her sister. She wore only a bit of foundation, blusher, and mascara to bring out the features on her heart-shaped face. Her large eyes tended to be a darker blue. But it seemed to depend on her mood. At times, they could even look gray. With them both looking so different, there was one feature the girls had in common: Their cute, slightly upturned noses.

"What are you staring at, Mom?" Sarah asked sharply, bringing Gloria out of her daze.

"Your noses." Gloria paused slightly before biting into her slice of pizza.

"Why?" Chrissy raised her eyebrows.

"I just realized you both have the same nose," Gloria stated flatly, then added, "except for Sarah's light freckles, you have identical noses."

"You're being weird, Mom." Sarah shook her head slowly and rolled her eyes.

Changing the subject, Gloria said, "Why don't you girls pick the movie you want to watch, and I'll grab some more drinks from the kitchen." She stood up from the floor, stretching out the kinks before heading to the kitchen.

They would stay up late watching movies and sleep in a bit the next morning. Gloria was not due to pick up the moving truck until 10:00 a.m. Alex had enlisted his brother to help them move the large stuff. It seemed everything was running as smooth as glass.

They turned out all the lights, except for the golden glow of one table lamp perched on top of a moving box, and laid blankets and pillows on the floor in front of the TV. Sarah settled in next to Gloria, lying on her stomach and propping up on her elbows. Out of the blue, she said, "You know, Mom, I support you leaving Dad."

Gloria had to do a double take, but the expression on Sarah's face was serious. Sarah had never actually expressed this sentiment aloud before, and when Gloria heard it, tears began to well in her eyes. Contentment overwhelmed her. She grabbed Sarah and wrapped her in a big bear hug, with Chrissy eventually joining in.

33

Gloria and Sarah could butt heads at times, but ultimately, she had always known she would have her support if she were to leave Charles. It was just so good to hear her say it—to hear the words actually coming out of her mouth.

"You are always going to be my little red-headed mother, aren't you?" Gloria looked into Sarah's eyes as she released her.

"You know that's right." Chrissy laughed as she let go of Gloria and Sarah. "She's my mother, too."

Sarah picked up a pizza crust and threw it at her sister. "Are you saying I'm bossy?"

"No," Gloria said. "You just always look out for your absent-minded mother and your crazy blond sister."

"Yeah," Chrissy agreed, smiling.

"Okay." Sarah grinned. "But you know someone has to do it."

Sunday morning, with all hands on deck, they made short work of loading the moving truck, and Gloria soon found herself driving down the familiar tree-lined street in her parents' old neighborhood. She took in the area, with its stucco houses in varying shades of tans and grays. Every lawn, as always, seemed manicured to perfection, as if there was a competition between the neighbors over who had the most immaculately maintained yard.

She pulled into the driveway of the single-story gray stucco home and stepped out of the truck as the kids pulled up behind her to the curb, in Chrissy's silver Ford Escort. She breathed in the smell of fresh cut grass as she shut the door, closing her eyes as that unfamiliar feeling of contentment overtook her once more.

Unlocking the front door, she opened it and looked over the familiar floorplan while the kids began to grab things to bring in. Directly in front of her, on the opposite wall of the living room, was the large rock fireplace spanning from floor to vaulted ceiling. She stepped in, walking across the hardwood floor to the cream colored curtains on the wall of windows looking out over the front yard. A flood of light immediately engulfed the room as she grabbed the pulls and slid them open. With no furniture in the house, the space seemed cavernous.

Heading toward the fireplace and turning left into the large double doors to the kitchen, she looked all the way through to the dining room, its built-in hutch covering one wall. She turned and walked around the breakfast bar, into the den and down the hall, looking into each of the three bedrooms. To Gloria's delight, the cleaning lady had been by and did a wonderful job of freshening up the place

Back in the den, she looked to the far corner and spied the built-in bar the girls had used as their little playhouse when they'd visited their grandparents so long ago. She could picture them there, and her heart warmed. The house had changed a bit since then. The blue carpet had been replaced with hardwood flooring, and there was fresh paint, in contractor beige, on every wall.

The smell of paint and cleaning fluid permeated the space. She would probably never have enough furniture to fill the place, and she would need to buy rugs and paint some accent walls here and there to give it a personal touch, but it already felt homey.

She stepped aside as the kids began bringing in boxes. "Do you want all of these in the den?"

She turned to see Alex, standing behind her and holding one of the large boxes. Turning back, Gloria said, "Oh, yes. Just put them all over there by the wall. I'll use this room as my staging area."

As they carried things in, Gloria stood directing traffic.

"Where do you want the sofa?" Alex yelled from the front door as he and his brother carried the large leather couch in.

Gloria hurried to the living room and saw Alex and his younger brother, David, paused in the doorway. The two could be

35

mistaken for twins even with their three year age difference. She directed, "Over here," pointing to the living room wall beneath the windows to the right of the front door she had opened up.

Boxes and furniture started coming in until finally, after David and Alex carried in the leather loveseat that matched the sofa. Alex said, "Well, that's the last of it."

"Great." Gloria gestured to the far wall. "Just put it over here, guys."

"I don't know what I would have done without all of you. Thank you so much," she said, as she began hugging them one at a time.

She found herself alone in the house Sunday evening. Sarah had decided to spend the night with her best friend, Cindy, and the rest had headed home after she had taken them all out for a late lunch.

She decided to cut open a box marked *Books* and spread the contents out on the hardwood floor. Selecting a book of inspirational quotes, she headed toward the master bathroom. The huge garden tub was beckoning her. With its wide, sloped back, it would be quite a luxury. She would be able to stay and enjoy this bath as long as she liked, and she had bought some vanilla bath salts just for the occasion. She smiled, thinking of how she could relax. Charles would not be walking in on her tonight.

Gloria continued slowly unpacking for the next week. Sarah had settled into her own room quickly. As promised, Gloria had given her money to buy drapes, a comforter, and décor for her to make it her own.

"It looks awesome," Sarah had said, looking her room over when she was finished.

Gloria had to admit, her daughter had a knack for interior decorating, as she looked over the room's palette of whites and grays, which Sarah had accented with pops of orange and red.

Gloria sat on the sofa watching an episode of *American Idol* Wednesday evening, a week and a half after she had dropped Charles off at rehab. Her phone vibrated on the end table beside her, giving her a start. She reached for it with a trembling hand as she held her breath, hoping it wasn't going to be who she thought it might be. Seeing an unfamiliar number, she thought of letting it go to voicemail, but eventually decided to pick it up. Grabbing the remote beside her phone, she muted the TV before grabbing her iPhone and answering the call.

"Hello," she said tentatively.

"It's me, Gloria." Charles's voice gave her a sudden sinking feeling.

After a slight pause, she said, "How are you doing?"

"It was horrible," he said, raising his voice, causing her to pull the phone away from her ear. Holding the phone out, she could hear him saying, "I was nauseated and throwing up for days. I couldn't sleep, I had the cold sweats, and I'm still shaking."

"It sounds awful." Gloria tried to sound sympathetic. She knew he was miserable, but after all the years of misery he had caused her, she had a hard time feeling sorry for him.

"It's still awful," he said dramatically. "You have no idea."

"I'm sure I don't," Gloria said.

Lowering his voice, he said, "I don't think I need to stay here much longer, though."

Feeling a twinge of panic at the thought of him leaving, Gloria's voice rose a bit. "You know you have to stay twenty-eight days to complete the program."

"I know, but I really don't think I need it," he said.

Gloria remained silent. She didn't want to agree with him, but on the other hand, she didn't want to upset him either.

"I'm going to have to go," he said. "Other people are waiting to use the phone."

"Oh." Gloria perked up, hoping the call would soon be over.

"Yeah, we aren't supposed to be on the phone too much, distracting ourselves from the program," he said, adding, "I think it's bullshit, myself."

"Okay." Gloria tried with everything in her to sound neutral.

"Well, I love you," he said, sounding down.

"Love you, too," Gloria said reflexively, before cringing.

After saying their goodbyes they hung up. She slid back on the couch with the phone in her hand. She was sure he would somehow know something was amiss. Irrationally, she thought he might have some kind of telepathy and know precisely what she had done after she had left him at rehab.

She tried to relax and slow her heart rate, which had risen sharply during their exchange. When she finally gathered her wits, she found the television show unable to hold her attention. Reaching over for the remote, she turned off the TV, switched off the light, and headed to bed, deciding to make an early night of it.

She decided for the rest of his stay, she would let his calls go to voice mail. She then would then delete the voice recordings before listening to them. She knew they would be irate calls, and she was just done with it all. She would worry about the consequences when he got out.

Picking up her phone on the day before Charles's release, Gloria dreaded the call she was about to make to his boss. She hovered over the last digit before finally pressing it and heard it ringing on the other end.

"Hello," Ed answered.

"Hi, Ed. It's Gloria," she was trying not to let the quiver in her voice show.

"Hi, Gloria. How's Charles doing?" he asked.

"Well, I don't think he's doing too well. He has been hating the program. Actually, I called to ask you a favor. I know you're his boss, but you're also his best friend, and I have a problem."

"What is it, Gloria?"

"It's just that I'm not feeling well and I don't think I'm going to be able to pick him up tomorrow in Long Beach." She paused a moment before asking, "I was actually wondering if you might be able to pick him up?"

"Sure. I can do that," Ed said.

She hated this little fib she was telling Ed, but there was no way she could pick Charles up. She was sure he was going to be livid when she didn't show up for him, but she tried to tell herself, she no longer cared. Attempting a brave front, she convinced herself it was no longer going to be her job to keep jumping to his every whim. Deep down; though, she knew it was going to take more than just a few days to break years of bad habits. All she could do was try not to sit and wait for the eruption to happen.

Chapter 4

March 2003

<u>After</u>

Bringing herself back to the present, or the past, or whatever the hell this is, she thinks, *I had better not check out now. I need to keep a clear head.* She had let her mind wander. She hasn't even made it past the first morning with Charles, and she wants to run out the front door. All she has to do is think of her little ones, and she knows she must stay for now. Still, she tries to think of anything to get away from him, even if for a moment.

As Charles sits sipping his coffee, Gloria looks up and says, "I need to go check in on the girls."

"Okay, but come right back," he demands, setting his mug heavily down on the kitchen table.

She feels suffocated. She is beginning to feel she can't catch her breath.

Still breathless, she rises from her seat and discreetly grabs Chrissy's apple juice from the counter as she heads through the bar doors and into the den. A few seconds later, she returns to the kitchen, apologizing to Charles, "There was some juice spilled on the carpet. I need to clean it up before it sets in and smells." She grabs a sponge and cleaner from under the sink. Hopefully, she can make slow work of this. "I'll be back as soon as I'm done."

"What was juice doing in the den?" he demands.

"I'm sorry," she says, stopping mid-step in the kitchen, not turning around to look at him; instead, she looks down at the floor in front of her. "I forgot. I set it down in there earlier, when I was with the girls. I'll get it cleaned up," she promises, as she slowly pivots to face him again.

"You better," he says, brows furrowed while raising both hands in the air in exasperation, before slamming them down on the table. "Do you know how much I pay for this house every month? Too much money to have the carpet ruined over stupid mistakes like that!"

Gloria jumps, then tries to recover. "I know. I'm so sorry," she says as she heads back to the den to slowly dab at the stain. How many times had she apologized during their marriage, she wonders. It has to have been thousands of times.

After a long day with Charles, Gloria feels her entire body drooping from exhaustion. How had she so quickly forgotten how draining it was to be around him?

Later, spying a calendar on the wall beside her vanity, she finally finds today's date. The calendar page is turned to March. The days are marked out with an X, up to the 15th, so she presumes the date to be the 16th. The year is showing 2003. She lets out a sigh when she realizes thankfully it's Sunday, so Charles will be going to work in the morning.

After putting the girls to bed, Gloria is hoping for some much-needed alone time. Charles has settled into his rocker in front of the TV in the den, and she decides to take a chance. "Do you mind if I take a bath?" she asks him as she stands behind his chair. She always had to ask permission to take a bath, and she seems to be falling into old habits quickly. He usually insisted she be by his side, watching TV in the evenings, but she knows she won't be up to it tonight.

41

Swiveling his rocker to face her, he says, "Don't you want to sit and watch the TV show with me?" It's more of a demand than a question, she can tell, and she realizes she usually wouldn't push it, but her nerves are frayed.

"I can join you when I'm finished," she suggests, hopefully.

"All right, but don't take too long. You'll miss half the show." He gestures, with a hand jutted toward the television.

She gives a timid agreement, before turning and quickly leaving the room. After closing and locking the bathroom door behind her, she places both palms on the counter and lets out a sigh. Slowly looking up into the mirror, she can see dark circles have formed under her bloodshot eyes, and what little color she had has drained from her pale complexion.

After running her bath and stepping out of her clothes, she glances at herself again. *How could I have ever had such a bad body image?* she thinks, and then quickly looks away. She has never been able to gaze at her naked reflection for long, but she forces herself to look again. She realizes she isn't perfect, but her reflection really isn't bad. If anything, she is a bit too thin.

She wonders how she could have been so hard on herself. Sure there are stretch marks here and there, but after having two children, everything still seems to be up where it should be. Even though she's thin, she still has curves, just smaller curves. Charles's quest for perfection always made her feel inferior and wreaked havoc on her self-esteem. She shakes her head as she runs her bath before stepping into the tub.

As she settles in, the warm water feels like a balm to her frazzled nerves. Taking some deep breaths, she relaxes her shoulders into the water. They feel as if they have been up to her ears all day, and it's wonderful to finally stretch them out, losing herself for a while.

42

She is startled back to full consciousness by a loud knocking on the door. She's not sure how much time has passed. It seems like only a couple of minutes.

"How long are you going to take in there?" Charles jiggles the door handle. "Why is it locked?"

Startled, Gloria jumps to attention, splashing water over the edge of the tub and covering herself reflexively, her pulse racing. "I'm sorry, Charles. I must have fallen asleep."

She realizes she has made two grave mistakes. She should never take more than ten minutes in the bath, and never lock him out. Privacy is something she has only gained since she left Charles two years ago - or, as it would stand now, many years in her future.

"I'll be right out," she promises.

"Well, don't take too long." She can hear his voice fade as he walks back down the hall.

Gingerly stepping out of the tub, she dries and slips on the ugliest nightgown she was able to find before coming in to take her bath. It's a faded, oversized yellow cotton gown, which falls past her knees, with half the hem coming loose at the bottom. She certainly doesn't want him getting any ideas tonight. She cringes at the thought, closes her eyes, and shakes her head vigorously as if that will get rid of the image starting to form in her head.

Gathering her wits, she shuffles toward the den planning to ask Charles if he would allow her to go to bed early tonight. She pauses before rounding the corner into the den. She can hear a slow scrape, scrape, scraping sound. When she slowly comes up behind him, she sees where the sound is coming from.

Charles is sitting with his hunting knife. In front of him, on the TV tray is a white stone sharpening block. He is holding the expensive Golden Amboyna Burle handle while pulling the blade across the block in slow, deliberate motions. Gloria immediately loses her nerve and decides to take a seat in the beige rocker beside him with no complaint.

He doesn't look at her when he begins to speak. "Do you know how sharp I keep this knife, Gloria?"

"Yes, Charles." She turns to look at him.

He turns to her, lifting the blade in her direction. He points at her left ear with the tip, and as he pivots the blade in a slicing motion to her right ear, he says, "It wouldn't take any pressure on my part to slit a person's throat from ear to ear."

Gloria holds her breath in horror, as his eyes become dark and threatening. He's speaking through a devilish grin. He's enjoying this, she can tell. She can't help herself, her entire body begins to tremble. All she can think to say is, "I'm really sorry."

"Yeah, well you would think a good wife would want to spend some quality time with her husband." He looks at the knife before returning his gaze to her.

She lets out a breath. "I'm sorry. I fell asleep in the tub, Charles. I don't know why I've been so tired lately." Tears of fear begin to prick her eyes.

With the knife still pointed in her direction, he says, "don't let it happen again."

She pulls her eyes away from the knife to glance at the TV. "I would really like to watch this movie with you." She is trying to sound enthusiastic, but it comes out as more of a whimper.

He tilts his head to one side, laying the knife on the table in front of him. "That's a much better attitude. You know Gloria, if you act like a child; I'm going to have to keep you in line like a child. Children don't know better, but you should."

That night, as they head off to bed, Charles carries the knife with him, laying it on his nightstand. Gloria finds herself wide-eyed until the wee hours of the morning.

44

Monday morning Gloria wakes with the hope that she is back in her own bed, in 2019. She longs to see her fiancé's kind face looking back at her. She wants to give him a great big kiss, morning breath and all. But, as she opens her eyes, her heart seems to stop. Charles is lying beside her. She closes her eyes again, trying to swallow the lump of disappointment that is lodged in her throat. Tears sting her eyes as she tries to grasp that this situation may never be over.

"Bye, Charles. Have a good day," Gloria calls from the front door as he slides into his car on his way to work. She knows this is expected of her, and she has complied.

"Bye," he calls back congenially, the night before seemingly forgotten. She knows she shouldn't have pressed her luck last night. She must be careful. It's just so hard this time around. The new Gloria wants to rebel.

She closes the front door and hurries to the den to check in on the girls. Chrissy is occupied with a coloring book and crayons spread out all over the floor, while Sarah is playing happily with her toys in her playpen. This gives Gloria some time to think.

First of all, she thinks, *I am going to have to call in sick to work.* She looks up at the clock over the fireplace mantel, which reads 7:30. No one would be in at Bradford Insurance Agency until after 8:00. She would usually arrive for work in accounts receivable by 8:30.

She decides she is going to have to fake a severe case of the flu in order to garner a few days off. She will need this time to come up with a plan for moving forward, having decided to think of this as somehow being her real life. She needs to figure out what to do.

She takes a seat on one of four high-back, swivel barstools at the breakfast counter, and picks up the handset from the house

45

phone. She hasn't even had time to find her cell phone since she's been here. Charles had the habit of hiding it from her over the weekend, and it would usually turn up on the kitchen counter Monday morning. She knows the only reason she has one is for Charles to get in touch with her throughout the weekdays, but it isn't there this morning.

She knows now that he is punishing her for last night by not returning her cell phone. She wonders what else he will do before he forgets the incident and moves on. She cringes, thinking about it.

Planning to try and fake a convincing raspy voice, she begins to dial promptly at 8:00. The old beige slim line rotary phone sounds like a coffee grinder as she slowly dials. It's a relic handed down from Charles's parents. She pauses slightly before taking a breath and dialing in the last number.

"Bradford Agency, this is Mickey," answers a cheery female voice. It's her supervisor.

Gloria thinks of Mickey and pictures her on the other end of the line. They always got along well. A rugged, outdoorsy woman, Mickey always sported a tan, her long brown hair usually pulled back in a low ponytail. Her other job, training show horses, had her in jeans most of the time. Even so, surprisingly, she was still able to pull off an evening gown quite well.

"Hi Mickey, this is Gloria," she chokes and then gives a little cough.

"Wow, you don't sound good," Mickey says.

"No." Gloria feels guilty for putting on this act. She rarely ever missed work, and would never call in sick, unless she felt it was an emergency. "I'm so sorry, but I'm not going to make it in today," she croaks.

"I can tell by the sound of it," Mickey says. "Take care of yourself, and don't come back until you feel better. We'll hold down the fort. You just rest."

"Thank you," Gloria says. After saying goodbye, she places the handset back in the receiver, leans her head on the counter, and sighs, not sure if she is ready for what lies ahead.

She counts herself lucky she has worked in such a great place for over twenty years, or eight years, as it would be now. Her coworkers were always her only friends, since Charles monopolized all her free time. The second time around seems unbearable, and this is only the second day.

As far as socializing goes, Charles expected her to attend his work functions. A large part of his job consisted of planning fundraising events throughout the year. She was expected to be at his side for all of these gatherings, at least as far as walking in the door went.

With her limited selection of clothing, Gloria tried to mix and match dresses, skirts, and blouses, but the reality was she had a small wardrobe, so she was often forced to wear the same things over and over. She would use inexpensive scarves and accessories to change them up, but her cheeks would flare with embarrassment when she tried to put together a different outfit for yet another event. She couldn't figure out why Charles didn't allow her enough money to buy a new dress here and there.

Gloria always steeled herself for the inevitable inspection at the front door before leaving. Looking her up and down, Charles would comment, "You've forgotten your earrings."

Feeling her earlobes, she would shrug apologetically and rush to pick out a pair she knew he liked, putting them on as she returned for him to complete his inspection.

"I'm glad you curled your hair, but you know I prefer it when you wear it down," he would say, and she would obediently return to her vanity and take the clips out of her hair, allowing curls to fall around her face. If she had worn it down, he would have wanted it up.

There were times when he would mention her limited wardrobe, as if she could magically make new dresses appear. She was just thankful she and Mickey happened to be the same size, and she was sometimes able to borrow from her closet.

Lost in her thoughts, Gloria is startled to hear a loud, "Mommy." She realizes Chrissy has been saying it over and over, and she has just now noticed.

"What's wrong, Mommy?" Chrissy's little blond head is cocked to one side, and her big blue eyes are looking up questioningly.

Nothing, honey. I was just daydreaming." Gloria tries her best to remove the startled look from her face, and put on a big smile.

"What's daydreaming, Mommy? Does that mean you went asleep in the day?"

"What a bright and inquisitive child I have," Gloria says, which only leads Chrissy to ask what *inquisitif* means.

Soon, it's down for naps. This again is some much-needed time by herself. There is no way she is going to live the next who knows how many years under constant stress with Charles all over again. And maybe she can prevent the damage done to Chrissy and Sarah, by not allowing them to grow up in this toxic household.

Chapter 5

February 2017

Before

Charles had returned home from rehab to find furniture and his family missing from the house. "What the hell have you done?" he said, when Gloria picked up the phone. "We've been together over twenty years, and you're just going to walk out on me."

Why had she even picked it up? Thinking she should hang up on him, instead she fell into her old pattern. Pacing from the rock fireplace to the front door and back, she said, "I just need a while to gather my thoughts."

Raising his voice, he said, "Gather your thoughts from what? Like I'm some kind of monster? Is that what you're saying? Have I just gone through hell in rehab for nothing?"

"I'm not saying that." She suddenly had the feeling of being thrown off a cliff once again.

Trying a new tactic, he lowered his voice. "I love you more than anything. I've done everything for you, and you do this to me?" He was using that pitiful tone she had heard many times before.

That snapped her to attention as her anger flared. *That's right,* she thought, *turn our problems around on me. You're good at that.*

With new resolve, she began to speak again. "Charles . . ."

He interrupted before she could say anything further, raging, "This is bullshit! That stuff you took belongs to me. In fact, lady, *you* belong to me!" The pitiful act sure hadn't lasted long.

"I don't belong to anyone," she fired back, before using a shaky finger to push the button to hang up. She had to try hitting the right spot a couple of times before she could disconnect the call. *So much for amicable*, she thought, trembling with rage. Normally she would keep her anger in check and bottle it up, but now she would allow it to run its course.

Turning off her phone, she threw it across the room, shattering it over the hardwood floor. She sat on the couch trembling and staring at her broken phone, almost in a trance, for quite some time before deciding to turn off the lights and head for bed, leaving her phone there in pieces.

Gloria stopped by Sarah's room before heading on to hers. She found her daughter sitting cross-legged on her bed with a school book perched on her lap, her auburn hair hanging around her face as she was bent over, studying.

"Sarah, honey, could you turn your phone off? I think your dad is going to be calling you tonight, and he's in a bad mood. I just think it would be better if you turned it off."

Sarah straightened up, a questioning look in her eyes. She had surely heard Gloria's side of the conversation, but she didn't ask. "Sure, Mom," was all she said as she reached under her pillow, pulled out her phone, and pressed the power button.

"Thanks, honey. I'll see you in the morning. Goodnight."

"Sure, Mom. Remember, I'm on your side."

"That means a lot," Gloria said, stepping into the room and over to Sarah's bed to give her a hug.

Sarah pulled back, looking her in the eye, a worried look on her face. "Goodnight, Mom. Try and get some rest."

"I will, but for now keep your phone turned off unless you need to make a call. We'll figure out a better solution later, but I don't want you having to deal with his rage."

Sarah smiled a sad smile. "I will, Mom. Don't worry, okay?"

Gloria looked at her daughter. "I love you so much, Sarah."

"I love you more." Sarah grinned.

"Impossible," Gloria said, before heading toward her bed.

After tossing and turning throughout a sleepless night, Gloria picked up a new phone from a different carrier the next day, hoping Charles would not be able to track it. She held on to this slight hope for only a day, before he found her number changed. Since he couldn't reach her by phone, he decided to show up on her doorstep, demanding to be let in. When she heard the pounding on her front door, she felt a knot beginning to form in her stomach. He began shouting as she ran to check the dead bolt, making sure it was securely in place.

Standing behind the door with her hand still on the lock, she said, "I'm not letting you in, Charles. If you don't stop yelling, and leave, the neighbors are going to call the police."

Gloria turned her back to the door and slid down to the floor as he yelled, "That's right, you can't even face me. You can't face what you're doing to our family. You're going to ruin everything."

With her head in her hands, she sat there silently. All she could do was hope he would go away.

"I demand you return home immediately and return all the stuff you took. I'm not going to let you get away with ruining our lives," he yelled, causing her to flinch as he began pounding on the door once more.

In the distance, Gloria could hear sirens. She wasn't sure they were coming her way, but she prayed they were. "Do you hear that,

Charles?" she said defiantly, through the door. "Someone called the police."

After a moment of silence, except for the sirens, she pushed herself up off the floor and moved to peer around the open curtains. To her relief, he was striding to his car, fists clenched. He climbed in and sped off as the sirens came closer.

Gloria turned to see Sarah, sobbing. She had come into the living room behind her.

"I'm so sorry, honey," she said as she reached out to embrace her distraught daughter.

"Why does he have to do that, Mom?" Sarah cried through muffled sobs against her chest.

Try as she might, Gloria couldn't think of an adequate response. All she could say was, "I don't know . . ." as she kissed the top of her daughter's head and smoothed her hair. "I just don't know."

Interrupted by knocking on the door, Gloria turned, her arm still around Sarah's shoulder. Together they approached the front door and greeted the two police officers who were standing just outside.

After the officers took their statements and suggested Gloria might want to file a restraining order, they headed back toward their patrol cars. Sarah immediately turned to her. "Can I call Dad and tell him the police were here?" she asked, her eyes pleading.

"Go ahead," Gloria said, reluctantly.

"Thanks, Mom," Sarah sniffled as she headed toward the kitchen, where her phone was charging on the counter.

She came back into the living room with her phone in hand and plopped down on the couch. Gloria sat down beside her and listened in as Sarah began to speak. "Dad, the police were just here. Please stay away. I don't want you to go to jail," she pleaded, as she began to tear up again.

After a pause, she said, "I know it's hard for you, but can't you guys work it out some other way? It's just so humiliating, having the police called and everything."

She sat nodding her head for a long while, before saying, "I know. I know. I'll try. Bye, Dad." She looked up at Gloria dejectedly as she ended the call.

"What did he say?" Gloria asked.

"He wants you to call him, so you can work stuff out," Sarah relayed, eyes downcast. "I know you probably shouldn't call him, but I said I would ask you to."

"I'm sorry, Sarah. I'll try to find a better way to handle things." Gloria tipped Sarah's chin up with a forefinger and gave her a halfhearted smile. "I think we should probably head for bed. You look as tired as I feel." Sarah nodded, eyes still downcast, as they both rose from the couch and slowly headed to their bedrooms.

Making her way back to her car from the police station, after filling out the paperwork for a restraining order the next day, Gloria looked up at the bright cloudless sky. It was going to be another beautiful Southern California day. Trying to enjoy the weather, she strolled slowly on her way back to the parking lot to find her used blue Honda Civic she had just purchased on credit.

She tried to have hope that the restraining order would have the desired effect and keep Charles away from her house. She would keep it a secret from Sarah and, if it worked, she would allow her to think her father had heeded her pleadings to stay away.

Over the next few days, Gloria found herself with some relief as Charles seemed to comply with the restraining order, but it

53

wasn't long before she found the hairs on the back of her neck standing on end once again. Keeping the curtains drawn at night, she would peek out occasionally, a familiar knot growing inside her stomach. She was never able to spot him, but she knew he was near. After so many years with him, her gut just seemed to know. She had surely lit a fuse under him that could eventually result in a massive explosion.

Chapter 6

March 2003

<u>After</u>

After much counseling, and finally admitting her inability to have a healthy life while still with Charles, she had decided to leave. But that was her future. In her future, she had left at almost forty, and, as they say, that's when her life began. It's all so confusing, thinking of the future as the past - but as long as this goes on, that's exactly what it is.

Her thoughts turn to her lack of money. She has only her secret bank account, with what little she is allowed after turning her paychecks over to Charles. Running to her bedroom, she begins looking for her purse. She finds it on the dresser, and then digs for her checkbook. Shuffling through her register, her heart drops when she sees she only has $34.73 in her checking account. The middle of the month has already passed. *Does that mean,* she thinks, *that he has already given me cash for the rest of the month?* She digs out her wallet and thankfully finds $150 in cash. She obviously hasn't made her deposit yet.

Knowing she has $184 to work with, Gloria begins to form a plan. *Okay,* she thinks, *where do Mom and Dad live in 2003? Is it Bakersfield, or have they already moved back to Dallas?* She tries to remember, but she's not quite sure. With so little money, she is praying they haven't moved yet. She doesn't need to be spending much-needed funds on a babysitter.

As the girls nap, Gloria falls onto the couch. As she sits there thinking, her eyes begin to droop. Her head begins to loll causing her to jump. Soon her eyes are heavy again and she decides to lie down for just a moment.

Immediately, she finds herself inside a box. Lifting her hands to push the lid open, she realizes there is something binding her wrists together. Frantically tugging and wiggling her wrists, she begins to feel panic rising. This causes her to strain even harder against the bindings. Unable to free her hands, she reaches her still-bound wrists up to push the lid open. It doesn't budge. She pounds and beats at it, but it won't budge.

Panting, she tries to take in her surroundings. It's so dark, but there seems to be a faint glow coming from somewhere. Willing herself to settle down, she tries to adjust her eyes, but the glow is too dim and she can't see. Panic and foreboding wash over her, and she finds herself struggling and flailing against the bindings once again. It's not only her wrists that are bound, it's her ankles too. She begins to register a throbbing pain in her head that causes her to stop thrashing. She wants to scream, but has a strong feeling she should stay quiet. She feels as if she can't breathe! *It's dark, and I can't move! I can't breathe! I'm going to die!* She thinks, just before waking with a gasp, trying to gulp in air as she comes around.

Her chest now heaving, she feels as if she has one foot in and one foot out of the dream. It's still so clear, and she finds it difficult to slow her beating heart. She hopes she hasn't cried out and woken the girls. She wouldn't want Chrissy to see her like this. There's something in the back of her mind, something relaying, "This wasn't just a dream."

The girls, she thinks; the need to go check on them is urgent. First she checks on Sarah, and then on Chrissy. Thankfully, she finds them both sleeping soundly. Her breath still coming too fast, she places a hand on the wall in Chrissy's room to steady herself as she tries to force her muddled brain to function fully. Finally coming to full consciousness, she realizes her clothes are wet and sticking to her body. She is covered in sweat from the dream, and knows she needs to take a shower and change. She hopes there is enough time before the girls wake.

Shuffling toward the shower with one hand on her chest, she is still trying to bring her breathing under control. Stripping off her clothes, she steps into the cold water of the shower, hoping to shock herself into the present. She gasps as the frigid water assaults her skin. Turning the hot water knob after the cold water has done the trick, she backs away, panting, as the water heats up. She steps back under the spray allowing the water to wash over and calm her.

Gingerly stepping out of the shower and grabbing a towel off the rail to dry off, she wraps it around her body. She sits slumped on her vanity bench and lets the tears begin to fall. All of the events are blurring together. She's having trouble keeping things straight in her mind, and she feels isolated. Letting out a long sigh, she contemplates how exhausted and alone she feels.

Trying to make sense of it, she asks herself the pressing question, *why am I still waking up in 2003? What does it mean? What do all the fragments mean?* It's strange how her mind is recognizing this as reality, and the future as also being real. Reality is a concept that's getting mixed up in her brain, until she feels as if she might go mad. If it wasn't for the girls, she might just curl up in a ball and wait for things to make sense. But because of them, she has to treat this as reality. She has to treat it as if God has given her a do-over.

Chrissy tiptoes into the room holding Pookie. Wide-eyed, she cheerfully jumps into Gloria's lap, giving her a hug around the neck and, thankfully, diverting her attention away from her confusion. She quickly wipes her tears, hoping Chrissy hasn't seen her crying, and holds her daughter close.

"I'm hungry," Chrissy says.

"Well, let me put some clothes on. We'll see if Sarah is up, and go make some lunch." Gloria smiles down while easing Chrissy's feet to the floor.

The afternoon passes quickly, and Charles comes home that evening to find Gloria in bed, with the girls lying beside her. "I've been sick all day," she croaks, lifting her left hand to warn him off, while covering her mouth to cough into her right. "You probably don't want to come too close. I think I'm contagious."

"No. It wouldn't be a good time for me to catch something. I have an important meeting tomorrow. Do you have a fever?" His question sounds like an afterthought.

"Yes," she lies.

"Okay, then just stay in bed. I guess I'll take care of myself." He huffs out a long breath as he pulls off his tie and heads toward the shower.

Heaven help him if he were to get sick, but would he watch the kids so they wouldn't catch whatever she had? Not in a million years. They will stay with Gloria, contagious or not.

She had truly tried to make Charles happy. She hadn't wanted to be the cause of his misery.

"I'll drive my car off a cliff, if you ever leave me," he had told her on more than one occasion. "I don't want to live without you."

"I'll never leave," she would find herself saying.

She hadn't wanted to be the reason for his unhappiness—or his death. She had always tried to do what was best for him, but no longer. It had never occurred to her, in all that time, to do what was best for her. That would be selfish, and she had been taught to

58

always put others before herself. She had tried. She really had tried her best, but trying to live up to that standard had almost killed her. *No*, she decides. *It's time to put the girls and myself first.*

She is awakened in the morning by Charles shaking her briskly. "Thanks for making breakfast this morning. I guess I'll have to grab something on the way to the office," he says, as she tries to get her bearings. She overslept!

"I'm sorry, Charles. I'm feeling ill." She pulls the covers up to her chin and buries her head in her pillow.

He shakes his head as he turns to leave, mumbling something Gloria can't quite make out. Hearing the front door slam behind him and his car engine firing up, she hops frantically out of bed.

Her hands are still shaking as she settles the little ones after breakfast. She plants herself on a barstool, rubbing her hands on her denim clad thighs as she tries to calm herself. Finally, picking up the phone, she begins to dial. She is not sure exactly how this is going to go, or what she will divulge, but she must reach out to her mother for some moral support.

She hears on the fourth ring - Dena's voice . . . her mom's. She slumps over the counter, releasing the anxiety that had been building; she had begun to fear there would be no answer.

Relief spreading through her body, she softly breathes, "Hi Mom, I'm so glad you're home."

"Of course, where else would I be?" Dena says, in her usual chipper tone. "I was going to call you this morning, but you beat me to it. I tried to call you at work yesterday, when you didn't drop off the girls." She continues, "I didn't know if you might have dropped them off at Sandy's. Mickey told me you were home sick. Are you okay?"

"Yes, I'm okay, and the girls are okay. I'm so sorry I forgot to call." She tries to reassure her mother.

"I didn't want to bother you yesterday, in case you were catching a nap." Gloria can hear the concern in her mother's voice.

"Thanks, Mom. I had a pretty bad day yesterday, but to be honest I'm not actually sick. Could I come over and talk to you about it?"

"Of course, you know you can come by anytime. That's why we gave you a key, but you never use it," Dena chides.

"Yeah, well, you know how Charles is about me visiting." Gloria begins to absentmindedly twist the phone cord around her finger. "It's just easier to keep him happy than to deal with his moods."

"I've always wanted to talk to you about that, but I didn't want to stick my nose into your relationship. You've never said anything about it before, but I've always been concerned that he doesn't let you visit, and I miss you." Dena softly sniffles.

Gloria can tell her mother is trying not to cry. She knew she had grown far apart from her parents, while living only fifteen minutes away. At this point, she would have been married about eight years. It seems that she had been slowly drawn away, into Charles's world.

It's hard to remember with exactness what happened. It just became easier to try and keep him happy and not rock the boat along the way. More than anything, she had longed for peace at home. In hindsight, though, it's clear she was never going to be able to obtain it.

"I know, Mom." She straightens in her seat and continues in a reassuring tone, "And please believe me, Mom, things are going to change from now on, but I'll be honest: I'm going to need some help."

"Of course. Whatever you need, all you've ever had to do is ask," Dena says.

"I've always known that, Mom, but I wanted you and Dad to be proud of me, and I didn't want to dump my marital problems on you." Gloria is trying unsuccessfully to keep up her brave front.

"Come right on over. I'm here all day. We can drink a pot of coffee and have a nice long chat." Gloria is not quite sure, but she thinks her mom might sound hopeful.

"I have to put myself together, and I'll see you in about forty-five minutes," Gloria says, before they say their goodbyes and hang up.

She is filled with a host of conflicting emotions. She is excited to be able to spend a whole day with her mom, but she also feels apprehension for what they must discuss. She feels the fear of Charles finding out she hasn't been home sick all day, after she sent him off without breakfast this morning. However, there is also the thrill of doing something she feels she shouldn't be, or, to be exact, doing something Charles thinks she shouldn't be doing.

Sitting in front of the mirror, she applies makeup for the first time since she woke up Sunday morning. Taking a long look in the mirror, she still can't believe how young she is. She's twenty-five years old again. *Wouldn't anyone give a fortune to be young again*, she thinks. All she feels, though, is lost. Reeling in her thoughts, she applies minimal makeup, tames her hair, and calls it good.

Venturing out feels unreal. As she walks out the front door, she can feel a light warm breeze on her skin. Thinking of the sweltering 110-degree summer heat in Bakersfield makes her thankful for the wonderful weather today. "Yeah, but it's a dry heat," Californians always seem to brag.

It's still dang hot, Gloria thinks.

Her face drops quickly, as her eyes settle on the ugly gold Oldsmobile parked in the driveway. It brings back memories, and not good ones.

The car is actually a new model. Charles had been so proud when he brought it home after trading in yet another car she had actually liked. All she can think about this one is, *it looks old and is the color of dirt*. Heaven forbid Gloria ever had a say in what she drove.

She guesses she should feel lucky Charles has a company car, so she is actually allowed to have a car to drive. She knows the only reason she is able to drive it is because he expects her to hold down a job to help support his lifestyle. Feeling a little petty, she tries to turn her thoughts around. It's just that every time she has something she likes, it is ripped away from her. She wonders if he does it on purpose. In the end, she figures it doesn't matter anyway. He will trade it in for a newer model as soon as it's a year old.

Gloria breathes deeply through her nose, taking in the clean air, thankful there is no smog today. She looks around at the stucco houses in different shades of tan, with their Spanish tile roofs and green lawns, and it hits her: She never really knew any of the neighbors. They never attended any of the neighborhood barbeques or parties. If Charles didn't have an interest in getting to know any of the neighbors, she was expected to feel the same. Chrissy would have loved to have had friends to play with. Gloria finds her eyes downcast as she thinks of how sad the situation is.

Her blue mood passes as she buckles the girls into their car seats. She finds herself brightening as she thinks about where she is going. Before she knows it, she is standing at the front door staring into her mom's living room, with its huge rock fireplace on the far wall and blue carpet. She is holding Sarah on her hip while Chrissy is waiting anxiously by her side. She can smell the coffee brewing in the kitchen as she gives Dena as much of a big one-armed hug as she can manage.

"Wow. Where did that come from?" Dena laughs. "Since when are you a hugger?"

Gloria steps back to look at her mother, who is smiling widely and causing lines to crinkle at the corners of her sky-blue eyes. Her blond hair is cut short and feathered back, in the style she has always worn. She is sporting a stylish black workout set. Standing a bit shorter than Gloria, she is just a bit heavier. The only features they share are pale skin and blond hair. She did not inherit her mom's cute upturned nose, and Gloria's eyes are a much darker blue.

That's right, she thinks, as she recognizes her mom's comment. She hadn't been a hugger when she was with Charles. He would hold onto her so tight and for so long, and wouldn't let go until he was good and ready. She shakes her head at the memory. It had made her shy away from hugging anyone for fear of them not letting go. Just thinking about it makes her cringe and step back slightly.

She quickly plants a smile back on her face and says, "Since right now," adding, "You look beautiful, Mom."

"Well thanks, honey! What brought that on?" Dena asks, with a look of surprise.

"I don't know, I guess I'm being weird," Gloria says self-consciously.

"Don't stop. I like it. I haven't ever seen you in this kind of mood. Well, come on in, you three." Dena smiles and makes a sweeping gesture with her left arm. "Are you going to stand on the porch all day?"

With Sarah still on Gloria's hip, Chrissy takes off to the den where her box of toys is hidden behind the built-in bar. Grandma takes Sarah, who giggles as she receives a great big bear hug and lots of kisses, while Gloria takes the chance to head toward the coffee pot. In the kitchen, there waiting on the white tile countertop, next to a dish towel that says, *An old bear and his honey live here,* is a large green mug ready to deliver some much-needed caffeine.

Her mom's coffee is already sitting on the large oak table in the dining room, just off the kitchen. After placing her own mug on the table, Gloria heads around the corner to the den to grab some toys from Chrissy's box. She finds Chrissy happily playing in her little cubby, and asks if Sarah might borrow some of her toys. Carefully picking a few toys to share with her little sister, Chrissy hands them over.

"Thank you. Sarah will like these," Gloria smiles down at her daughter.

"Are you happy, Mommy?" Chrissy giggles.

"Yes Chrissy, why do you ask that?" Gloria is taken aback, by her daughter's question.

"You look like you're happy, Mommy," Chrissy says, with a big grin.

Gloria ponders this and realizes she must be smiling more than usual. She regrets she used to be so serious all the time, and feels a pang of guilt that Chrissy has noticed the difference.

"I'm going to try to be happy a lot more now." Gloria ruffles Chrissy's hair.

Chrissy smiles and returns to playing with her toys as Gloria turns to head toward the dining room. Rounding the corner into the dining room, she scatters the toys around on the blue carpeted floor and sets Sarah in front of them to play. She takes a seat next to her mother and does her best to keep her voice down. Chrissy has big ears at times, and there is no telling how much a seven-month-old can understand. As they sit, they both turn their chairs so their knees are almost touching.

Through the tears starting to well up, Gloria begins. "Mom, my marriage is not good right now. In fact, it has never been good." She pauses and looks up at her mother, before continuing, "I've just tried to make it work because that's what I feel like I'm supposed to do, you know, with the kids and all."

Looking down at her lap, she attempts to hold back the tears as she sniffs and continues, "I've watched you and Dad for all these years, through good times and bad, sticking together and making it work. But. . ." Try as she might to contain it, the dam seems to burst as she explains, "I feel like a failure sometimes for not being able to make mine work. You just don't know what it's like." She begins to sob, dropping her face into her hands.

Dena stands and pats her on the back before stepping into the kitchen for a moment and coming back with some tissue. Handing a couple of tissues to Gloria, she returns to her seat and listens quietly, moving closer and putting an arm around Gloria's shoulder. They sit knee to knee now as Gloria cries. "Only you know what you're going through, and you are not a failure," Dena says. "So just get that out of your head."

"He's not at all like Dad." Gloria looks up, dabbing at the tears streaming down her face. She can see her mother has tears beginning to brim in her eyes as well. "I'm sorry to dump this on you, Mom," she says, beginning to choke up from the guilt she feels for springing this on her mother.

"It's okay, honey. You need to get it all out." Dena pats Gloria supportively on the shoulder.

After a pause, Gloria decides to go on. "He has real problems and issues I can't help him with. He always says I'm the one with all the problems, and he doesn't believe in counseling."

"Honey, we never knew. I'm so sorry. You know you can confide in us anytime." Dena lifts Gloria's chin to look sincerely into her eyes. "I want you to know that."

"Thank you, Mom." Gloria smiles through her tears, her heart beginning to feel lighter, knowing her mother is by her side.

Dabbing at her tears with the tissue, she looks down at her lap again, thinking of what she needs to say next. Finally looking at her mom, she says, "You know, he takes things out on the girls and me. Mostly I try to take the brunt of it, but I'm not always able to protect them from the yelling." She begins to twist and untwist the tissue, hands balled up in her lap, gathering the courage to go on. "He doesn't let me see you, and I don't have any friends. I feel like a prisoner."

"I know, honey." Dena's voice is calming.

Gloria knows her mom will sit and listen as long as she needs to talk, and relief begins to wash over her. With encouragement from Dena, she feels safe to go on. "Charles doesn't know it, but I've been seeing a counselor." Looking up, with regret she admits, "I haven't been totally honest in my sessions. I gloss over it. For some reason, I make excuses for him to the counselor, to you, and to everyone." Screwing up her face, she admits, "I don't know why I do it. I think it's because all these years, he has made me feel like the one in the wrong. And if I could just get my act together, we would be fine." She wipes at her face with the back of her hand, and Dena can see the tissue is now shredded and covering her lap.

Dena steps away to retrieve more tissue. She brings the whole box this time. Handing it to Gloria, she says patiently, "I'll be right back. I'm going to check on Chrissy. Don't go anywhere. I want to hear everything."

Dena rounds up Sarah, who has crawled around the table. With Sarah on her hip, she heads toward the den to see how

66

Chrissy is doing. "Everything is fine," she reports, as she returns. Gloria gets up from her seat to pick up Sarah's toys, and puts them back in front of her, placed on the floor once more by Dena.

"I'm so sorry, Mom. Thank you. I feel like such a bad mother sometimes." Gloria shakes her head dejectedly.

"Don't say that. You're a great mom. You do everything for those two. Right now, you need to focus on you." Dena's mouth is set with determination. "I will make sure they're all right. Don't you worry about that right now."

"I feel like I say I'm sorry a hundred times a day. Something is always my fault. I swear, he can make the weather into something that's my fault. I'm not kidding," Gloria says. "Seriously." Shaking her head in disbelief, she gives a chuckle. "Mom, I know it's ridiculous, but he can make the weather my fault."

"I believe you. I'm glad you felt like you could be honest with me. You know we are on your side, no matter what," Dena says, before emphasizing, "Maybe you should be a little more honest with your counselor. That's what he's there for. He's there to help you." Thinking for a moment, she adds, "If you need to get away, you should stay here with the girls until you get things figured out. You know you're welcome as long as you need to stay."

Relief flooding over Gloria, she begins to feel her muscles relax as she leans forward and rests her head on her mother's shoulder. "Oh, thank you, Mom. I didn't want to ask. Are you sure Dad would be okay with it?" Thinking quickly, she sits up and adds, "I know it wouldn't be good in the long term, but it might give me some time to regroup."

Dena looks at Gloria with a confident gleam in her eye. "We don't even need to ask Jack. He will definitely be okay with it."

Gloria straightens up and wipes at her eyes with a tissue.

Turning serious again, Dena says, "You know, we've always known something is not right between you two. We could tell he wasn't letting you see us, but we weren't going to stick our noses in your business." She reaches out with her forefinger and taps Gloria on the nose, and, with a sincere smile on her face, adds, "We've been waiting for you to confide in us, and now I'm glad you have."

Gloria knows she hasn't even begun to tell her mother what is actually going on. She decides she will broach the worst of it later. Checking her watch, she wipes at her face and announces, "It's already lunchtime, and after that it's naptime for the girls."

Sarah, having been rounded up by Dena several more times, is starting to fuss, and Gloria feels she can use a nap herself. She hates to waste her time napping when she could be with her mom, but all this emotional stuff is exhausting.

"Do you mind if I borrow the guest room after lunch?" she asks. "I was up late last night, and I really need some sleep."

"Of course not, go right ahead," Dena has a look on her face that relays, *As if you have to ask.* She reaches out to give Gloria a tight squeeze, before standing up and heading into the kitchen to prepare lunch. "You just wait here. I'll make sure everyone is fed."

"Thank you, Mom. Really, thank you so much."

After lunch, Gloria rocks Sarah to sleep in the old rocking chair Dena used to rock Gloria in when she was a baby. The sturdy white rocker with its paisley print cushion, sitting in the corner of the guest room, has rocked many a baby to sleep over the years. Slowly rocking back and forth, Gloria is comforted by this familiar piece of her history. Soon, Sarah is asleep, and she places her in her crib on the other side of the room, while she and Chrissy take the queen-sized bed in the middle.

She lies contentedly on top of a quilt her grandmother made out of her dad's old bowling shirts, visiting with Chrissy while Sarah naps. She dreams of the new lives the three of them might be able to forge for themselves. Before long, Chrissy has fallen asleep as well, with Gloria not far behind.

Gloria wakes a short while later, in a cold sweat. She had that dream again, the one where she is locked in a dark box, unable to move her arms or her legs. Even more frightening were the flashes of bright light and a man's shadow looming over her. As she recalls the dream, an ice-cold shiver runs through her body.

Her cheeks flare with embarrassment as she registers she has soaked her mother's bedding, along with her own clothes. She can't believe she had such a violent dream and neither of the girls were disturbed. She must have been crying out or thrashing around. How could she not have been? The dream was so vivid, so lifelike, leaving her with a feeling of familiarity, which is more disturbing than anything else.

With Chrissy still sleeping beside her and Sarah napping in her crib, Gloria quietly leaves the room. Dena is sitting on the cream-colored, tufted sofa in the den, working on one of her drawings, with a sketch pad and pencils spread out over the glass-top coffee table in front of her. She takes one look at Gloria as she walks in, and gasps. "What's wrong, Gloria? You look like you've seen a ghost."

How can she tell her mom she was dreaming about something happening in the future, but at the same time, she feels like it has already happened? She knows she would sound crazy.

"It's just a nightmare I've been having lately." Gloria tries to dismiss it as nothing.

"That must be quite a nightmare. Do you want to talk about it?" Dena's eyes are wide.

"No, I would rather forget it. I'll be okay." Gloria doesn't budge from the spot.

"Come sit on the couch. You look like you might pass out," Dena instructs, with more than a little concern in her voice. She pats the seat beside her, inviting Gloria to sit.

Gloria, not feeling she wants to be near anyone in her condition, says, "Mom, do you mind if I take a shower and borrow some clothes to wear home? I'm afraid I'm drenched from the dream, and I've soaked your sheets." She can feel her cheeks flushing bright red as she adds, "I promise it's only sweat, and none of us wet the bed."

"Don't worry about it." Dena's brow is furrowed. "I think you apologize way too much. You don't need to be sorry for everything."

"I know. I'm sorry," Gloria says again, before catching herself.

"Go to my closet and pick out whatever you think might fit, and feel free to take it." Dena points a pencil toward her bedroom. "And of course, go take a shower if it will make you feel better. You know you don't have to ask."

With a thank-you, Gloria heads off to her mother's room, emerging a short time later in a pair of gray sweats she found folded on a shelf in the master closet. They hang on her and she had to pin the waist, but she feels much better after her shower. She takes a seat by her mother. "Mom, I think I'm going to have to pick the right time to leave Charles. He's like a powder keg, ready to explode; I don't trust him. I want to make sure I do it the right way, at the right time, if that makes sense."

"Do whatever you need to do, in your own way. You know best." Dena seems confident in Gloria's ability to handle the situation.

70

"I'm going to have to make up an excuse for today. I'm sure he has tried to call home several times by now. He still hasn't given me my cell phone back from when I made him mad the night before last. I'm going to have to figure out something he will believe." Scrunching her brow and pursing her lips, she concentrates while trying to come up with a believable excuse.

After a long moment, Gloria says with disgust, "You know, Mom, I was just thinking . . . he has turned me into a liar. I am so ashamed that I have to lie all the time. I always thought of myself as an honest person. Mom, I'm not honest now. Not anymore."

Dena pulls Gloria's head to her shoulder. "You're doing what you have to do to survive. You're always doing what's best for those girls. Don't be ashamed." She gently strokes Gloria's hair.

"I will help you with this one," Dena says, seemingly unconcerned. "How about you say that you were at the doctor's office, and there was a long wait. After that, you had to go to the pharmacy. And, between all of that, you had to drop the girls off with me and pick them up."

Gloria sits up straight and looks into her mother's eyes. "Now he's made you a liar through me. It's awful, the power he has. I'm so sorry for putting you in the middle of this."

"Don't worry about it. I'm not. And, I think I'm a pretty honest person; he has no power over me. Soon he won't have any power over you either. Believe me, Gloria." This serves to bolster Gloria's confidence.

"I appreciate it, Mom. I think your idea might work."

"You're going to figure this out, honey." Dena gives Gloria a confident smile.

Contemplative for a moment, Gloria says, "I guess I'd better not push my luck. When the girls wake up, I should head home."

With her mom rubbing her back gently, she tries to relax and soak it up. There will be plenty of time to worry later. For now, she just wants to be a little girl again and allow her mother to comfort her. It's been so long since she's felt soothing hands on her body, and she feels about a hundred years old right now.

Dena breaks the lengthy silence. "There is no pressure from us to do things, one way or another. We'll be here for you whenever you need us."

"I could sit here like this forever, Mom. It's been so long since someone touching me has felt good, except for the girls of course. Every time Charles touches me, I want to run. If it weren't for the girls, I think I would run somewhere he would never find me."

"I understand. As it is, though, you have us, and you don't have to run." Dena continues to rub Gloria's back.

"Thanks, Mom." Gloria begins to calm and relax.

"It will be nice, not having to ask permission for everything. I have to ask his permission for anything I want to do, even taking a bath. I feel like a child. I've never been on my own or made my own rules. I long to be free, out from under his thumb. I just want peace." Gloria can feel her muscles begin to tense once more, thinking about his hold over her.

"You're tensing up again. I can feel it," Dena says.

"I know, Mom. That seems to be my default state, unfortunately."

Sitting in silence for a while, Gloria feels she is all talked out. There is so much more to tell, but that will have to wait for another time. For now, she has no more words.

When Gloria walks into her kitchen, dropping her keys on the counter, she cringes as she sees there are three messages left on the answering machine. She knows they are all likely from Charles. As she presses the play button on the machine, sitting next to the

72

phone on the kitchen counter, it beeps and gives the time, 11:35 a.m. She tenses as she hears Charles demanding, "I'm not sure where you are, but give me a call as soon as you get this."

She presses erase and then listens after another beep, to the time of 12:43. "Where are you, Gloria? Give me a call." Of course, it's Charles again. She presses erase. The last call was left at 2:19. It is now 3:30. "Well, since you don't seem to want to answer my calls, don't expect me home until late tonight. I'm going out after work with Ed." He sounds as if he is talking through gritted teeth. She begins to rub her temples, trying to ward off a headache that seems to be brewing. She takes some deep breaths, knowing that relaxing will be the only way to ward it off.

After Sarah is asleep and she has read *Horton Hears a Who* to Chrissy, Gloria cuddles up on the couch and loses herself in a book for a few hours. Looking up to see the clock, she groans as she registers the time: 10:45 p.m. It's not unusual for Charles to be out drinking at this time of night. When he's with Ed, there's no telling what hour he will come crawling in, but she wants to make sure she is asleep when he finally does come home. Hoping if she is, he won't bother her and will just fall into bed and pass out.

As she readies herself for bed, she grimaces at her reflection in the mirror. She doesn't look well. She has huge circles under her bloodshot eyes, which are puffy and pink from crying all day. Looking closer, she realizes she must be forgetting to eat again, due to all the stress. She had only felt like eating a couple of bites of her sandwich earlier, and hasn't had dinner. Her normally full face looks sunken and hollow. She thinks the worst of it must be from all the crying today. She falls into bed promising herself she will make an effort to eat tomorrow.

Gloria is startled awake a couple of hours later by Charles pawing at her. She can smell a combination of liquor mixed with

73

sour breath and body odor, a rancid combination that almost causes her to gag. The smell seems to ooze out of his pores. "Not tonight," Gloria pleads, as she begins to feel a familiar panic rise. Her protests go unheeded, as she tries to fight him off. It's no use. He's too strong, and too drunk to reason with.

Trying to calm herself, she begins to think of anything that might stop him. She tries kneeing him in the groin, but he has her legs pinned. He obviously feels her trying to kick, and she knows it has made him angry. She can feel the force of his anger, even in the dark, as he places his hands around her neck.

"Do you know how easy it would be for me to just press a little harder, Gloria? You are my wife, and this is my right," he says, spitting in her face. She cringes and turns away, trying to wipe at her face. She knows he's not used to her putting up such a fight, but she is determined to get out of this.

She wiggles, squirms, and claws at his face. He takes his hands from around her neck to tame her clawing fingers. He pins her arms above her head with one hand, and begins tearing at her gown with the other. He is going to have his way. She is just not strong enough. At this point, Gloria allows her mind to leave. She knows she does not want to be present for what is to come.

Retreating deep inside, she can hear his muffled voice. The sound is fading out, first fuzzy around the edges, until she is slowly enveloped in a fog. She can't feel her body anymore. She feels utterly detached as things go quiet and then finally everything completely disappears. The other Gloria is handling this tonight, and she will not have the memory.

The next thing she knows, she is waking the next morning with no memory of what happened the night before. She remembers a struggle, but not anything definite she can put her finger on. Her thoughts are hazy, and then there's just the utter blankness where a memory should be. She is just thankful that she is actually present this morning. The dissociation hadn't lasted long this time.

Looking into the mirror, she can see what looks like finger marks on her neck. She has bruises on her arms, and feels sore all over. *I must have put up a fight last night*, she thinks, but try as she might, she can't remember what happened. Not being able to remember chills her to the bone. Even though the memory would not be good, it leaves her feeling ungrounded, not being able to mentally latch onto something concrete. For Gloria, it's the unknown that terrifies her.

Chapter 7

July 2017

<u>Before</u>

Slowly, Gloria seemed to be gaining what felt like control over her life, when her peace was completely shattered one Saturday evening in July. Sarah and Gloria were watching *The Wedding Planner* on Netflix. She was enjoying being camped out on the couch with her teenage daughter, sharing a bowl of popcorn.

Startled, they heard what sounded like a car backfiring. At seemingly the same instant, something hit the wall beside the TV. Not thinking, Gloria jumped up to investigate, her mind not quite able to register what had just happened. Running her finger over a hole in the wall, realization finally hit. "It's a bullet . . . Sarah . . . call the police!"

Instantly, Sarah screamed and hit the floor. "Get down, Mom," she cried, her eyes pleading, as Gloria stood like a deer in headlights. Snapping out of it enough to recognize what Sarah was shouting, Gloria hit the floor alongside her daughter. Sarah, having crawled to her cell phone charging in the kitchen, began speaking to a 911 operator. Gloria, moving to crouch by the fireplace, near the kitchen door, could hear Sarah's end of the conversation.

"We've just been shot at!" she said, frantically. "Send the police."

She heard Sarah give their address and add, "Please, please hurry."

"No, no one is injured. Please hurry," she begged.

Sarah covered the mouthpiece and said breathlessly, "Mom, she said to stay on the phone until the police arrive."

Crawling to Sarah and taking the phone, Gloria identified herself to the operator. Sarah gladly relinquished phone duty.

"Did you see anything?" the operator asked.

"No, we had the curtains closed. The bullet just came through the window and hit the wall."

"Your daughter says no one is hurt. Is that right, ma'am?"

"That's right, but we're pretty shaken up," Gloria said breathlessly, her voice trembling.

"Just stay on the line with me, and the officers should be arriving at your door any time. Let me know when they arrive," explained the operator, in a measured tone.

"Okay." Gloria's shock was beginning to wear off as she began to shake violently.

Within minutes, there was a knock at the door. "Kern County Sheriffs," a male voice said gruffly from outside the door. Gloria and Sarah could see flashing blue and red lights reflecting through slits in the curtains.

"They're here," Gloria reported to the operator, as she motioned to Sarah to open the door. Sarah, seemingly unable to move, stayed crouching inside the kitchen door.

"Okay, they will take care of you. You can hang up now," Gloria heard before disconnecting.

Bending as she walked toward the door, Gloria hoped it would make her less of a target. She straightened up a bit as she opened it. She was greeted by a sheriff's deputy, who identified himself as Deputy Wells. He was a broad-shouldered man, clean-shaven, with short cropped dark hair; a reassuring figure standing at her front door. Glancing out past him, Gloria saw there were several police units arriving, reassuring her, and she finally stood up straight.

"Do you have any idea who might have done this?" Deputy Wells asked.

"I might," she said, pulling her pink bathrobe tighter around her body. "But I can't talk about it here," she added quietly, with a head gesture toward Sarah, who was presently crouching on the floor, near the fireplace. She sat clutching her knees to her chest, while looking up timidly.

Deputy Wells asked if there was a place where they might talk freely. Gloria invited him in, and led him to the kitchen. Sarah tried to follow, but Deputy Wells asked her to stay with his partner, Deputy Sanchez, a shorter man with a serious countenance.

Once in the kitchen, he asked again, "Who might have done this?" as he took a tablet and pencil from his shirt pocket, poised to take notes.

Gloria said, "I think it could be my estranged husband."

"Do you think he would do that, with your daughter inside?" Concern darkened Wells' features.

"Unfortunately, I do, and he was probably drunk." She began to shift from one foot to the other, seemingly unable to stay still.

"Do you have someone you can stay with tonight?" He looked up from his notepad.

"Um, yeah, I guess I could call my daughter," she mumbled.

"Excuse me?" Deputy Wells strained to hear.

"Oh, I'm sorry, I guess we could stay with my older daughter," Gloria said, louder this time.

"Does she live here in Bakersfield?" He looked at her, his pencil poised over his notepad.

"Yes. She does," Gloria replied.

"You might want to give her a call," he suggested, a kind expression replacing the concern on his broad face.

"We're canvassing the neighbors, to see if they might have seen anything, and we will be talking to your husband. I will need his information," he said, while scribbling a note on his notepad.

After giving Deputy Wells Charles's information, Gloria headed to the den, still devoid of furniture and with a few boxes still left to unpack. Deputy Sanchez had taken Sarah there, away from windows for safety. Gloria wrapped her arms around her shaking daughter, and tried to reassure her everything was going to be all right. While the deputies and technicians finished up, Deputy Wells suggested the two women pack a few things for the night.

"Where are we going?" Sarah asked.

"To Chrissy's." Gloria hugged her daughter as she relaxed back into her arms.

"Do you think you will be okay to drive?" Deputy Wells asked, with a note of concern.

"Yes" Gloria nodded. "I can drive."

"I will give you an escort then." He tucked his tablet back into his shirt pocket.

After arriving at Chrissy's apartment, Deputy Wells escorted them to the door. He filled Chrissy in on what had transpired that night, and urged them to call if there was any further incident.

"Oh my gosh," Chrissy said with a look of astonishment. She turned to Gloria and Sarah. "Are you going to be all right?"

"I'm not," Sarah said, frantically, eyes wide in disbelief. "Someone just tried to kill us."

Placing an arm around Sarah, who was beginning to shake and tear up, Chrissy led her inside. Turning back to her mom, she gently asked, "How are you doing?"

"I'm okay." Gloria waved dismissively. "I'm just very tired. I think we should both go to bed. We can talk in the morning."

Chrissy led Sarah to the spare room, which was bare except for a twin mattress made up on the floor. She pulled some sheets and a blanket out of the closet to make a bed on the couch for Gloria. As Chrissy tucked in the sheets, Gloria took her daughter's hand and a somber expression clouded her face. "Don't tell Sarah, but I'm sure your dad did this."

Chrissy did not look the least bit surprised. "I know. I was just thinking the same thing."

Making sure Sarah was able to fall asleep, Gloria shut the door and headed to her makeshift bed. Chrissy sat beside her for a while, worry etched on her face.

Gloria knew Chrissy had always wished she could protect her, even when she was small. Her eyes began to sting with tears, thinking of her little girl feeling helpless as her parents fought.

"Mom, are you sure you're going to be all right?" Chrissy's voice was thick with concern.

"Yeah, I'm just somewhat in shock right now." Gloria yawned.

"If you need to talk, I'm here for you." Chrissy patted her arm.

"Do you need to talk, Chrissy?" Gloria sensed her daughter bottling things up again, as she usually did.

"I'm just so angry with dad," Chrissy said. "I don't know how to let it go."

"Maybe you, Sarah, and I should go to counseling together as a family," Gloria suggested tentatively.

"I actually think that's a good idea. I know Sarah is going to be messed up from this, and I'm already messed up anyway."

"Are you able to talk to Alex about any of this?" Gloria was hopeful that Chrissy had a strong shoulder to lean on.

"Yeah, he's pretty open, but he hasn't been through anything like we have, so he doesn't understand. It's not that he doesn't try, because he does. It's just that you and Sarah are probably the only ones who can really relate to what I'm feeling." A lost expression seemed to cloud Chrissy's eyes for a split second, before it was gone. "Here I am talking about my problems, after what you two have been through. I'm going to shut up now."

Gloria wanted to encourage her daughter to keep talking. This was a rare opportunity, for her to hear what Chrissy was feeling. It was also helping to take her mind off what had happened that evening. "I don't want you to shut up," Gloria said. "You never talk about your feelings. Please know I'm always here for you."

"I know, but we're all tired." Chrissy pulled the covers up over Gloria's shoulders.

"Okay, but please remember I'm here," Gloria said.

"I will," Chrissy promised, as Gloria closed her eyes and quickly drifted off to sleep.

Gloria sat at the breakfast table the next morning with Chrissy and Sarah, all still in their pajamas. Alex had left for work before any of them had gotten up. They each sat with an empty bowl and spoon, passing a box of Rice Krispies around followed by a jug of milk.

After pouring milk over her cereal, Gloria announced, "I'm going home today. Sarah, if you feel safer here, you can stay."

"I definitely want to stay here, Mom. You should too," Sarah said, between bites of cereal.

"I'm not going to give into fear. I have to go home for my own reasons, but that doesn't mean you have to." Gloria reached out a hand across the table to Sarah.

"You should stay here, Mom. It's okay with us," Chrissy said. "Alex and I talked about it last night, and you and Sarah are welcome to stay here as long as you need to."

"Thanks honey, but I need to conquer this fear, and I think going home is the best way to do it. I've let fear rule my life for too long." Gloria looked resolutely into Chrissy's eyes.

"Well, I guess there's no talking you out of it." There was a hint of frustration in Chrissy's voice.

"Yeah, she's stubborn." Sarah shook her head, before spooning another bite of cereal into her mouth.

"I'll be leaving as soon as I finish my cereal." Gloria gave both of her daughters a decisive glance, before dipping into her bowl with her spoon.

Midmorning, as Gloria drove up to the house, she began to wonder if she had made a wise decision to return. She pulled into the driveway and quickly exited the car. She couldn't seem to get through her front door fast enough. Once she was in the door and the dead bolt was locked, she hurried to her room. She stayed there huddled on the bed for awhile before she figured out she was doing exactly what she had promised not to do: Cower. Forcing herself to get up, she walked slowly to the kitchen. Seeing dishes in the sink, she decided to try to act as if things were normal. She began cleaning the kitchen.

Chrissy stopped by in the afternoon to pick up some clothes and supplies for Sarah, who had been too frightened to come along, so she'd sent Chrissy with a long list of things she thought she absolutely needed.

Chrissy sat with Gloria on the edge of Sarah's full-sized bed, putting her arm over Gloria's shoulder. "I'm sorry this happened to you. I'll watch after Sarah for a while, so you can recuperate. I can

82

keep her as long as you need." She gave Gloria's shoulder a supportive squeeze.

"Thank you, honey. I'm glad she has a place to stay until she feels safe to come home." Gloria turned to give Chrissy a hug.

"I'm concerned about you," Gloria said, sitting back to look at her daughter. "How do you feel about all of this?"

"To be honest, I haven't had time to process it. I'm sure Dad might be capable of doing it, especially if he was drunk." Her head was down, her shoulders beginning to sag. "I don't even know how to feel about him. I know he never cared about Sarah or me."

"Oh honey, I'm sure he did . . . in his own way," Gloria said, trying to be reassuring.

Chrissy's head popped up. "Mom, when I was five years old, he told me he had never wanted me. That kind of sticks with you, you know." Chrissy looked at Gloria and began to cry, before burying her face in her hands.

Gloria felt as if someone had slapped her in the face. She pulled Chrissy toward her and held her tight. "I'm so sorry. I never knew, Chrissy. I can't believe it." She began to tear up along with her daughter, as she rocked her back and forth.

"I knew you wouldn't believe me. That's why I never said anything." Chrissy looked wide-eyed at Gloria.

"No, honey, no. That's not what I meant. I do believe you. I just can't understand how he could do such a horrible thing to you. I wish I had known." Gloria choked, trying to fight back her tears.

"Mom, I'm sorry to tell you, but there's a lot you don't know. You've protected us from so much over the years, but we've tried to protect you, too." Chrissy bowed her head, her blond hair hanging around her face. She began rubbing her hands on her jeans as tears spilled onto her Cal State–emblazoned T-shirt.

83

"I'm so sorry." Gloria reached reflexively and tucked Chrissy's hair back behind one ear. "I won't push you, but if you ever want to talk about it, I will be ready to listen." She wanted more than anything for Chrissy to open up. What did she not know? How bad was it? Telling a five-year-old child she wasn't wanted seemed about as bad as it could get. Then she wondered. .

Turning to face her daughter, Gloria's voice rose as she asked, "Chrissy, did he ever molest you?" She couldn't help but cringe in revulsion, hoping more than anything the answer would be, "No."

"No, Mom. Don't worry about that. It never happened. It was more psychological," she said, visibly shocked at the suggestion.

Gloria knew she shouldn't feel relief that her daughter had only been psychologically abused, and not physically abused. After all, the psychological stuff could sometimes be worse, couldn't it? How must Chrissy feel? What does it do to a girl, to be told she isn't wanted by her own father? Gloria needed to know the rest, but she was resigned not to push. She just held her daughter and cried with her.

"I'm sorry I couldn't protect you, Chrissy. I love you so much. My heart is breaking."

"I know, Mom. I love you, too. You've been my rock. Now I have Alex, and you can rest for a while. I will probably tell you things someday, when we are both in a better place." She wiped at her tears with the back of her hand.

"I'm here, no matter what place I'm at in my life. Please, please come to me if you need to talk," Gloria pleaded.

"I promise I will, Mom, but now I need to get Sarah's things together and head off to class before I'm late." She released Gloria and stood up from the bed.

Both wiping tears, they set to the task of gathering the obscene amount of things on Sarah's list. "I wonder how long she's planning to stay," Gloria said. "From this list, it looks like you might have her for a year." At that, they both agreed and laughed, still wiping tears from their faces.

"Don't worry, I'll send her home before she grows roots." Chrissy laughed.

Before Chrissy left, Gloria had one last request. "Could you help me move the TV from the living room to my bedroom?" For all her promises to the contrary, that's where she would end up hiding for the next week, only venturing out to the kitchen when necessary. Leaving the house was difficult for the first few days. Her senses on hyper alert at all times. Her head seemed to be on a swivel, always checking her surroundings.

She called again, to see if there were any updates on the case. It seemed to take forever for Deputy Wells to pick up his line.

"Hello Deputy Wells. This is Gloria Davis again. I'm sorry to keep bothering you, but it's been a while and I was wondering if there might be an update on the shooting."

"Unfortunately, Gloria, there isn't much to report. There were a couple of neighbors who witnessed a car speeding away, but neither was able to get a good enough look at the vehicle to describe it."

"As I told you, I spoke to your husband. He told me he was home all evening, but I felt the hood of his car and it was warm. He had obviously been out very recently. When I brought this up, he changed his story and said he'd gone out for some beer. I'm sorry, Gloria, but even though I highly suspect him, there was nothing I could do. He was in his own home, and there was no evidence."

"He doesn't even drink beer." Gloria slapped her forehead in exasperation.

"Like I said, he's probably guilty, but at this point there is nothing we can do. Hopefully, I might have scared him enough to stay away from your house and not try something like that again. We'll keep an eye on him."

She realized that was all he could do and thanked him before hanging up.

Sarah finally decided to return home after a week, but insisted on sleeping in Gloria's bed. They both watched TV in Gloria's bedroom during the evenings, propped up on pillows against her gray padded headboard. She tried to be strong and calm for Sarah, explaining away the incident as a random event.

"We're just playing it safe for a while," she told Sarah. "We will eventually put the TV back in the living room . . . when you're comfortable with it."

"It will probably be a long time before I'm comfortable with it. That was so terrifying, Mom."

Gloria knew what she had to do. She would have to confront Charles. This hiding and cowering had to stop. She would show up at his office if she had to, and in front of all his coworkers, she would accuse him of trying to shoot his daughter and her. She would confront him with the evidence the police had that pointed to his being guilty. He was so proud of his standing in the community; she would like to see how proud he was when everyone knew what he was capable of. She reasoned this would also put him on notice that if anything happened to her or the girls, he would be the prime suspect.

Chapter 8

March 2003

<u>After</u>

Charles went about getting ready for work Wednesday morning as if nothing had happened last night. He never mentions Gloria's visible bruises before leaving for work. It was all Gloria could do to make his breakfast and attempt to act as if nothing had happened.

As soon as 8:00 rolls around, she puts in a call to her counselor, Dr. Dyson. As she dials, she prays he will have a cancellation. The pressure of living under Charles's thumb, and fearing the things she can't remember, is beginning to make her feel as if she is losing her mind.

"Dr. Dyson's office. This is Camille," the receptionist answers Gloria's call on the second ring.

"Um, yes. Would Dr. Dyson happen to have any cancellations this week?" Gloria asks tentatively.

"As a matter of fact, I just had someone cancel a 2:00 appointment today. Would you like to take it?"

"Yes," Gloria says a little too enthusiastically.

"Okay then. We'll see you at 2:00," Camille says.

Promptly at 2:00, Dr. Dyson settles into his large navy blue wingback chair, sitting to one side of his massive oak desk. Tall and fit, with sandy, slightly tousled blond hair, kind brown eyes, and a handsome angular face, Dr. Dyson had made Gloria slightly unnerved when she first met him. She had thought she might have felt more comfortable spilling all her secrets to a kind, grandfatherly looking man. Today the doc is wearing a pinstriped, long-sleeved button-down shirt, his sleeves rolled up to his elbows, his top button undone, and dressed down with a pair of jeans. Casual clothes, to go with his casual manner.

His chair sits opposite Gloria's; she has just plunked herself down in the cozy, oversized floral print chair with two matching accent pillows. She picks up a pillow from one side and clutches it to her chest. She does this every session, feeling it gives her some kind of protection. Protection from what, she's not quite sure. Thankfully, so far he has not mentioned said pillow clutching. She knows it might veer the session off into why she feels the need to do it. She sits there, hoping she is not the only one of his clients with this habit.

She doesn't know how she remembered so easily that she had been seeing Dr. Dyson back in 2003. Her brain seems to have picked up on the time frame and taken over from there.

Even though she had felt a little off balance, before she knew it that first session, she was answering questions, carefully revealing only what was comfortable for her at the time. He never pushed, although she knew he could tell she was not divulging everything. He was surprisingly patient, allowing her to reveal things as she felt up to it. Yet, he had said one thing that first session that had really caught her off guard. After asking her about Charles, and what kind of husband he was, she had answered, "Perfect." She has no idea why she said it, but she meant it at the time.

He had replied flatly, "We will eventually have to work on that."

What does that mean? she'd wondered. At the time, she wasn't even being sarcastic. She actually thought everything wrong with her life, and her marriage, was her fault. Now, sitting here, with so much hindsight, she feels quite stupid.

She has no idea how long she has been sitting lost in her thoughts, when Dr. Dyson clears his throat and begins to speak.

Startled, she jumps. Seeing him leaning toward her, elbows on knees, she blinks frantically, before saying, "I'm sorry, could you repeat the question?"

He sits back in his chair. "I was asking how you've been doing, since our last visit. You cancelled two sessions since I saw you last," he adds. "I can see you were a little lost there. Can you tell me where you were just now?"

"Oh, I don't know," Gloria replies, somewhat confused. "Zoned out, I guess. I'm sorry. I do that a lot."

"It's okay, and it's normal. Everyone does it at times, but if you find you're doing it quite often, it could become a problem." She can see he has picked up his notepad off the desk beside him, and has begun to write a few notes.

Thinking over what he has just said for a second, she begins to say she's "just fine." This is what she is used to saying to the question of, "How are you?" But, catching herself, she shakes her head and decides to be honest with him.

"I'm doing terrible, actually." She looks down at the pillow her arms are wrapping. "I'm beginning to realize what an unhappy marriage I'm in. I'm feeling a bit panicked, because I'm realizing . . . I am going to have to leave him." As she says it, she looks up and expects to see shock on the doctor's face, but he doesn't even seem surprised.

A bit taken aback, she continues, after some contemplation: "I feel like the more I work on me, the more I am unable to visualize

89

myself staying in the marriage." She frowns as she looks down and notices a snag on the front of her black knit skirt; she has to resist the urge to start picking at it.

After glancing up, she tries to forget about the snag and continues: "I've made a list of what I think I need to do. Well, really, half a list, but I'm unsure when exactly to do it." She is back to the spot on her skirt, and forces herself to look up again. The doctor, with a neutral expression, is sitting back in his chair, and all she can think to say is, "Wow, I can't believe I just said all that."

She mumbles to herself, after it has all poured out.

"What was that last part?" he asks, leaning forward again.

Concentrating on his question, she admits, "Dr. Dyson, I have no idea what I just said."

"That's all right. I was wondering when you would feel safe enough to start opening up," he says reassuringly. "Why don't you tell me what's really been going on?"

She's not quite sure, but she thinks she might have just heard a little enthusiasm in his voice. She has to admit, the neutral tone was beginning to unnerve her.

Feeling somewhat relieved, she continues, clutching her pillow tighter and trying to look up at him. "I haven't told you this, but Charles doesn't know I've been coming here." She waits a moment, expecting to see a giveaway expression on his face. As usual, she can't read him, so she goes on: "He doesn't want me talking to anybody."

"I told him many times I felt like I needed counseling, and he has always refused to allow me to make an appointment. He says our lives are private, and I have it so good, I shouldn't need to see a shrink. Her voice trembles slightly: "If he knew I was here, he would explode."

"You know," he says, leaning toward her and speaking firmly, "these sessions are private. Unless I feel you are a danger to yourself, or to others, I can't reveal anything you say here, without your permission. You don't need to worry about that."

He doesn't seem upset about the fact that she is lying to Charles. And, he seems to support her coming to counseling behind Charles's back. Gloria is beginning to feel, maybe, she can trust him after all.

Relaxing back into her chair, she decides to place all her trust in this man. She begins to tell him everything. She tells him about checking out, after Charles forced himself on her the night before; how she knew something had happened because of the bruising. She rolls up the long sleeves of her ivory blouse to show him.

"I think I see a little on your neck, too." He leans forward for a better look. Gloria pulls self-consciously at her ruffled collar. "This is not okay. I hope you know that, Gloria. I don't mean the blacking out. I mean these bruises, and being forced. In fact, it's called rape."

His mouth is set in a straight line, and she is startled by his reaction, by his calm demeanor becoming quite serious.

"But he's my husband." She shuts her gaping mouth quickly when she becomes conscious of her expression.

"It doesn't matter," he says firmly, a serious look in his eyes. "What he's doing to you is never okay. You always have the right to say no."

Gloria sits for a few seconds staring off into space. The thought that it was okay to say no had never crossed her mind. Not that it would stop Charles. Even so, she begins to feel empowered by these words. She might not be physically able to fight him off, but she has the absolute right to say no. Why was she never told this, in all the years she was with Charles?

91

She cannot remember a time - past, or future - when this was mentioned. It could have made so much difference. The problem, she realizes, is she never told anyone about this part of her marriage. She never gave anyone the chance to relay this knowledge to her.

"We can revisit your blacking out when you feel more stable, but right now I think you might need it to cope with what's going on." Dr. Dyson becomes contemplative as he sits back, before picking up the notepad from the desk beside him and again jotting down notes.

"It just bothers me. I can't remember so many parts of my life. I don't remember the bad things that have happened, and I have lost many good memories as well. Why can't I bring myself back, after the bad stuff is over?" She sits, dumbfounded.

"Right now, your brain is trying to protect you. We can practice mindfulness at another time. This may help you to stay more in the present, and that might give you a bit more control over it," he says calmly as he begins scribbling again.

She contemplates this, and is hopeful. There seems to be so much work to be done with Dr. Dyson, and she decides to ask if she might see him more than once a week.

Looking up from his notes, he says, "Sure. We can do two sessions, if you would like. In fact, I would encourage it."

The session goes by in a blur, and when time's up, she is physically and emotionally wiped out. She stands slowly and says, "Thank you," as she begins to walk to the door.

"Sure, but before you leave," he begins. Gloria turns around, and he continues, "I want to make sure you are going to be safe. If you feel you and your girls are in danger, you must promise me you will get out."

"I will," she promises.

He sits looking into her eyes for a moment, seemingly contemplating whether he should trust her answer.

Finally, he says, "I'll see you at your next appointment. Be sure to stop and make one on your way out."

While driving home, Gloria decides to treat herself to a coffee. She stops at a quaint little coffee shop downtown she has driven by many times, but has never visited before. The shop is tucked in the middle shops on the bottom floor of a vintage four-story building. Gloria passes under the awning and in through the single-pane glass door, with trim painted bright red. There are colorful plush chairs scattered throughout, with high tables and stools intermingled. The smell of coffee is enticing. Once she has purchased her cup, she spies a red wingback chair by the window.

She settles in with her steaming cup and stares out the window, watching as people walk by. She reaches down and tugs at her skirt and smooths her blouse before leaning back and grasping her cup with both hands. She tries to imagine what their lives must be like—the people strolling by outside the window. When did she lose touch with the world, and with other people? It must have been shortly after she met Charles.

She recalls the day her father had introduced her to his new employee, at the Bakersfield office of Multi-National Oil Company, where Jack had worked as a geologist. Charles had just been hired as Jack's assistant.

Her father had recently been transferred to the Bakersfield office, from Dallas. He had started in his new position four months earlier. Being the new girl in town turned out to be difficult for Gloria. She had grown up on a ranch, outside of Dallas. It was a commute to the city for her dad, but he wasn't a city boy, and was determined to keep their rural life intact. She had horses, motorcycles to ride, and friends in the small school she attended.

Her life had been happy there. She was a complete and utter country girl, her preferred wardrobe jeans and T-shirts.

When Gloria first spied the San Joaquin Valley, as they descended from the Tehachapi Mountains, her heart had soared for a moment. "Dad, I thought you said there's hardly any rain here. Why is it so green?"

"Well," he said, "this valley is fed by the California Aqueduct. It's a huge man-made cement river that runs from Northern California to Los Angeles. This is actually one of the most fertile valleys in the world."

"Oh," Gloria said, fascinated by the sight. It looked green and rural, like her home in Texas. They passed orchards, vineyards, and an abundance of crops, as they drove on down into the flatlands, before reaching the city of Bakersfield.

But, after moving to Bakersfield, things didn't go smoothly. She was fifteen years old, with braces on her teeth, and was shy to boot. She had started Bakersfield High School as a sophomore, at the beginning of the school year. She found it difficult to make friends in a school much larger than the one she was used to. Being shy didn't help her efforts to fit in; after a couple of months, she just stopped trying. That was about the time she met Charles. She realizes now, he spotted her from a mile away.

Before she knew it, he was down on one knee proposing marriage. When she sputtered and didn't answer right away, he said, "I don't think I will have a reason to live if you say no."

She didn't know what to do, so she said, "I guess so." She wouldn't want him to do anything drastic. She reasoned she could just get out of it later, but later never came.

She finds her coffee half-empty and cold, when she snaps out of her reverie. It's getting late, and she had better head home. She will either face a very angry husband, or an answering machine full of irate messages, when she walks in the door. She hopes it will be the latter.

Chapter 9

October 2017

<u>Before</u>

Gloria began thinking she might not have to confront Charles at his office after all. Everything had been pretty quiet since Deputy Wells visited his door. She couldn't quite get the night of the shooting out of her mind, and Sarah was still skittish about going out. After the shooting she found herself constantly looking over her shoulder and she was sure it was Charles who'd fired that shot.

With Thanksgiving fast approaching, Gloria finally assembled the computer desk that had been laying in pieces in the corner of the den. Deciding she was going to be in a festive spirit for the holidays, she found herself surfing the Internet, trying to come up with ideas for inexpensive Christmas gifts.

As she was poking around the web, an annoying link popped up. She moved to clear it from her screen, but stopped short, as PerfectDate caught her eye. As she read further, she could see it was an advertisement for a dating site, for singles over thirty-five. She gave a little laugh at this, before getting rid of it and continuing to shop.

The next evening, it happened again. PerfectDate was sitting in front of her, tempting her to take a look. Gloria hadn't even thought of dating, but still, this seemed to plant a seed in her mind. It was coming up on a year since she had left Charles, and

Someone to talk to might actually be nice, she caught herself thinking. *Forty is not too old, is it?* she mused as she found herself staring at the screen for a few seconds longer. She took a deep breath, rolled her eyes, and found herself clicking on the link.

When the site loaded, she could see they were having a free trial offer. She would be able to check out and contact her matches right away. She was not so sure about the contacting part. *But, it would be interesting to see who's out there*, she thought, butterflies beginning to flutter in her belly.

After a while she found herself checking over her shoulder, waiting to be caught in her illicit activity by Sarah. When she looked. There she was. Sarah was standing right behind her causing her heart to skip a beat. "Don't do that," Gloria squeaked, trying to recover her voice and catch her breath.

Looking over Gloria's shoulder at the extensive profile she had been working on, Sarah reached out and shook her shoulder. "Mom, what the heck! You know those people are crazy on there!"

"I'm only going to look out of curiosity." Gloria knew she was being defensive, which made her look even more guilty. "I have to fill this whole thing out before I can look." She was just digging a deeper hole. She knew Sarah wouldn't drop this, so she caved in. "I know. You're right, honey." With a dramatic click of the mouse, she removed the site from the screen. A long lecture ensued for the next half-hour, from Sarah, about the dangers of meeting people online.

"Shouldn't I be the one giving this speech?" Gloria said as she strolled toward her bedroom.

"Obviously the daughter is wiser than the mother, in this case," Sarah admonished from behind her.

"Okay, I get it." Gloria stepped into her bedroom and shut the door behind her.

97

As she undressed, she decided that she was not going to give up yet. Her curiosity was too strong. She would make sure that Sarah was away the next time she went to the site. At least when she was thinking about PerfectDate, she wasn't thinking about Charles.

Friday morning, Sarah sat at the breakfast bar, picking at her scrambled eggs while Gloria stood washing dishes. "Can I stay at Cindy's tonight?" Gloria turned to see Sarah looking up from her plate.

"You're over there more than you're at home since we've moved." Gloria worried that Sarah might never be comfortable in their new place. "You'll have to invite her over sometime."

"She's my best friend, Mom. Of course we spend a lot of time together. I'll invite her over next time, I promise."

Gloria put dish she was rinsing down on the counter and gave in as usual. "Yeah, that's fine."

Sarah came around the bar with her dish. Scraping the leftover eggs into the trash can, she handed the plate to Gloria and gave her a big hug. "Thank you, Mom," she said, beaming, before heading off to her room to get ready for school.

Gloria found herself working through her lunch hour at the office. She sat typing at her computer terminal from the time she sat down at her desk, until after 5:00 had come and gone. She had been promoted to head of the accounting department a few years back. However, at the moment, she was the only one there. Her accounts receivable clerk, Keisha, had called in sick, and the accounts payable position was still unfilled after a month's vacancy. This had put all the work squarely on her shoulders. She had no time during the day to obsess about PerfectDate.

Sitting on the edge of her bed after a long day at work, she found herself taking another one of Charles's calls.

"Remember the old days, when we were so happy?" he slurred.

"Not really, Charles." She flopped back onto the bed in frustration.

"We were happy, weren't we?"

"No we weren't, Charles." She rolled her eyes. "Remember how I used to make you angry all the time?"

"It wasn't all the time. And besides, that was your fault. We could be so much better if you would just come back." He sounded pitiful, but Gloria had heard it all before.

"I need more time, Charles," she insisted.

"But don't you remember?" he said.

"This call is going nowhere, Charles. You need to sober up." She slapped her hand to her head, exasperated once more.

"I'm not drunk. You are always accusing me of being drunk. Well, I can handle my liquor."

"I'm hanging up now, Charles. This conversation is going nowhere." Pressing the end call button, she screamed in frustration under her breath before throwing the phone on the bed. She would have to calm down or there would be no sleeping for her that night.

Trying to get her mind off Charles after Sarah left for the weekend, Gloria pulled up PerfectDate and completed her profile. After her last conversation with Charles, she found herself more determined than ever. Hitting the *next* button, she was now able to scroll through profiles of men seeking women.

She was deep into her illicit activity when matches started popping up. *These are matches we have found for you*, it read, and below were three profiles. She reminded herself she would not be contacting anyone.

As she read through the matches, she had to admit they were interesting, but not "Mr. Right." Even so, it didn't take her long to fudge on her rules. She eventually decided she would not contact anyone unless he could possibly be, "Mr. Right." She doubted with this new rule, she would ever contact anyone at all, so basically, to her way of thinking, the rules had not changed.

It dawned on her that she was actually making rules for herself. Charles had made the rules for so long, and she began to feel empowered to be making her own. And, she could break them if she wanted. She could break her own rules. She could modify them, too. The freedom felt like a rush. Like a prisoner being paroled after so many years behind bars, her mind swam with possibilities for her new future.

She was jolted back to reality when she heard a loud knock on the door. She glanced at the time on her computer; it read 11:35. It could only be one person at this hour. Charles, and he was most likely drunk. With only a desk lamp and the computer dimly lighting the room, she thought she could pretend to be asleep. The rest of the house was dark.

As she ran to the front door and peeked through a slit in the curtains, she could see Charles illuminated by the street lamp. He was leaning with one hand on the door and knocking with the other. She held onto the knob and let out a breath she didn't know she was holding; she laid her head against the door, praying he would go away. The doorbell rang over and over, and he pounded continuously.

"I'm not answering the door," she finally said. "If you don't go home, I'm calling the police. You don't want to end up in jail. You might lose your job."

"You're not getting away with this," he said in a low growl against the door.

Peeking out again, she could see that, thankfully, he was leaving. Thinking quickly, Gloria hurried to her phone she left

100

charging on the kitchen counter and found herself dialing 911. She would report a drunk driver on Charles's route home. She hoped they might catch him before he reached his destination. There was a part of her that felt guilty for doing this, but she reasoned, *He could kill someone.*

Hanging up, her heart was racing. She headed back to turn off the computer, before falling into bed. She placed her phone on her nightstand. She still hadn't fallen asleep by 6:00 a.m., when she received a call. She knew who it would be, as she rolled over to grab her phone. Why was she picking it up? She couldn't seem to help herself. So many years of jumping to Charles's whims had taken a toll. She had terrible habits she needed to break.

"Hello," she said groggily.

"You have a call from an inmate at the Kern County Jail," an automated voice said. "Will you accept the call?"

She knew who it was. Charles had been arrested the night before. She couldn't help her curiosity, so she accepted.

Of course, he asked her to come bail him out. Feigning ignorance, she asked, "What are you in jail for?"

"They say I was driving drunk. I wasn't drunk," he insisted.

This was a worn-out record Gloria had heard thousands of times. No matter how much he had to drink, he would declare it had only been two, and he was never drunk.

"I don't have any money to bail you out, Charles. You will have to call Ed."

"I'll just call Chrissy, then," he said, defiantly.

Her mama-bear instincts kicked in at that moment, and with a sternness she had never heard in her voice before, she warned, "You better not. She doesn't have money to bail you out, either."

Furious now, she hung up the phone. *Hopefully*, she thought, *he might just get some jail time*. She was looking for any way to get him out of her life.

Things became eerily quiet after Charles's arrest. Gloria was so used to being on edge, she didn't quite know how to react to the sudden peace. She kept looking around, waiting for something to happen. Trying not to think about him, she found herself spending an evening on PerfectDate, after Sarah had gone to bed. Perusing profiles and matches passed the time and was a welcome break from thinking about when Charles might strike next. That it was forbidden fruit proved only to drive her on.

She had herself convinced it was all harmless fun to sneak a peek at PerfectDate profiles every evening. She was sure to wait until Sarah was fast asleep. It cut into her own sleep, but it really did take her mind off all the Charles crap.

After about three weeks, "He" popped up in her matches. His name was Richard Gaines, and his picture all but leaped off the screen. Gloria smiled, her heart seeming to skip a few beats. She could see from his profile picture he was ruggedly handsome, with dark brown hair graying a little at the temples, an olive complexion, broad face, brown eyes, and a salt-and-pepper beard cut closely to his face. His smile was huge and infectious.

Continuing to read his profile, she saw he was 44 years old, 6'1", divorced, and looking for . . . she couldn't believe what she saw: "Ms. Right." Then she saw the one downfall. He lived in Ontario, which happened to be two-and-a-half hours away from Bakersfield.

She continued to read that he loved travel, motorcycles, boating, water-skiing, Jeeping, hiking, skiing, and anything John Wayne. He was looking for a lifelong partner to share all these things with, as well as cuddling up on the couch with a good movie.

Is this guy real? Gloria thought, shaking her head. She had never done any of those things before, except the motorcycle and movies, but she was sure up for adventure. From the looks of it, life with him would be just that. Could she dare hope that he might be attracted to her? Could she dare hope he really could be a good guy?

Reading further, she saw they seemed to share the same values. It also appeared he liked blondes, which was a plus, and her medium build fit as well. She thought of how she had tried to keep in shape over the years but had filled out from the skinny girl she used to be. So it seemed, physically, she might be his type.

She had been told she had aged well and was often complimented. She never truly believed it, brushing the compliments aside while blushing self-consciously. Inside, she was still that shy, awkward teenage girl who had never really dated.

With trembling hands, she found herself writing:

Hello Richard,

I see PerfectDate has matched us. My name is Gloria, and I enjoyed reading your profile and seeing your amazing pictures. Oh dear, did I just sound a little too enthusiastic? Sorry about that. Anyway, it looks like we enjoy the same things. Please read my profile, and if you think we might be a match, I would love to hear from you.

Have a great evening,

Gloria

Not knowing the first thing about online dating, Gloria had no idea how she would come across. She sat debating whether to press send for a half-hour, reading over and over what she had written.

Finally, she figured, *what the heck*, closed her eyes, and made the keystroke that sent the message off.

Before she sat at her computer terminal at work the next morning, she looked at the two other desks in the back office, which were still vacant. With a sigh, she sat down. It looked like it would be just her again today. Before she began her work, though, she took a moment to take in a deep breath. She couldn't help but wonder if she would have a reply in her inbox on PerfectDate that evening when she logged on. She admonished herself, thinking, *for all I know, he could be an ax murderer*. But, alas, it did no good. She was smitten and hoping against the odds that something good might come out of this.

Gloria felt guilty as she spent time with Sarah that evening. She was only half paying attention as Sarah discussed her day and filled her in on who said what and about whom. The TV was muted as they sat on the couch and she tried to keep up, but she needn't have worried; Sarah was on a roll. All Gloria had to do was nod and say uh-huh here and there, and Sarah filled in the rest.

Peeking into Sarah's room for a second time later that evening, Gloria finally found her asleep. She practically skipped to the computer, to boot it up. The wait seemed interminable until she finally saw she had one message. Feeling the butterflies begin to flutter in her stomach once more, she opened it.

Thankfully, the message was from Richard:

Gloria,

Thank you for your flattering response to my profile. I have read your profile, and I must say you look gorgeous in your picture. You should post more. You sound quite interesting, and we seem to share a few things in common. I am tempted to ask you for your phone number, but I know it's probably not something you would give out on this forum. If you would like to talk, though, my number is (760) 555-0574. I understand if you would rather message me, but I would certainly like to hear from you again.

Regards,

Rick

Gloria was on cloud nine, flush from his compliments. She pondered whether she should really call him so soon, but her gut was urging her on. She reasoned that it would be easier for them to get to know each other over the phone, but not wanting to seem too eager, she sent a note back instead of picking up the phone.

Rick,

I would probably be able to call you after 10:00 tomorrow night, if that works for you.

Have a great evening,

Gloria

She received a response almost immediately.

Gloria,

Sounds great! Talk to you then.

Rick

Gloria found Keisha sitting at her desk when she walked in the next day. "How are you feeling," she asked, a relieved smile on her face.

Keisha slowly shook her long black braids. "Not great, but I'm here."

"I'm glad to see you, but go home if you're not feeling well." Gloria could now see Keisha was struggling, still not recovered from the flu that had put her in bed for the past few days.

"No," she said. "I want to try and do this today. I've never been able just to lie around. It drives me crazy. I might cut out early, though, if that's okay."

"Sure." Gloria smiled sympathetically. "Just do whatever you feel up to today. I hate that you're still feeling so poorly, but I have to say, I'm glad to see you."

Keisha smiled back before turning to her work and diving right in.

Gloria crawled into bed that evening at 10:00 p.m. sharp. Plumping her pillows and propping them up against the headboard, she settled in comfortably. As she began to dial on her iPhone, her stomach started doing flip-flops. Luckily for her stomach, Rick answered on the second ring. This gave Gloria hope that he might have been as excited as she was, sitting by his phone, waiting for her call.

"Rick?" Gloria asked tentatively.

"Yes," he replied, in an amazingly smooth, deep voice.

"This is Gloria."

"It's good to hear your voice," he said.

For the next hour, they talked easily, and when he explained he was a computer network engineer, with his own company, Gloria laughed.

"I'm sorry." She tried to recover. "I would have never pegged you as a computer nerd."

"I get that all the time." He laughed. "Don't apologize. By the way, you have a cute laugh."

Gloria was sure he must have been able to see her blushing through the phone line. This annoying habit of hers drove her crazy. She would turn beet red at the smallest things. She couldn't imagine what she must look like when she was really blushing; probably like a tomato, with long blond hair. The crazy picture this elicited in her head caused her to laugh even harder.

"What's so funny?" He sounded concerned. "Did I say something?"

"No." Gloria choked and coughed as she tried to recover. "I was just picturing something in my head. I must sound crazy." she said. "I'm sorry. I'll stop now. I must be exhausted. I'm giddy."

"Please share," he said. "I could sure use a laugh."

After taking a moment to compose herself, she described the blond-headed tomato to him - and he busted up. "I bet you didn't know you would be talking to a tomato tonight." Gloria barely got it out before laughing again.

"Okay," Gloria said, after clearing her throat. "We can talk about something serious now."

"Okay, if you say so." He chuckled.

"Your profile says you have a daughter." Gloria cleared her throat and deliberately changed the subject.

He explained that he did indeed have a daughter, Megan, who was ten years old. Gloria could tell he was a proud daddy. He talked about taking her boating in the summers and skiing in the winters. He explained he had been divorced for seven years and had split custody, having Megan every other week.

"It sounds like you and Megan have a lot of fun together." Gloria smiled at the thought.

"We do, for sure," he agreed.

Informing him that she had two daughters, one still at home, she remarked, "My girls would have loved to have had such adventure growing up. It sounds amazing. We've never even been on a boat or skiing."

"It sounds like something we're going to have to remedy," he said, jovially.

"Really? That would be great. I've always wanted to ride on a Harley too," she admitted. "I see you have one. I grew up on dirt bikes, but I've never ridden on a street bike. I love adventure, but I'm afraid I haven't had much of it in my life."

She explained how she had been married when she was seventeen, and the only trips they had taken were to visit relatives. She added: "Well, we did spend days in Morro Bay and Pismo Beach. I wouldn't count those as trips, even though I do love the ocean. Your life sounds adventurous."

"That's my middle name. Wow, you were married young," he added as if it just hit him.

"Yeah, I wouldn't recommend it," she said, trying not to let her thoughts drift to Charles.

"I know this is probably way too soon, but would you consider meeting in person? I was thinking, maybe after the first of the year. That would give us time to get to know each other a little more, over the phone," he said, before adding, "Please feel free to turn me down. I know it's out of the blue."

"Actually, I would like that, but my daughter will flip out. She's warned me about this internet dating thing, and I'm sure she's right, but I just have a good feeling about you. I do think we should talk more first, before meeting." She hoped she was sounding reasonable.

"That's great, and I agree. Sorry if I'm being too pushy," he said. "I don't mean to be, but I seem to be coming off that way, unfortunately."

"No worries, I think I understand. I'm anxious to meet you as well." She couldn't help smiling.

"We will have to set a date later." He sounded tired.

Neither wanted to hang up, but they both had to work in the morning, so they reluctantly said goodbye. Afterward, Gloria was beaming. They hit it off amazingly well, she was sure.

She lay awake for hours that night, eyes wide looking up at the ceiling in the dark. This seemed to be her MO lately . . . not sleeping. Then the thought hit her: *How am I going to explain this to Sarah? She has always been too mature for her britches. Now I'm lying here worried about getting in trouble with my daughter.* As Gloria thought about it, though, she realized she was probably acting like an impulsive adolescent herself. Her emotions had taken over, and her brain seemed to be in neutral.

She began to rationalize. *If we do meet, I will be sure it's in a public place. I will travel in my own car and take all the precautions I've researched on the Internet.* Hopefully, this would placate Sarah. *No,* she thought, *this is going to be a serious battle.*

She would definitely not let on about her plans, until closer to their meeting time. They hadn't even set a firm date yet, so she was probably getting ahead of herself. On the other hand, Chrissy would definitely be excited for her. She had always been the wild child, and now Gloria seemed to be taking lessons from her.

Remembering she hadn't shut down the computer, she hopped out of bed. If Sarah were to see what she had been up to that night, things would not go well. While shutting it down, Gloria spied a message in her inbox. It was from Rick, wishing her a good night, and saying he had enjoyed their conversation. Her heart fluttered in her chest. Flushed, she typed a quick reply;

Rick,

I really enjoyed our conversation, too. Have a great day tomorrow.

Chapter 10

March 2003

<u>After</u>

As Gloria pushes through the heavy glass doors of the Bradford Agency Thursday morning, she approaches the granite-topped reception counter to greet Samantha. It's her first day at work after feigning sickness.

She tries to stifle a chuckle as she sees Samantha looking just as she remembers from so long ago. In her early forties, Samantha's long chestnut hair is permed, with voluminous bangs, and is half-piled on top of her head. Her sunny yellow blouse, sporting shoulder pads, is tucked into a black pencil skirt. Samantha is quite the flamboyant character, with a fondness for anything eighties.

"How are you doing?" Samantha flings her arms around Gloria.

"I'm a lot better," Gloria says, giving Samantha a hug.

"You look really tired," Samantha says, stepping back to take a look.

"Yeah, that's pretty much how I feel." Gloria gives her a half-smile.

The commotion at the front of the office has drawn everyone out to the entrance of their cubicles, and they all seem to be standing and waiting for Gloria to come by and say hi on her way to the back office. As Gloria moves on, she greets everyone with a

110

hug at their station. It was such a rare occasion, her being out sick. They are all fawning over her, making her feel guilty for her lie.

When she nears the entrance to the back office, she can hear the hum of the computer tower and the clicking of keys on Mickey's keyboard. As she rounds the corner into the office, Gloria announces herself, trying not to startle her supervisor. Heading toward Mickey's desk in the far corner, Gloria reaches down to give Mickey a hug as she swivels around in her chair.

They are all acting as if she has been gone for a year, instead of just a couple of days. But, that's the way it is at the office. Everyone is family here, and Gloria has always been happy about that.

"So glad to have you back," Mickey says, giving her a hug and a pat on the back. "I'm not used to you being away from work. I missed you, girl."

"I know what you mean. I'm not used to being away, either. I miss the place when I'm gone," Gloria says, as she moves over to her desk in the opposite corner of the office.

As Gloria takes a seat, Mickey asks, "Are you sure you're feeling better? You look a little peaked, still."

"Yeah, I'm okay. I just need to take better care of myself." Gloria manages a tired smile.

"I hear you," Mickey says. "You probably ran yourself into the ground, taking care of Charles and the girls. You need to make time for yourself."

"If only I could figure out how." Gloria smiles halfheartedly. "But, right now I probably need to get to work. I see I have quite a pile on my desk to catch up on."

Mickey chuckles and returns to her keyboard as Gloria settles in and puts the letter opener to use on the stack of mail currently sitting in front of her. She looks over at Mickey and smiles, an

111

envelope in one hand and the opener in the other. Steady, reliable Mickey is such a comfort and has always been there for her. With her hair pulled back in a ponytail and wearing jeans, Mickey, Gloria knows, will be going home directly after work, as she does every day, to train her horses.

Gloria places the envelope and opener on her desk and makes a quick decision to confide in her friend. "Mickey."

"Yeah." Mickey turns to look at her, fingers still perched on her keyboard.

"I've decided to leave Charles," Gloria blurts out.

She can see the corners of Mickey's mouth begin to turn down. "Wow. You've never mentioned you were having trouble."

Gloria can tell Mickey is a little hurt, probably because she never confided in her about her marriage, and now here she is saying she's leaving. "I'm sorry, Mickey. I know I should have said something to you, but honestly, I didn't even tell my parents until yesterday. I guess I just always hoped things would get better." A tight smile curves her lips, as it finally dawns on Gloria—she had friends and family in her corner all along, if only she had let them in.

She figures she might as well continue since she seems to be on a roll. Mickey has turned and rolled her chair closer to her, and Gloria can tell she now has her full attention. "I'm going to need to take some time off. I will need to pack and move while he's at work. I'm sorry. I know I've just taken sick time, but this is something I need to do sooner rather than later." Gloria is trying to get it all out before she changes her mind.

"Turn around and go home now." Mickey points to the door. "We'll manage here."

"I'm not quite ready yet, and I do want to catch up with some of this work first, but I think I'll be ready next week," Gloria says. "But thank you, your support means more than you know."

"Whenever it is, just let me know. You can take time whenever you need," Mickey says.

"It's good to be back." Gloria's smile grows wider as she looks into Mickey's eyes.

The day at work flies by and, during the evening, Gloria finds Charles in a decent mood. So far, she has not upset him; her goal is to keep it that way. After her ten-minute bath, she joins him to watch *Whose Line Is It Anyway* on TV. Thankfully, he is engrossed in the show, and she actually enjoys the silliness as they laugh along to the cast's corny antics.

A few minutes into the show, he says, "Be ready at 5:15 tomorrow, for Tavern," his eyes still glued to the TV.

That's right, she thinks. Friday nights are their date nights at Tavern by The Green. She enjoys the view from the second-story dining room overlooking the golf course, but it's way overpriced, and when the dining room shuts down, they always move on to the bar. Friday nights were always long and tedious. After about four hours of him drinking wine and her drinking Diet Coke, she was always ready to pull her hair out.

She feels like running away before tomorrow. Instead, she says, "Okay, I'll be ready.

They arrive at the Tavern a little later than usual Friday evening, and Gloria finds herself in a pretty testy mood. No telling how this is going to go over. She orders her usual bowl of clam chowder, while he orders the prime rib with crisp green beans, a baked potato, and his first glass of wine. Gloria glares at the glass, knowing she isn't going to be able to contain her anger tonight. This new Gloria doesn't seem able to keep her emotions in check

113

like the old Gloria did. She remembers how she used to hold her anger in so well until the only feeling she had left was numbness.

Rick, ever patient with her, taught her to feel her anger again. She has been plenty angry with him, and the world didn't fall apart. They always made up quickly. But that was another life. She must keep her mind on the here and now.

Gloria sits closed mouthed through dinner while he consumes four glasses of wine. He decides to go ahead and move into the bar early. There's a singer he apparently likes performing. Go figure: She's blond, and wearing a skin-tight, very short black dress with plenty of cleavage showing. As soon as they sit down, Kasandra steps down from the small stage on the other side of the room. She comes directly over to put a hand on Charles's shoulder, asking if he would like to make a request, and, by the way, "I don't think I've met your wife."

Charles introduces them. Gloria certainly isn't pleasant, and Kasandra just smirks, rubbing Charles's back before stepping back on stage, picking up her guitar and singing his request. *This is going to be a lovely night*, Gloria thinks. She's not jealous. She just doesn't like women like Kasandra. She couldn't care less about her fondling Charles, but she knows Kasandra must do this with other women's spouses, and it raises her ire.

Charles is up and down all night, putting tips in Kasandra's jar and requesting songs. He must know her pretty well and seems familiar with her repertoire. Gloria knows he probably follows her around like a puppy, wherever she's performing during the week. It irks her that so much money is going into Kasandra's jar, yet she and the girls have to live on a ridiculous budget. What really gets her blood boiling is part of that money is money she earned.

114

After two hours, she has had enough and announces she is leaving. Charles stares at her, seemingly stunned. "What do you mean leaving?" he says, wide-eyed.

Gloria shocks herself by standing up and saying, "I'm calling a cab, and I'm leaving."

"The hell you are," he says, a little louder than she would have liked. Everyone is looking their way.

"Keep your voice down." She looks around nervously. "People are staring."

"I don't care," he slurs. "You are my wife, and you will stay as long as I do."

Kasandra just smiles down at them from the stage, and Gloria has the feeling if she stays any longer, she will have to strangle her.

"I'm exhausted, and I need to go home. You can take me if you like, or I can call a cab." Gloria continues to stand.

He grabs her wrist and squeezes. She yelps. Thankfully, as people turn to look, he lets go.

"Have a seat," he says through gritted teeth, but she stands defiantly. She doesn't care if she's making a scene.

She turns quickly before he can grab her again, and walks toward the phone in the lobby. He is right on her heels. He grabs her shoulder and swings her around. "You will come back in the bar with me, or you'll be very sorry."

There are no people in the lobby to back her up, and she's not quite sure what to do. He has never seen her like this before, and she's afraid it might push him over the edge.

"Okay, okay." She puts her hands up in surrender. "Just let me go to the restroom, and I'll be back in."

Thankfully, he releases his grip as she heads toward the restroom. She is sure he will be hanging outside the door when she is through. She's hoping if she stays long enough, he will go back into the bar and wait. Surely he'll want a drink, and he'll have to go back into the bar to get it. Sitting on the lid of the toilet in one of the three stalls, she stares at the glossy wooden stall door, determined to wait him out.

She can't believe she is doing this after the knife incident, but she can't seem to help herself. She has herself convinced that Charles just wanted to scare her. He wouldn't actually kill her. She tries to reassure herself that this is going to be one of those nights where he blacks out and doesn't remember anything by the next morning. After all, she has lost count of the drinks he's consumed.

Fifteen minutes later, she looks at her watch and decides to exit the stall. She washes her hands, and pulls some paper towels out of the dispenser to dry, before throwing them in the trash. Tentatively, she pushes the door open, afraid of what she will find on the other side. To her surprise, he's not there. Now all she has to do is make it to the payphone, and then get out the door before he comes back.

Hopping on one foot at a time, she removes her heels before sprinting to the phone hanging on the far wall. She fumbles with the phone book on the shelf below. He still hasn't returned her cell phone, and she hasn't dared to ask for it. It seems to take forever to find the number. When there is finally an answer, she asks how long it will take for a cab to arrive.

"Twenty-five minutes, ma'am," the man says.

Thinking quickly, she says, "Meet me at the Chevron station, on Ming." She will not wait around in the Tavern parking lot, and the gas station is only a few blocks away.

"Okay, ma'am," she hears the man say, before she hangs up.

Keeping an eye on the door to the bar, she hurries past it to the exit, praying Charles doesn't see. Soon she is down the stairs, and she quickens her pace toward the gas station with her shoes in hand.

She decides she probably should stay with her parents tonight and let Charles sober up. He is going to be livid when he discovers her missing. She doesn't even want to think of what his reaction might be when he finds she is not home.

She hands the cabbie a twenty and tells him to keep the change. She is in front of her parents' house. She strides to the door and uses her key to let herself in. Picking up pen and note pad sitting on the counter, she begins a note to let her parents know she is there. When she finishes, she heads to the guest room. As she switches on the light, she can see Sarah is fast asleep in her crib, and Chrissy is sprawled across the queen-sized bed. She shrugs off her dress and places it over the back of the rocking chair. Sitting on the old cedar chest at the foot of the bed, she removes her shoes and stockings, torn from her sprint to the gas station. Leaving on her slip, she turns off the light and gently moves Chrissy so she can crawl in on her side of the bed.

Saturday morning, Gloria is awake early. A large part of her is disappointed to keep waking up in 2003. The other part is happy when she sees Chrissy and Sarah, her heart simultaneously aching and glad. Her feelings seem to be on a perpetual roller coaster.

She wishes Rick could be her knight in shining armor today. Even though most of the future is fading, everything about him seems to remain crystal clear. If it weren't for Rick, she is sure her future would cease to exist. It seems a double-edged sword. If she would just let go and let it fade away, she could pour all her energy into now. She wouldn't be disappointed every morning when she wakes up. She wouldn't have the guilt over being disappointed.

She does want a do-over with her girls. She yearns to make a better life for them. If she would just forget Rick, she could do it. If she would only take a foot out of the future and put them both into now, she could do it, but her heart won't let go.

Saturday morning, she slips on her dress from last night, quietly steps out of the room and makes her way to the kitchen. She can smell the coffee already brewing. Dena, in her pink silk pajama set, is seated at the dining room table, nursing her first cup. Gloria grabs her green mug and soon joins her on the same side of the table, facing the built-in china hutch. It looks like her mom has just read her note.

"Well, fancy seeing you here this morning," Dena says, smiling brightly.

"Yeah, things went a little sideways last night." Gloria shrugs and slowly stirs her coffee. "He was so drunk, I decided to call a cab. He wasn't too happy about it, to say the least. I'm hoping he doesn't remember it when he wakes up today." Looking up, she lets out a long sigh. "Anyway, I'm hoping not to walk into a minefield this morning."

She can see the worry in her mother's eyes. "I can't believe you hid this for all these years." Dena places a supportive hand on Gloria's arm.

"I guess I'm a pretty good actress. I'm really sorry for all the deception. I didn't want to cause you grief." Gloria looks down and stirs her coffee again, absentmindedly.

"Does he drink like that often?" Dena is unable to mask the concern in her voice.

"Yeah, pretty often. It seems to be more and more, as time goes on." Gloria has decided not to try and sugarcoat it this morning.

"I can see your reasons for leaving, in a clearer light now," Dena says, as the crease between her brows becomes more prominent.

Gloria shrugs and grimaces, before confessing, "I think I might have stepped in it last night. I've never stood up to him like that before. I just hope he doesn't remember what happened." Attempting a hopeful smile, she continues, "Thankfully, sometimes he completely blacks out and has no memory of the night before. I'm hoping that will be the case this time."

"You can always stay here," Dena almost pleads.

Laying her spoon on a napkin and grasping her mug with both hands, Gloria turns to her mom. "I was thinking, if I go home now, he might still be asleep. I'm sure he tied on a good one last night after I left. Maybe, if I'm there when he wakes up, he might not even know anything happened," then she quickly adds, "I could leave the girls here, if that's okay."

Dena seems disturbed, but if she thinks Gloria is making a mistake, she doesn't say so. "Yes," she agrees, "the girls should probably stay here."

"I'm going to go ahead and leave after I finish my coffee. I don't want to be wearing this dress when he wakes up. I'll have to change." Gloria looks down at the navy blue A-line she wore last night.

Returning home, Gloria slips quietly into their bedroom. She finds Charles lying crossways on top of the covers, with his feet hanging off the side of the bed. He is still in last night's clothes. His shoes have been thrown off on the floor, and his suit jacket is crumpled in a heap beside him on the bed.

She sneaks slowly by and heads to the closet. After pulling off her dress, she picks out a pair of jeans and an emerald tank top. As she is pulling the top over her head, she hears Charles breathing behind her. She freezes before pulling the top down slowly and turning around to face him. He is standing in the middle of the doorway to the closet, looking disheveled—so unlike him. He stinks of alcohol.

"So you finally decide to come home." He is seething.

"Ch....Charles, you scared me," Gloria stutters. Then for some inexplicable reason, she lets out a nervous laugh.

"Oh, so you think this is funny, do you, Gloria? How dare you humiliate me, leaving me at the bar like that?"

She can't bear to look at him, so she looks down at her feet. "No, Charles. I don't think it's funny. I'm just nervous."

She's trapped with his form filling the doorway. For some inexplicable reason, she takes a step forward and quickly kicks out, grazing him between his legs. It wasn't a solid hit, but it seems to have done the trick. As he drops to his knees, moaning, she leaps over him.

She hears herself cry out as he reaches out and grabs her right ankle. Crashing to the floor, she lands on her side behind him, her head bouncing off the carpeted floor. He is still holding onto her ankle as his moan turns into a growl. "I can't believe you just did that. Don't you know better than that by now, Gloria?"

"Yeah, well I hope you can't pee for a month." She slaps a hand over her mouth, wishing she could take it back.

She knows she has to follow through now. What had she been thinking? Fighting back only ever makes things worse in the end. She quickly turns onto her stomach and kicks him in the back with her left foot, causing him to release her ankle, sending him toppling over into the closet. As he lets out a roar, she quickly pushes herself up to standing and then stops as her head begins to swim. The blow to her head must have been harder than she thought.

She turns to see his swimming form crumpled in the closet, and she knows she must get out of here. She takes a step toward

120

the bedroom door and then another as the room spins around her. She stumbles into the wall, holding herself upright. Feeling her way along the wall, she reaches the doorway to the hall. As she steps out into the hall, a crushing hand grabs her arm from behind. She can hear his heavy breathing in her ear as he limps in front of her and pulls her along the hall.

He doesn't say a word, as he drags her toward the hall bathroom. She stumbles along the way, trying to get her bearings. She knows she can't escape from his iron grip. When they make it to the toilet, he says, in a low guttural tone, "Get down on your knees."

It's no use fighting. When he's enraged, he seems to have superhuman strength. Her head is still swimming, and she knows there is no way she will be able to get away from him. She obeys and slowly drops to her knees as he lets go of her arm. "Now, turn around," he orders.

She scoots herself around on her knees as he commands her to lift the lid. She reaches out a trembling hand and does as he says. He grabs a handful of her hair at the nape of her neck and shoves her head down, pulling her knees off the floor. Her face is only an inch from the water now.

"You will never, ever do that again," he warns. "Now if you know what's good for you, you won't move. Your face is going into that water. I will hold you down there as long as I like. You may still be breathing when you come up, or you may not. Who knows?"

With a sudden shove, her head hits the porcelain as her face goes under the water. She closes her eyes and holds her breath as her ears start to ring. She begins to chant in her head, "*I will stay present. I will stay present. I have to stay present.*"

He shoves harder, and she begins to see shooting stars behind her eyelids. He is silent as he holds her under, but she can feel the rage radiating through him. She dare not struggle. Her lungs are beginning to feel like they will explode, and she prays he will let her up soon. The need to take a breath is becoming overwhelming. Her will seems to leave her body, the chanting leaves her head. No matter how hard she has tried to stay present, everything begins to fade.

Gloria wakes to the alarm. She looks at the illuminated red numbers on the digital clock on her nightstand, displaying the date and time. She sees that it's Monday morning. She's lost two whole days, she thinks as she slaps her hands over her face in frustration. This time she remembers why it happened. The humiliation of it all begins to burn hot on her face. She had stayed present long enough to know, which should be a victory. But, she can't help but be disgusted with herself for letting go.

As she tries to swallow, her throat feels raw. She lets out a cough which makes the pain worse, radiating all the way to her lungs. She knows she must have swallowed water Saturday morning when he held her head under. She grimaces and reflexively gags thinking about it. How long had he held her under? She has the sudden realization, she is probably lucky to be alive.

At work that morning, Gloria can barely speak through her sore throat as she asks Mickey for two days off. She is too humiliated to tell Mickey why her throat is so raw, and Mickey seems to buy her story of having a slight cold.

She knows she must have these two days off. She can't see herself staying in that house with Charles any longer. After what happened, she knows things are escalating. She cannot be with Charles and remain present. Being herself seems to anger him even more. The Other Gloria knows how to handle him. She can't seem to keep her mouth shut and take it anymore.

She will go home tonight and behave herself. Tomorrow, she'll start packing. Two days should be enough, and hopefully, she'll be out by Wednesday evening. Only two more evenings with Charles. Surely she can make it two days without setting him off.

Chapter 11

December 2017

<u>Before</u>

Gloria was having a wonderful Christmas morning with Sarah, their first on their own. She couldn't believe how much she had enjoyed the company of her teenage daughter during the past few months. Chrissy and Alex had arrived in the afternoon to share in a large Christmas dinner. Gloria had always gone all out for the Christmas meal. She had prepared turkey, dressing, mashed potatoes, a green bean casserole, and pumpkin pie. She would be sending lots of leftovers home with Chrissy and Alex when they left.

That evening, after Sarah was asleep and Chrissy and Alex had gone home, Gloria made her nightly call to Rick.

"Hello Gloria," he answered brightly.

"From the tone of your voice, it sounds like you must have had a good Christmas," Gloria said.

"Back at ya. You sound pretty chipper yourself," Rick said. "So, how was your Christmas?"

"It was great. Chrissy and Alex came over for Christmas dinner. As usual, I made way too much food, and they had to take a lot of it home." She laughed.

"Wish you could send some our way. Megan and I had pizza." He sounded sheepish.

"What? You had pizza for Christmas dinner?" Gloria teased.

"I know. I know. But it's my specialty." He laughed.

"So you and Megan had a good Christmas together."

"Oh, yeah, we had a great day. She got some new skis and boots. She was thrilled. We're going to hit the slopes tomorrow." He yawned.

"Sounds like I had better let you get your rest tonight. I wouldn't want to ruin your big day." Gloria began to yawn herself.

"Well, Megan did keep me up pretty late last night. She was so excited about Christmas, she couldn't fall asleep."

"We can catch up tomorrow. You're probably as exhausted as I am," she suggested.

"Sounds like a plan," he agreed. "We should probably both get some rest. Before we hang up, though, I wanted to run a date by you."

She raised an eyebrow. "A date?"

"Yeah, I was wondering if you might be able to meet the weekend of January thirteenth."

"Oh, I'm sure that would work for me," she answered quickly, with a smile.

"Great! I could come to Bakersfield, but we can discuss the particulars later," he suggested.

"Sounds good." She threw a fist in the air and grinned.

After hanging up, Gloria could feel a little fluttering in her stomach. She began to experience a heightened anticipation. It sounded like they had finally set a date to meet. Her tiredness seemed to fade away, and she found herself wide awake, looking forward to their conversation the next day.

Sunday, Gloria found herself alone again. She enjoyed reading on the couch, covered in a fluffy white blanket, with a cup of hot chocolate sitting beside her on the side table. Sarah was once again at Cindy's house, and Chrissy and Alex were spending time with his family for the day. The quiet time alone was a welcome respite, although it didn't do much for taking her mind off when Rick would call during the evening.

"So, how was skiing?" she asked, after picking up the phone.

"It was great. Megan got used to her skis right away. She does have a couple of blisters from the new boots, but she's a happy girl." He sounded happy, but tired.

"That sounds wonderful." Gloria was glad for them both.

"Yeah, I have to send her home to her mother tomorrow. It really sucks," he said.

"Sorry about that. Thankfully, I don't have a shared custody agreement with Sarah."

"Yeah, I wish I could have full custody. Veronica doesn't even want custody. She only fought for it to get back at me." He sounded agitated.

"I can't imagine a mother not wanting custody." Gloria was shocked at the thought.

"Well, part of that is my fault. I fought with her to have a baby in the first place since I wanted one so badly. I never should have done it. She has been resentful ever since. It was a deal we made when I finally agreed to marry her. She wanted to get married, and I wanted a baby. In hindsight, we should have never been together at all."

"How long were you married?" Gloria hoped her curiosity wouldn't scare him away.

"Ten years," he replied frankly.

Since he had answered that question so easily, it gave her the courage to ask her next question. "And you've been divorced for seven years?" She adds, "I hope I'm not asking too many personal questions."

"No, it's okay to ask. How else are we going to get to know each other? I hadn't been looking for another relationship until recently. It was so volatile with Veronica, I shied away from women for years."

"I have to admit, I was curious as to why you were single," Gloria found herself blurting out.

"My ex really screwed me up," he admitted. "I began seeing a counselor shortly after we split. There was a lot of work I had to do on me before I could think of getting into another relationship. I asked her many times to go to counseling with me, but she refused, so I ended up going by myself. I hope that doesn't scare you off."

"Actually, I think it's great. I see a counselor as well. My relationship with my husband really screwed with my head, and I'm trying to work through things myself. Charles wouldn't go with me, either. He said I was the one screwed up." She smiled at the thought of Rick being so open with her - a man who could admit his weaknesses. It just made her care for him more.

"I know what you mean. She always said I was the one who was screwed up. There was nothing wrong with her." At that, he gave a sarcastic chuckle.

"I know. My husband said the same about me. I've always heard the ones who don't think they need help are the ones who really do." She chuckled herself.

"Yeah, that's probably true," he agreed, laughing.

After their conversation, Gloria felt she was beginning to get to know this man. He had been so open with her, and it made her want to open up to him even more.

They continued to get to know each other during their phone calls throughout the week before New Year's Day. Gloria's ritual every year had been to take down the Christmas tree on New Year's. It was usually a depressing job, with celebrations in the past and a new year looming. This year; however, she was singing as she put away the ornaments she had spirited from the house she shared with Charles. Snoopy on his dog house in a Santa hat, baby's first Christmas, Santa Claus, and all the little trinkets she had gathered over the years were placed carefully and cheerfully away in plastic bins. Gloria was looking forward to this new year. She couldn't help but be optimistic, after all her conversations with Rick.

Her thoughts were interrupted as the phone chimed.

She picked it up and heard, "You are receiving a call from an inmate at the Kern County Jail. Will you accept?" For some reason, Gloria found herself doing the inexplicable and accepting the call.

"Hi, Gloria," Charles said flatly.

"Hi, Charles, what's up?" She held the phone on her shoulder while sitting cross-legged on the living room floor wrapping ornaments.

"It really sucked, being in jail for Christmas," he said.

"I'm sure it did. How long are you going to be in there?" She set aside her task and straightened up. She took the phone off her shoulder and held it tightly against her ear, hopeful he would be in jail a while longer. She supposed this is why she took the call in the first place. She needed to know how much more time she had without him showing up.

"I have forty more days to finish my sixty-day stint." He sighed heavily.

"Are you going to have a job to go back to when you get out?" She couldn't help her curiosity.

"Yeah, I still have a job," he said, perking up a bit.

Gloria couldn't believe it. What would it take for him to hit rock bottom? Gathering her nerve, she said, "You had better stay out of trouble from now on. I'm sure they won't keep letting you come back if this keeps up."

To Gloria's surprise, he didn't sound angry when he answered, "I know. I'm going to have to be more careful. Anyway, I have to go now. Someone else needs to use the phone."

"Okay. Bye, Charles." She was happy to hang up.

"Bye," he said, sounding a bit beaten down. She had never heard him like this. She was so used to him always having things under control, or *thinking* he had things under control.

Hanging up, she pondered how she might approach her complicated marital situation with Rick. Even though they'd had some deep conversations, she hadn't been quite brave enough to bring it up. What would he think when she explained that she had been afraid to file divorce papers because of Charles's unpredictable temper? Or, if she told him Charles was in jail? She was sure he might want to run, as fast as he could, in the opposite direction. She wouldn't blame him. Even though Charles had sounded beaten down, she knew it would only be temporary.

Chapter 12

March 2003

<u>After</u>

Tuesday morning, Gloria drops the girls off with her mom. A rush of adrenaline hits her, and she begins to feel giddy with excitement. Cranking up the volume on the stereo, she sings along with Kelly Clarkson as she packs her little one's rooms. Charles won't notice if some of their stuff is missing. He probably wouldn't notice if she removed all of their things. The only concern he has about them is that they don't receive too much of Gloria's attention. She could swear he keeps a scorecard, and his score must always be higher than theirs.

She spends the morning dancing around and packing, unable to believe how much of the girls' stuff has to be packed. They have outgrown many of their clothes, and Gloria makes several piles for charity. With family sending cute clothing to the girls regularly, their closets are filled to overflowing.

Gloria also makes a charity pile from her closet, but it's not very big. She doesn't have that much to begin with. She will have to take a portion of each paycheck and buy herself some decent clothes, knowing it could go a long way toward building her self-esteem.

Dena is a bit surprised to see her daughter on her doorstep at noon, with six full boxes. "So I guess you're really doing it," she says, as she begins helping to move the boxes from the front porch to the guest room. "Is this all of it?"

"Not even close, Mom. I'm going home to pack more, and I'm moving the final stuff out tomorrow. I hope it's okay to bring the girls by again in the morning?"

"I don't know why you even ask. I would have them anyway if you were at work." Dena shakes her head, seeming a bit annoyed.

"I know it's ridiculous." Gloria looks away. "I've been so used to asking for permission for everything, I guess it's just habit. And, I don't want to be rude."

"Not that it's a bad habit. I mean, you don't want to take advantage of anyone, but Gloria, it's me. Relax." Dena places a hand on her shoulder and looks her in the eye.

Gloria drops off another load later that afternoon, which they move into the garage. She has just enough time to go home, pick up the donation boxes, and deliver them to the Goodwill. On the way home from Goodwill she stops by KFC to pick up some chicken for dinner. She had been so busy packing all day, she completely forgot about putting something in the oven. She knows it will be okay with Charles, though, since she is paying.

During the evening, she is glad to find Charles smiling, but this only serves to make her feel guilty for what she is doing. The guilt she always feels when "Good Charles" shows up.

When they are gathered around the kitchen table, with a sincere smile, Charles asks, "How was your day?" before choosing a piece of chicken out of the KFC bucket.

Confused by his mood, Gloria tentatively says, "Fine," as she sits in her chair beside him, spooning mashed potatoes into Sarah's bowl before placing it on the highchair tray.

"That's good," he says, after chewing a bite of his chicken. "How is Mickey doing?"

Does he know something's up? she thinks nervously, before answering, "She's fine." Her tone is a little more high-pitched than she expected. "How was your day?"

"It was great. Guess what," he says with a broad smile.

Gloria turns from Sarah, a quizzical look on her face. "What?"

"I just got a raise," he says, triumphantly.

"That's wonderful, Charles." She smiles back at him. She finds herself truly happy for him. Her emotions, when it comes to him, seem to be all over the place.

Logically, she knows she has plenty of reasons to leave, but in this moment, with things going well, a little doubt slithers into her mind. That slimy snake that invades the crevices of her brain, hissing that she is wrong and maybe Charles is in the right after all. It's a negative, ugly thing that shows up any time it pleases, making Gloria doubt everything about her actions. That rotten snake Charles let loose in there the day she met him. It has grown into quite a monster over the years, and he seems to feed it by keeping her off-kilter.

Remember, she admonishes herself, *this is all part of the pattern. It's part of the inevitable cycle we dance through every time. Good times never last!*

Stopping to think for a moment, she realizes her problem is three-pronged. She has to stop apologizing. She needs to stop feeling guilty for everything. And, she needs to stop checking out. She must remember the rest of her life, and wonders, *is that why I'm here?* There is so much of her life she can't remember. *Is that what this is? Can it really be a do-over?*

She is startled out of her trance when Charles raises his voice, "Where are you? I was asking you a question."

"Sorry, I was daydreaming again." She looks around the table, wondering how long she has been sitting in a daze.

132

Chrissy looks up while biting into the last of her drumstick. She pauses when she sees Gloria looking at her, and grins a huge greasy grin. Sarah has managed to rub mashed potatoes into the tray of her highchair, and now she is slapping the mess with both hands and giggling, causing her bowl to jump with every slap.

"Yeah, well, could you refill my drink?" He's irritated, she can tell.

She obediently gets up and brings the iced tea pitcher to the table from the kitchen counter. She smiles sweetly while pouring tea into his glass.

She returns the pitcher to the counter and grabs paper towels to clean up Sarah's mess, before eating her first bite of chicken. With everyone finished except her, she quickly eats and begins picking up the dishes to take to the sink. She makes slow work of washing the dishes, before giving the girls a bath.

Wednesday morning, after dropping the girls off, she is back home packing again. She pulls her clothes off the rack and stuffs them into boxes, hangers and all. After packing all her personal things from the top shelf of the closet, she starts filling another box with shoes.

Continuing, she moves to her vanity and hastily grabs her makeup and personal items, being careful not to break any of the bottles. She wraps things quickly and stuffs them in a box. Next, she turns to her dresser drawers, pulling them out and dumping bras, panties, nighties, and stockings—not feeling she has the time to make sure things are placed neatly inside the box. She is able to fit six more boxes into the car, and she takes another load over to her parents' house.

Thankfully, Jack has arranged for the loan of a pickup from his work this afternoon. He will be taking a long lunch hour to help her move the girls' furniture. Gloria has taken the crib apart, carefully saving the nuts and bolts in a Ziploc bag, which she tapes to the rail. She has taken all the drawers out of Sarah's dresser and moved it to the driveway. She has moved Chrissy's bed, dresser, and toy box as well. All the furniture will be ready to load when her dad arrives with the truck.

She is waiting outside in the sunshine when Jack pulls into the driveway. Watching his stocky frame get out of the white oilfield truck, she can visualize him playing ball for his high school football team. She smiles as she sees the little bit of belly he is always worried about losing. She definitely inherited his skin coloring, blue eyes, and blond hair. Wearing a lime green golf shirt tucked into black slacks, Jack strikes Gloria as young and handsome. His broad face sports a wide smile, as he approaches and gives her a hug.

"It looks like you've been pretty busy." He raises his eyebrows.

With her tools in hand, she can tell from his expression that he is impressed with her ability to take charge and get things done. She hopes he is realizing she is stronger than he gives her credit for. But, being the strong and silent type, she knows he has a difficult time expressing it. With a look of admiration, he begins to help her load the furniture; a short while later, it's all unloaded into her parents' garage.

Returning home, she begins to pack the kitchen, taking things she knows she will eventually need when she moves into her own place. She is careful to leave enough behind for Charles. Moving to the hall closets, she packs linens and towels, making a partial carload to take over.

At 3:30, she is searching the house for miscellaneous knick-knacks and keepsakes. Some of these things are sentimental. Charles has broken so many of her precious things, she knows he will break more if she leaves them behind. Satisfied she has all she needs and has left Charles a fair share, she takes a seat on one of the barstools at the counter and begins to write a note on the yellow legal pad sitting by the phone. Her hand trembles as she begins.

Dear Charles,

I am so sorry it has come to this, but I have decided to leave. I don't feel that our fighting and arguing is healthy for the children. I know you try, but I always seem to be pushing your buttons, and this can't be healthy for you either. I know you love me in the only way you know how, and I am not blaming you. We married way too young, and I feel we have grown apart. I don't feel I was old enough to know anything about real love, but now I have decided that love is not what we have shared these past years. I don't know what you would call what we had, but I'm sure you can agree, it hasn't been easy.

I think by doing this, it will be a gift for you as well. You can find someone who will be able to love you the way you want to be loved. It's not that I don't care for you. I have always cared for you in my own way. It's just that we are not good together.

I hope you will agree that we should both move on.

Gloria

Reading the note back to herself, she thinks she has been far too nice about it. If she were to put her real feelings down on paper, it would probably scare her. She has so much bottled up inside, she is afraid for it to come out. She would never want to put it on paper for the world to see. If she's honest, she wouldn't put it on paper for herself to see. She decides to save it for Dr. Dyson to pull out of her during another session. Thinking about it, though, it would take a whole group of sessions, to bring it all to the surface.

Closing the front door for the last time, Gloria's heart is filled with a host of emotions. She feels the hope of freedom, and, for some reason, a sadness for Charles. No matter what he has done, she still cares about his welfare. Her heart has always been in a tug-of-war when it comes to him. One part of her wanting so badly to please him, while the other part wants to run to the ends of the earth. *How stupid am I?* she thinks.

Arriving in her parents' driveway, she begins to have a vision of her new future. As she walks in the door, Chrissy runs into her arms, and she is filled for now with awe. She will worry about the problems that are sure to arise, later. Right now, she is back with her mom and dad, and her girls are here with her. Her heart fills with warmth, and she feels ready to weather the storm.

She needs to be honest with her parents about everything that has been happening in her marriage. She can't have them falling for Charles's manipulations. She knows all too well how convincing he can be.

That evening, Gloria sits humming as she rocks Sarah to sleep in the guest room. She looks over at the quilt on the bed, covering Chrissy's sleeping form, and smiles. She thinks of all the hours her grandmother had put into each quilt she lovingly made for the family, and she knows there are more in the cedar chest at the foot of the bed. She looks up at the large oil painting framed above the bed, a mountain scene her mother had done before she took up drawing. She remembers fondly all the time her mother had put into the picture, sitting and painting at her easel.

Looking down at Sarah, who has been asleep on her chest for quite a while, she knows she can't put off talking to her parents any longer. She stands up and pads around the foot of the bed to the crib. Laying Sarah down gently on her back, she slips out of the room quietly.

She finds her mom and dad settled into their recliners in the den. She takes a peek over Dena's shoulder to see the drawing she is working on.

"That's beautiful, Mom," she says, looking at the husky puppy lying beside a pair of intricate beaded moccasins. "Is that one spoken for?"

"No, would you like it?" Dena smiles, as Gloria moves around the chair to stand in front of her.

"If it's not spoken for, I would love it." Gloria looks it over.

"Well, as you can see, I'm almost done with it. If you want it, it's yours." Dena hands the drawing to Gloria, so she can get a better look.

Gloria stares at the thousands of tiny pencil marks her mother has made to make up the image in front of her, and marvels. "Thank you, Mom. I wish I had inherited some of your artistic talent."

Handing it back for Dena to complete, Gloria moves over to the couch and plops down, resting her forearms on her thighs. "I have something I need to talk to ya'll about," she says reluctantly.

"What's going on, Gloria?" Jack turns to look at her, his forehead creasing. "This doesn't sound good."

Dena looks up from her drawing, "Go ahead, we're all ears," she says, worry lines etched on her brow.

After a moment of hesitation, Gloria knows she has to begin. "First of all, I know Charles is going to try and appeal to you both, saying we need to be together, and I'm breaking his heart." She shakes her head.

Her parents look toward her expectantly, and she knows she has to continue. "I considered not telling you this, but Charles has been abusive. He has never hit me," she emphasizes. "But, he gets drunk and forces himself on me. He threatens me and leaves bruises from manhandling me. Sometimes he chokes me." Her voice begins to quiver as she feels the heat of shame begin to rise in her cheeks.

Jack stares, open-mouthed, before closing it and shaking his head. "Why wouldn't you tell us this?"

Gloria can't tell if he is upset with her or with the situation. "I'm sorry, Dad. I just always thought it was my job to work out the problems in our marriage. I wanted you to know, in case he calls trying to garner your sympathy, saying I'm breaking his heart." She can feel her flush of shame begin to burn hotter.

"Well," Jack says, almost snarling, his face beginning to turn crimson. "He's not going to be getting any sympathy from us." He pounds a fist on his thigh. "My younger, more impulsive self would have headed over to beat the living daylights out of him. That's exactly what I would like to do, but I know that would just cause more problems. Believe me, he is going to get an earful when he tries to call."

"We'll let your dad handle all the calls." Dena reaches over to give Jack's hand a reassuring squeeze as he attempts to calm down.

"I'm so sorry to bring all this into your home." Gloria puts her head into her hands.

"We're family. It's okay. We are going to be right here for you and the girls." At this moment, Gloria is thankful for her mom's calming presence.

After a long, drawn-out silence, she announces, "I'm exhausted. I would like to go to bed if you two don't mind. It's been a long day." She looks up at her parents and can feel her eyelids begin to droop as she begins to feel quite drowsy. She stands and gives them each a hug goodnight, before heading off to bed.

"Get a good night's sleep, and don't worry too much. Things have a way of working out," Dena says over her shoulder as she walks away.

She stops and turns around. "Thank you both so much."

The phone was eerily silent during the evening. Gloria chalked it up to Charles being out drinking with his buddies. *He will definitely be blowing up the phone line tomorrow*, she thinks before falling into a deep sleep.

The same nightmare strikes her again, seemingly as soon as she drifts off. She can't wake herself from it this time. The dream is now more vivid. It's so dark, and the panic sets in immediately. She finds herself again locked in a box. Finally, she has the startling realization that the box she's locked in is a trunk. The trunk of a car, and it seems to be traveling fast! She discovers her arms and legs are bound. She begins to flail, but her head is aching, and she has to stop. She tries to free her hands, which seem to be tied together in front of her, but the bindings are tight, and she can't break free. Again, she sees the bright flash of light and the figure of a man looming over her.

The dream takes a turn, and she is driving frantically. Then, all of a sudden, she's trying to run, but she can't make her legs work. Is someone following her? The feeling of being watched is overwhelming, but she can't see anyone. There's no one there! There are lights ahead in the distance, and she tries to reach them, but she is moving so slowly. In a moment, she is back in the dark trunk. The dream keeps going in circles until she wakes, gasping for air.

She does suffer from claustrophobia, but so far, she has managed her fear of tight spaces well, she thinks. In the dream, though, she is not managing it at all. She is allowing panic to take her over. She wonders if she might be able to calm herself next time she has the dream. When she finds herself in the dream again, can she will herself to be calm?

Still panting in the dark, a thought comes out of the blue: *Is this what happened to me in 2019? Did I die and somehow come back to 2003?* It seems ridiculous to think such a thing, but isn't being in the past ridiculous? There seems to be no explaining the crazy situation she finds herself in.

If she sat and did nothing but wait, what would happen? She turns over to look at the clock on the nightstand. It reads 4:30 a.m. She can't get up and take a shower now. The pipes are too noisy. She would wake everyone up. Lying there uncomfortably, she waits an hour before finally calming herself enough to fall back to sleep.

Her parents, having risen with the girls Thursday morning, were careful to keep them quiet so she could sleep in. Finally, at noon, feeling like death warmed over, she heads toward the shower, unable to believe she slept so late.

After a shower, she enters the kitchen. She finds her dad and Chrissy sitting at the breakfast bar. He is helping her color a picture of a hummingbird. She smiles at the sight.

Her mom is just coming into the kitchen. "I just put Sarah down on a pad in the spare room," she says, reaching out for a hug.

"Thank you for taking care of the girls this morning," she says, hugging her mom, before going around the bar to hug her dad and Chrissy. "I didn't even hear them. I was out cold."

"Dad, what are you doing home?" It's just dawned on her what day it is.

"I decided to take a day off and keep an ear out for the phone. I don't want you having to deal with Charles today. I'm hoping I might be able to defuse the situation," he says, seeming to have calmed down from last night.

"Thank you, Dad," Gloria gives him another hug. She knows he would like to beat the living daylights out of Charles, but she also knows he will handle him in the right way.

Finding the coffee cold, she rinses out the pot and prepares another. She feels desperate for caffeine this morning, or afternoon, or whatever the heck time it is. She takes a seat at the table after pouring her first cup of coffee, thinking she should probably slow down on the caffeine. It can't be good for her nerves.

"Don't worry about the girls," Dena says. "They've been good. We took them to McDonald's for breakfast."

Jack chimes in from around the corner, "I've fielded a few phone calls from Charles this morning."

"Oh," Gloria says, her heart sinking into her stomach. "How did that go?"

As she looks up, she sees her dad standing beside her, fists clenched and resting on his hips. He seems to grow taller as he speaks. "I told him you two would have to work on things later. He asked how much later that would be, and I tried to explain you just needed some time. I was pretty proud of myself for keeping my anger in check."

Feeling somewhat more confident from her dad's posture, she asks, "And he was okay with that?"

"Well, that was only the first call," Jack says. "He sounded like he was pretty hungover. He must have let it sink in a little after we hung up the first time. The second time he called, he asked if he could just talk to you for a minute. I told him you were still sleeping, and I thought it would be best if he waits for you to call him."

Gloria sighs, thinking her dad has just taken care of her problem for a while. She's surprised at how civil he was with Charles. A small part of her had hoped he would unload on him and get rid of her problem for good. She knows there is really no getting rid of Charles, and realizes she is actually glad her dad held his tongue.

"Oh, but that's not all," Jack says. "He called a third time and asked if I could get a message to you. I was pretty upset by then, and I think he got the message by the tone of my voice. I told him to wait for you to call, and don't call again. It's been an hour, and he hasn't called back, so hopefully, he got the message."

"You know it's not going to be that easy," Gloria says, already feeling exhausted from Charles's calls, and she wasn't even the one who took them.

"We will deal with it as it comes." Jack takes a seat at the table. "We won't have him disrupting all our lives. Trust me to put a stop to this, honey."

"Thank you, Dad. I'm sorry I put you and Mom in this position."

"In a way, I feel it's my fault." Jack shakes his head. "After all, I was the one who introduced you two."

"It's not your fault, Dad. There's no way you could have known his true character." Gloria gives her father a reassuring tight-lipped smile. "I'm the one who needed to put a stop to it early on. I think I was just swept under before I realized what was happening."

"Let's not worry about it. What's done is done. We will just move forward from here," Jack says, before standing to head back to the kitchen.

A few days later, Gloria sits looking at her parents' answering machine. The number on the machine is showing fifteen calls. She is beginning to feel it isn't right to saddle her parents with the duty of keeping him at bay. As she sits at the breakfast counter, by the phone, she is startled when it begins to ring.

When Charles hears her voice the first time, he is contrite. "Hi, Gloria, thank you for taking my call."

"I just needed some time to think, Charles." She picks up a pencil from the counter and begins twirling it absentmindedly.

"I'm so sorry for everything, Gloria," he says, sounding dejected. "I would do anything. Just bring the girls and come home. We can work this out. We always have."

"I know you mean it right now, but it all goes out the window when you decide to have your next drink." She startles herself when the pencil she is fiddling with snaps in her hand. She drops the pieces to the counter.

"I'll quit drinking," he says.

She leans forward, putting both elbows on the bar, and something in her snaps, "You have said that a thousand times before. What makes this time different?"

"You've never left before," he says. "Now that I realize how upset you are, I'll do anything to make things right again."

"I need time to think, Charles. If you leave me alone and give me some time to think, I might talk this over with you. If you don't give me time, I'm afraid my mind is already made up. Please hear what I am saying. I'm going to hang up now, and you are going to give me time to think."

"I hear you. How long do you think you need?" he asks.

"I will let you know. I will call you," she says in frustration.

"Okay," he says, quietly.

She knows as soon as they hang up, he is not going to be dejected. He is going to be angry, and he is going to break things.

"Bye, Charles," she says finally and hangs up.

She will have to ask Dr. Dyson for guidance. She wants things to go differently this time. Not like her memories of the future that had gone so terribly wrong. She is slowly accepting this as her life

143

now, as the future is becoming quite fuzzy around the edges. Sitting back in her seat to contemplate her life, she runs her fingers through her hair, then clasps her hands at the back of her head. She has to admit she has made some drastic changes. After all, she did leave Charles. This gives her hope she will be able to make some real changes in her life. She might not be able to control Charles's reactions, but she can certainly control her own.

As she expected, it only takes a couple of days for him to begin calling again. He didn't give her long to think, but with Dr. Dyson's help, she eventually begins to exert some control over their conversations. She slowly cuts the calls down to every other day, and he has to stay on neutral topics, or she will hang up. *This is all feeling so familiar*, she thinks. *This is going to buy me a little time, but he's not going to settle for it much longer.*

Chapter 13

January 2018

<u>Before</u>

Finally, it's here, Gloria thought, as she woke on Saturday, January 13, 2018. *We're going to meet.*

Rick had asked her what there was to do in Bakersfield, and Gloria had suggested horseback riding. "I know you aren't afraid of the cold. You're skiing all the time," she said.

"Bring it on," he fired back. She knew Rick was active and she thought riding might be a good icebreaker for their first date.

The night before, as Gloria sat scrubbing her face in front of her bathroom mirror, Sarah came in and leaned against the doorjamb. "Mom, I know you've been talking to someone. I haven't always been asleep when you make your nightly calls," she said flatly. When Gloria had decided to wait until the last minute to tell Sarah, she really had pushed it to the limit.

"I hear you talking sometimes. I know you two are planning to meet, but what can I do? You won't listen to me, whether I'm the only sane person in this house or not," Sarah said, in frustration, as she leaned in the doorway and began to twirl her auburn hair around one finger nervously.

Gloria turned to Sarah. Trying to appear confident, she looked her daughter in the eye. "I'm sorry, Sarah. I go crazy, stuck in the house. You spend so much time with Cindy. Not that I want you to stay home. Of course I want you to have a life, but I need a life too."

"So when are you going to meet?" Sarah raised an eyebrow.

"Tomorrow at noon." Gloria turned back to the mirror, scrubbing her face a little harder than she should.

"It's okay, Mom. You are going to do what you're going to do."

Gloria stopped rubbing her face and tried to come up with something to soothe Sarah. "What if I call you during my date, so you can put your mind at ease that I'm all right," Gloria suggested, as she turned back to look at herself in the mirror, her face crimson from scrubbing.

"How about I go with you for the first meeting? Two of us would be safer than just you," Sarah countered.

Gloria's head whipped around, eyes wide. "I'm not taking my fifteen-year-old daughter on a date. Are you being serious?"

"Yes, Mom. I'm worried." Sarah continued to stand defiantly in the doorway.

Gloria had to take a moment to calm down. She considered the sincere concern she could clearly hear in her daughter's voice and countered with another suggestion: "How about I call and check in with you every hour while I'm out, and let you know I'm not lying in a ditch off Highway 99 somewhere. I give you permission to call 911 if you don't hear from me." Gloria winced a little as the last part came out of her mouth.

Suggesting Sarah call 911 was going a little too far, but it was out now, and, to her surprise, she could see Sarah slowly begin to smile. More like half a smile, but a smile nonetheless.

Sarah began to nod, "We have a deal. You have to call me every hour on the hour," she said, with one hand on her hip and the other with her hair still wound around it. "Better yet, I will call

146

you." Screwing up her freckled nose, she added, "It just goes against the natural order of things, you know, Mom. I mean, you guys are so old."

"I know, Sarah. We're ancient." Gloria suppressed a laugh.

Sarah just kept shaking her head, and Gloria could hear her saying, "Ewww," as she turned to leave the room.

Gloria had to apologize when she finally called Rick, later than usual, that night.

"I told Sarah we are meeting, and I had to calm her down." She sat nervously on the edge of her bed waiting for his reply.

"Oh, okay." He sounded relieved. "I thought you might have changed your mind."

"Are you kidding," she said. "I've been looking forward to it."

"Is Sarah going to be okay with it?" he asked.

"Don't worry. She thinks she's my mother sometimes, but she'll warm up. I have to let her call me every hour on our date, though. I hope that's not too weird. She wants to make sure I'm not dead somewhere." She cringed, waiting to hear his reaction to their crazy arrangement.

"That's quite all right. I'll just have to take care of business on the half-hour." He laughed. "No, seriously," he said, "let her know I will take good care of you, and I will send you home safely."

"Thanks for understanding." She laughed as relief began to flood through her veins.

"Do you still have the directions to Mickey's ranch," Gloria asked.

"Sure do. I'll meet you there," he said.

As Gloria backed out of the driveway Saturday morning, Sarah waved from the back door and pointed to a watch that wasn't on her wrist. She knew what that meant: Sarah would be calling in precisely one hour if she didn't check in.

She headed out of town on Highway 119. As she passed over I-5, she began to leave the farmlands behind. In front of her stretched out the flatlands which so far had been left natural with only dirt, scrub brush, and weeds. Closer to the foothills dotting the landscape in the distance were pump jacks and oilfield roads crisscrossing just about everywhere.

In Bakersfield you never knew where you might see a pump jack, with its horse head bobbing up and down, the counterweights turning slowly behind. You might see one in the middle of the city between commercial buildings, or you might see one in the middle of a cotton field on the outskirts of town.

She took a left off the highway onto a gravel road just before reaching the foothills. She was soon driving alongside the rusted pipe rail fencing cordoning off Mickey's ten-acre property. Turning onto the dusty drive, she traveled under a rusted, arched metal entrance, from which hung a plank with the Lazy M brand burned into the wood.

Passing the white clapboard ranch house on the left, with its white picket fence enclosing a lawn that lay dormant for the winter, she drove on to the back of the property. Junipers lined the road to the twelve stall, gray metal-sided barn in back. Two yellow tabby cats scurried into the barn as she approached.

She could see Mickey at the hitching rail near the arena situated across the road from the barn. Her brown hair was pulled back in its usual long ponytail. Wearing a denim jacket with her jeans and western boots, she looked every bit the horsewoman she was. She already had two horses saddled up. It looked like Gloria and Rick would be riding Suzy Q and Hot Shot today.

Suzie was a beautiful golden palomino filly, with a snow-white mane and tail. Gloria knew she was a little green. Mickey usually liked to pair her up with Hot Shot, who despite his name was quite a gentle, seasoned bay quarter horse gelding. Suzie stood stomping an impatient hoof, kicking up little puffs of dust underneath her as she waited.

Like Hot Shot, the horses Mickey raised for show, were American Quarter Horses. She also kept other breeds she used for her riding students and horses she would train for friends, so her stalls were always full.

On the other side of the arena, Gloria could see Mickey had one of her show horses hooked up to the hot walker, slowly walking around in a circle, as the mechanical device churned. A beautiful sorrel mare, her coat gleaming red in the sun. The remainder of her show horses were in their stalls covered in blankets to keep them from growing shaggy winter coats. She knew Mickey spent hours brushing each one of them to an amazingly glossy shine.

Gloria stepped out of her car and pulled on her light nylon jacket. The day hadn't turned out to be so cold after all. Looking up, she could see there were only a few puffy white clouds in a clear blue sky. She had parked near the door to the barn and could smell the sweet smell of alfalfa bails stacked inside. She turned and headed across the dirt road toward the arena.

"Hi, Mickey," she called out, as she waved a hand high in the air.

Mickey smiled and waved back. "Hi there, stranger."

"Are you missing the Insurance Agency yet?" Gloria said, jogging over.

"Are you kidding? I would rather be training horses and teaching lessons any day of the week." Mickey flicked her ponytail back over her shoulder and smiled.

"I don't blame you. I would rather be doing the same." Gloria reached out to rub Suzie on the muzzle, saying, "Sorry, no carrots today, girl."

"You know this is going to cost you," Mickey said, tightening the cinch on Hot Shot's saddle.

"Oh yeah, and what exactly would that be?" Gloria eyed Mickey suspiciously.

"You have to tell me every juicy detail about this new guy of yours." Mickey looked up with a smirk.

"I knew I was going to have to do that anyway." Gloria looked nervously toward the entrance for Rick's black pickup. She turned back and said, "So it looks like I'm riding Suzie today. You're keeping me on my toes."

"Yeah, you're doing me a favor. I try and take her out as much as possible. I just put her through her rounds in the round pen. She should be ready to go." Mickey gave Hot Shot a pat, once she finished with the saddle. "Does your man ride?"

"He said he's ridden a few times. He thinks he will probably be pretty rusty," Gloria nervously glanced over her shoulder at the entrance again.

"Ooh, you're nervous," Mickey teased.

"Yeah, I never know what might come out of your mouth," Gloria said, chuckling.

Mickey just laughed as she came around and pulled on Suzie's stirrup, checking to see if the saddle was snug. They both heard the truck coming down the drive at the same time and turned to look. "Now Mickey, behave yourself," Gloria chided.

Gloria's phone began to jingle in her pocket. She pulled it out and could see it was Sarah. She answered quickly, knowing Sarah would worry if it took her too long. "I'm fine," she said as soon as she picked up. He's just now coming down the road. Don't worry, Mickey is here with me."

"Okay," Sarah said. "But, I'm calling again in an hour.

"What was that all about," Mickey asked, as Gloria put the phone back in her pocket.

"Don't even ask." Gloria rolled her eyes, not wanting to explain the strange arrangement she and Sarah had come up with.

Rick parked next to her car and stepped out of his truck. Her heart skipped a beat. He looked quite handsome in boots and a gray button-down Western shirt tucked into jeans.

Gloria stepped forward and gave him a hug, which he returned. "It's so good to finally see you in person."

"Same here," he said, giving her a big squeeze.

"Hi, I'm Mickey." Mickey reached out her right hand for a shake.

"I'm Rick, so good to meet you. Gloria's told me some stories about you two," Rick said, reaching out to shake Mickey's hand.

"Well, she hasn't said nearly enough about you." Mickey clasped her hands behind her back and rocked back on the heels of her boots.

Laughing, Rick said, "Well, this is the first time we've met in person. We've just been getting to know each other over the phone."

Gloria was trying not to turn crimson. She could see some shenanigans erupting between these two if she left them to their own devices, and she knew she would be the butt of those shenanigans.

"Okay, you two. We best be getting along with what we came here to do today," Gloria said.

As they headed on back over to the horses, Mickey explained, "You'll be riding Hot Shot today, Rick. He's the bay."

151

"Sounds good, Mickey. Thank you for letting us ride." He approached Hot Shot, then appreciatively stroked his long black mane.

"Gloria here has Suzie Q. She's a bit green, but Gloria can handle her. Hot Shot, despite his name, is a pussy cat," Mickey explained.

Gloria took Suzie's reins and hopped up into the saddle. Suzie backed up a bit. "Woah girl," Gloria said.

Mickey held Hot Shot's reins as Rick stepped up into the stirrup and swung his leg over the saddle. Once he was settled in, Mickey handed him the reins. "Well, have fun, you two," she said, smiling.

"We'll probably see you in a couple of hours," Gloria called over her shoulder, as side-by-side they walked the horses toward the gate.

"You're a natural," Gloria said, as they took a right onto the gravel at the gate.

"Thanks," Rick said. "It feels good."

Gloria pointed up ahead. "We'll just take that dirt road and ride out through the oilfields. There are roads crisscrossing all over up there in the foothills. It's great for trail riding, or I guess you might call it road riding." She chuckled.

They both became quiet for a moment, and all they could hear was the crunch crunching of the horses' hooves on gravel until they stepped off onto the dirt road. Soon they were coming up beside a pump jack, its horse head bobbing slowly up and down, pushing the rod into the well and pulling it out again. The large counterweights on the back were turning around in a slow circle. The unit would squeak as the head bobbed up, and make a thunking sound as it hit bottom.

"I've never been up close to one of these before," Rick said. "I've just seen them while driving by on the road."

A jackrabbit darted out from the sagebrush up ahead, causing Suzie to sidestep quickly. Hot Shot pricked his ears but held steady. Suzy, taking cues from Gloria and Hot Shot, decided it wasn't a danger after all, and fell back into step.

"Well, that was exciting," Rick said.

"Yeah," Gloria said. "She's a little green, but Hot Shot keeps her pretty steady most of the time."

Gloria pointed to the foothills ahead. "On the other side of the hills is a little town called Taft. In the old days, it used to be named Moron."

"You're kidding." Rick laughed.

"Nope. Just a little trivia," Gloria said, chuckling herself.

He appraised her, sitting tall on Suzie Q, and commented, "It looks like you really are a country girl."

"I have to warn you, I'm a real get-down-and-dirty country girl at times, and I'm not afraid of critters."

"Actually, it sounds like it could be a lot of fun." He smiled over at her. "I like it."

Gloria winced as her phone began to ring. "That would be my daughter. Sorry." She answered the call; Rick just laughed.

"Hello," Gloria said.

"Mom, thank goodness you answered," Sarah said dramatically. "How's it going?"

"Great." Gloria looked over at Rick and smiled. "I promise I will tell you all about it when I get home."

"Okay Mom, but I'm calling again in an hour," Sarah warned.

"Okay honey. Talk to you later." Gloria hung up and placed the phone back in her pocket.

"Was that your rescue call?" He raised an eyebrow.

"I've read about those. Actually no, as I told you, she insists on calling every hour to make sure I'm alive."

"You mean you aren't going to exit, stage left, right about now?" he asked, with a chuckle.

"No exiting. She's just my little worry wort, who half the time thinks she's my mother." Gloria reached down to pat Suzie on the neck.

"That's okay, I understand." He was obviously trying to put her at ease. "She loves you and worries about you. There are worse teenagers in the world, believe it or not."

"I know. She's really a great kid. Thanks for understanding. Tell me about Megan," she said, hoping to change the subject.

He looked over at her as they plodded along the path. His brown eyes lit up as his full lips stretched into a wide grin, before beginning: "Well, the thing is, I thought I wanted a boy, but as soon as I laid eyes on Megan my heart was hers. I never looked back. I'm thrilled we had a girl," he said wistfully. "We do everything together. She's my little shadow. She's ten years old and in the fifth grade now. It seems like she's growing so fast." He leaned over and pulled his wallet out of his back pocket with his right hand while holding the reins with his left. He pulled out a picture and reached over to Gloria.

Gloria reached out to take the picture and couldn't help but stare down at the beautiful, olive-skinned girl with long flaxen hair. She had his large brown eyes and full lips. "She's absolutely beautiful," Gloria said with a sincere smile, as she passed the picture back to Rick.

"I guess I'm a little biased, but she has the heart to go along with it." He smiled and tucked the picture back into his wallet. "I look forward to my weeks with her. We always try to do something

154

fun on the weekends. I try to get all my work done during the week, so we can just play."

Half the afternoon was gone, by the time they returned to the ranch. Sarah had called again, but after Gloria assured her that everything was fine, she let them be for the rest of the day.

Mickey was working one of her show horses on a lunge line in the round pen when they arrived. "Just hitch them to the post," she called. "I'll put them away."

"Are you sure," Gloria said.

"I'm sure. You two have better things to do. Just get on with it." Mickey laughed.

"Thanks, Mickey," Gloria said, waving goodbye before they turned and walked toward her car.

"Yes, thanks, Mickey. It was good to meet you," Rick called over his shoulder.

"Same here," Mickey called back.

Gloria couldn't help but think they seemed to get along as well in person as they had on the phone, and there was an undeniable attraction between them. She didn't believe in past lives, but it seemed there was an uncanny familiarity.

Rick checked his watch. "It's 3:00, I should see about checking into a motel. Would you like to try and meet for dinner tonight?"

"That sounds great." She snickered. "But I will probably have to go home and clear it with the boss."

"Do you want to meet somewhere around 6:00?" He smiled and looked down at his watch again.

"That works," she said, sliding into her car.

"Where would you suggest we go?" He stood looking down at her as he held onto her car door.

"Would you like to try the Chrystal Palace? That's Buck Owens' place. There will be country music and dancing. I know you like country music," she said with a hopeful smile, quickly adding, "They have pretty good food, too."

He nodded in agreement. "Sounds like a plan."

"I'm really looking forward to it." Gloria grinned from ear to ear as Rick closed the door.

Driving home, she tried to remember the last time she had been dancing. She remembered being fourteen when her best friend's father had taught her a couple of country steps. She hoped she would remember and not step all over Rick's toes. She had been feeling pretty brave to suggest dancing, but she had decided to let the chips fall where they may. The chips might be falling all over the dance floor tonight, but so be it.

She hoped Sarah was not going to be too difficult over them going out again. She would just have to explain that Rick had driven all this way, and they'd hit it off so well. *Look at me. I'm feeling like the child again*, she thought.

It took a bit of assertiveness and a bit of compromise, but she and Sarah eventually came to a mutual understanding. Gloria would do everything she could to ease Sarah's mind, but she was going to date using her own best judgment.

Later that evening, as she entered the lobby of the Crystal Palace in a form-fitting black dress and heels, Gloria rocked back and forth from one foot to the other, her jacket flung over one arm, she clasped her hands nervously in front of her, waiting for Rick to arrive. She glanced around at all the Buck Owens memorabilia, encased in glass. Owens' bigger-than-life bronze statue stood in the middle of the lobby.

As she gazed at Buck's famous red, white, and blue guitar, Gloria felt a gentle hand on her shoulder. She couldn't help but jump, before turning around to see Rick. Dressed in jeans and a black Western dress shirt and denim jacket, she swooned a little before giving him a hug and they headed off hand-in-hand. Walking through the doors and into the dance hall, they headed off to one of the tables set on tiers facing the stage and dance floor. As they climbed to the second tier, they were seated in a large U-shaped booth.

Rick leaned forward and asked, "Do you want to move closer together?"

"Sure," she said, sliding toward the middle of the booth as he did the same.

Above the bar, to Gloria's left, actually hanging on the wall, was Elvis Presley's white convertible Pontiac with steer horns mounted on the front. She heard that Owens had allegedly won the car in a poker game. She had seen it before, but she still stared in amazement, wondering how they must have mounted it on the wall. There were a few people at the bar and a few more sitting at tables and walking around, but the action hadn't yet started.

"I believe the band starts playing at 7:00, but I've only been here a couple of times," Gloria explained. "I actually like the quiet for a while, so we can visit."

"That works for me," Rick agreed, taking Gloria's hand in his underneath the table.

Turning slightly in her seat to face him, she asked, "Do you dance?"

"Actually I do," he said, turning toward her and winking.

She didn't feel nervous, being so close to him. It felt right somehow like they had known each other forever. Still, she felt the butterflies being let loose in her stomach again when he winked at her.

Blushing, she said, "I hope you're a good lead. I haven't danced in years. Your feet might be in peril."

They both laughed as he reassured her, he was sure she would be great.

When the waiter came around, a good-looking young man in very tight Wranglers, they both ordered chicken fried steak with mashed potatoes and green beans.

"I'll have to take a carry-out later, I hope you don't mind," she said, smiling shyly after the waiter left.

He looked at her quizzically. "Why would I mind?"

"Charles never allowed me to take food home. He said it was too tacky." She shrugged. "I never used to order a large meal. I hate wasting food."

"That's ridiculous. You should order whatever you want," he said.

Just then, their drinks arrived. Rick had ordered a draft beer, while Gloria ordered her usual Diet Coke. "It's not that I don't want a margarita. Alcohol gives me migraines. I might be a dull date, but if you like, I can try to act tipsy." She smirked.

"Oh no," he said dramatically. "I had it all planned out. I was planning to get you drunk, take you back to the motel, and have my way with you."

Gloria laughed; she was beginning to recognize his sense of humor and knew he was joking. She felt at ease and enjoyed his witty comebacks.

"Well," she said, "now you will have to drag me there kicking and screaming." At that, they both laughed.

"No," he said seriously. "I only plan to have one since I have to drive back to the motel." That was music to Gloria's ears.

They began to discuss music they liked, which in his case was classic rock and country. Gloria agreed she liked the same but was a fan of just about all music. "Except bluegrass, and rap." She chuckled. "Lucky for you, tonight it will be country music."

As they visited, Gloria took notice of how the place was filling up. Even though they were sitting close to each other, they were beginning to have to speak up to be heard over the din of conversations going on around them. She mentioned this to Rick, who said he had been so busy looking into her big blue eyes, he hadn't noticed. Gloria blushed and wondered how many times she had done so since they'd met. As she thought about it, she blushed again.

"I'm sorry." She was embarrassed at not being able to hide her feelings. "I keep blushing like a schoolgirl. I'm not used to this much attention."

"No worries," he said. "I think it's cute." Then she blushed once more, hiding her face in her hands.

The food arrived, and Gloria felt hungry after not eating much of anything all day. She unfolded her napkin and laid it across her lap; Rick did the same. She waited a couple of seconds, not wanting to tear into her food too hungrily. After he began to eat, she slowly cut into her steak and took a small bite. She closed her eyes in delight. She didn't know if the food was actually that good or if it was the company.

They were eating in silence when the band began to file on stage. All dressed in tight jeans and western shirts, and wearing cowboy hats, the band members began doing mic checks and tuning their instruments. Tonight it looked like there would be a lead guitarist, a bass player, a keyboard player, and a drummer.

Gloria looked up and smiled after barely putting a dent in her food and said, "I'm afraid I'm full."

"Already?" he said, placing his fork down on his plate.

"Yeah, I can't eat much at one time. It used to infuriate Charles, so I quit ordering full meals when we went out. It's been forever since I've had a meal out like this."

He shook his head. "That's just not right."

"I'm sorry. I shouldn't have brought him up." She looked down at her lap.

"It's okay. He was a big part of your life for so many years, he's bound to come up sometimes." He gave her hand a squeeze. "Really, I don't mind."

Finally set up, the band began to play. Gloria recognized the song as "Can't Break it to My Heart," by Tracy Lawrence. Rick slid smoothly out of the booth and reached for Gloria's hand before leading her to the dance floor. She followed nervously but fell easily into step as he took her in his arms. They fell into a smooth two-step as goosebumps began to form on her arms, and she felt as if she were melting into him. Not thinking about the steps, she allowed herself to let go, and she couldn't imagine a more intimate moment. For her, there was no one else on the crowded dance floor; before she knew it, the song was over.

She looked up at him and smiled dreamily as he gently bent down to kiss her. She didn't resist, forgetting where she was for the moment. Her brain seemed to take a back seat, and the sound of the busy dance hall faded away. Before she knew it, they were dancing again. Finally hearing the music, she recognized the song as "The Dance." She had to admit the lead singer was doing it justice, and that was a hard thing to do with a Garth Brooks song, she thought as they twirled around the floor once more.

As the last strains of music faded away, Rick led her back to the table through a throng of people; they bumped shoulders as they went. Usually, such a close crowd would be uncomfortable for

Gloria, but with Rick's strong arm around her, she was quite content.

Moving back to the middle of the booth, their conversation flowed easily. When the band played a song they both liked, they would get up and dance until the dance floor became too crowded.

Finally, looking at his watch, Rick asked, "Would you like to get together tomorrow?"

"Yes. That sounds great." Gloria was thankful he'd brought it up.

"What would you like to do?" He took the last sip of his drink as she thought about it.

"How about driving to Pismo Beach for the day?" She looked at him quizzically.

"Sounds perfect." He smiled and nodded his approval.

"I guess I had better be getting home tonight, though," she said, looking down at her watch.

He agreed, and Gloria grabbed her box of leftovers as they both moved out of the booth. After escorting her to her car, he bent down for another kiss. This one was deeper than the last, and Gloria's legs seemed to turn to rubber. She could feel a strong electricity between them as he held her close, both not wanting to let go.

"Is this what they call chemistry?" she said, looking up into his deep brown eyes.

"I would say definitely," he assured her as they stood in the moonlight, looking into each other's eyes. He was the first to move. "We had better get you home." He reached around her to open the car door. After helping her into the car, and with a gleam in his eye, he bid her goodnight.

Gloria swayed a bit as he helped her in. Apologizing, she said, "And that's me without anything to drink. Imagine me with alcohol."

Laughing, he closed her door as she attempted to gather her wits.

Sarah was up watching a movie on Netflix when Gloria walked in at 10:30. She and Rick had stepped outside around 9:00 to call Sarah and tell her things were alright, and that she would be home in about an hour and a half. She had nailed it, walking in an hour and a half later.

Explaining that they would be spending the day together tomorrow, and would be meeting for breakfast, Gloria headed off to bed. She left out the part about riding in his truck to Pismo Beach. *No need to worry her*, she thought.

If Sarah was upset by all of this, Gloria didn't know. She really hadn't given her time to react before heading off to bed. Sarah would be in bed when Gloria left in the morning, so hopefully, problem solved.

After breakfast Sunday morning, they headed off in Rick's Chevy truck to Pismo. Yesterday had been such a good day, and Gloria was anticipating what might come. Rick invited her to slide to the middle seat. She happily accepted, buckling in beside him.

It was a beautiful day at the beach, as they pulled into the public parking area just off the boardwalk. To the north was a street lined with touristy shops, but they decided instead to walk south toward the entrance to the beach. The breeze was cool, and they quickly grabbed their windbreakers, putting them on before heading off.

The golden sand was sparkling under the sunlight as puffy cotton-candy clouds floated by in a beautiful blue sky. They walked down to the beach, arm in arm, trekking through the soft sand to make their way to firmer ground near the surf. Heading south, they jumped back as the tide rolled in, trying to avoid getting themselves tangled up in kelp left in the wake of the tide as it rolled out.

Gloria bent down, picking up shells she found along the way, handing them to Rick to put in his pocket. Turning back toward the boardwalk after a while, they eventually found a bench there and decided to have a seat and take in their surroundings.

They took in the salty sea air as Gloria tried to tame her hair, which was blowing wildly in the wind. When it blew across her face, she wished she had remembered to bring a hair tie to tie it back. Rick pushed it out of her face and laughed. She decided she would have to find a hair tie in one of the shops later.

As they looked down on the beach dwellers lying on blankets, building sand castles, and running in and out of the surf, Rick settled in by resting his feet on the weathered wooden railing. When Gloria tried to do the same, her legs were unable to reach the rail, so she turned sideways on the bench, resting her back against Rick's side. Listening to the waves roll in, Rick shared adventures he and Megan had experienced, while Gloria sat transfixed. She couldn't help but think he had done so much in life, and she had done almost nothing.

Gloria sat up to look at Rick. He turned to her, taking her hand in his. "It just occurred to me, I haven't heard anything about your childhood," she said, a quizzical look in her eyes.

After a pause, a cloud seemed to descend over Rick's face, as he said, "I try not to dwell on my childhood."

"I'm sorry." Gloria shook her head. "I didn't mean to . . ."

"It's okay," he interrupted. "You've told me all about yours. It's something you need to know. I understand that. It's just, my childhood was very different from yours."

"I'm sorry . . ."

"No," Rick said. His brows knitted as he looked off into the distance. "I want you to know." Pausing a bit before continuing, he said, "You see, my dad was an alcoholic. He used to beat my mom. They would have real knock-down, drag-out fights . . . My sister used to take me out of the house when things got really bad. She's three years older than me," he explained. "Anyway, my mom didn't seem to know when to quit arguing with my dad, when he had had too much to drink. He would hit her, and she would just keep going until he knocked her out. I remember one Thanksgiving, he threw a frozen turkey across the kitchen and knocked her out cold."

Gloria's eyes grew wide, and she gave his hand a squeeze, before saying, "I'm so sorry, Rick."

"It's okay. It's all in the past. Both my parents are gone now." His eyes seemed to refocus on the present. He shook his head. "Let's think about happier things today."

"Of course." Gloria nodded. "I'm sorry if I ruined your day."

"No, no," he said, a smile beginning to return to his lips. "We'll just dwell on good things for the rest of the day."

They both agreed and decided they were a bit hungry, so they headed off to Brad's for lunch. It was a couple of streets over from the boardwalk, and they browsed in many of the touristy shops along the way. Gloria found a surfboard keychain with Megan's name on it and insisted on buying it for her. Rick seemed touched by her thoughtfulness.

They eventually made it to their destination. Gloria had been to Brad's a couple of times and loved their clam chowder. They both settled into the same side of the booth. Gloria slid in all the way on the bench, inviting Rick to slide in beside her. Again, they both ordered the same thing, a hollowed-out bread bowl with clam chowder poured inside.

"The best part is at the bottom." Gloria poked her spoon to the bottom of her bowl and grinned. "The soggy clam chowder-soaked bread, at the bottom."

He laughed. "I haven't had a bread bowl before, but I'm glad we are being environmentally conscious and eating our bowls." At that, they both chuckled.

Just as they began walking across the street, heading back to the beach, they found themselves being bombed by a flock of seagulls. Running for cover, they began to laugh. Gloria doubled over laughing, while Rick tried to wipe the white sticky bird crap off her shoulder. Rick had a bit on his cheek, and when she saw it, she doubled over again. Finally, she composed herself enough to wipe it off with a finger, before heading to the boardwalk restrooms to wash up.

"Well," Rick said, laughing again as he emerged from the restroom, "I guess we'll always remember the bird-bombing incident of 2018."

"That's true. They must have all eaten something bad at the same time. Oh well, it's our first memory together." Gloria tried to rub out the stitches that had gripped her side from all the laughter.

He frowned. "How about the dancing and the kisses?"

"Oh yes, we will definitely remember those, so this is like our fourth or fifth memory." She grinned.

Evening came quickly, and Rick dropped Gloria off to pick up her car in the restaurant parking lot where they'd had breakfast that morning.

"Call me when you get home," Gloria called out her open window, as she passed his truck in the parking lot.

"I will," he said, leaning out his window before pulling away.

Chapter 14

May 2003

<u>After</u>

Gloria and Pam, the rental agent, pull up to a quaint little cottage in the downtown area of Bakersfield. It had only taken Gloria two months to save enough money to move out of her parents' house, and she is taking her lunch hour to see this property. Upon first sight, she is sure she has found what she's looking for. The little gem sits on an oak-lined street with branches fanned out over the road, forming a canopy over passing cars.

The little wood-sided cottage is painted white with forest green trim. As Pam opens the front door, she explains that the house had been built in the 1940s. Walking in the door, they find themselves directly in a tiny living room, which is painted lavender. It's not a color Gloria would have picked, but it's whimsical and somehow suits the house. She can see the hardwood floor has been restored and looks great.

As she continues to explore the interior, she finds all the rooms are painted in a different pastel color, Champagne pink in the tiny master bedroom, pale yellow in the kitchen, the slightest hint of blue in the second bedroom, and a cream-colored bathroom with Jack and Jill doors to each bedroom. Somehow the colors brighten Gloria's mood. When she spies the little playhouse, painted to match the main house, at the end of a rose-lined path in the back yard, she knows she is sold.

Returning to the living room, she stares at the little stone fireplace. She could swear it sparkles. Upon closer inspection, she can see there are tiny crystals throughout the rockwork. She can't help but think, *Whimsical, just like this little house*. She moves her head this way and that, watching the light refract off the glistening surface.

She asks about the appliances in the kitchen, which are all white and seem to be from the 1950s. Pam assures her they all work, and Gloria is glad. They suit the place. There's not much cabinet space, but she can see there would be room in the corner for a portable pantry. *Yes*, she thinks, *this will do nicely*.

"I'll take it." Gloria looks over at Pam smiling.

"Great," Pam says. "I have the paperwork in my car. You can make a deposit to hold it and return the paperwork to me tomorrow."

"That would be wonderful," Gloria says, as they step out the front door.

Sitting around the dinner table that evening, Gloria is too excited to eat. Her dinner sits untouched as she tries to wait, before describing the little house to her parents and Chrissy. The excitement seems to spread as Sarah, sitting on her mom's lap, starts to giggle and clap her hands together.

"You won't believe the house I found." Gloria beams, as she looks back and forth between her dad and mom across the oak table, bouncing Sarah on one knee.

"It's tiny but so cute. You would have to see it. Now don't laugh, but the rooms are all painted a different pastel color. The living room is actually lavender." Quickly she adds, "I know it sounds weird. Like I said, you will have to see it to understand. And, there's a playhouse for Chrissy in the backyard."

"Yay," Chrissy says, her hands in the air.

Jack turns up his nose a little at her description, but recovers when Dena gives him a look, her head cocked and eyes squinting in his direction.

"It definitely sounds interesting," he finally says, in between bites of green beans.

"I'd love to see it." Dena pats Gloria's shoulder.

"I was hoping we could all go see it this weekend," Gloria says.

Before heading to bed, she spends time completing the rental application; she is anxious to return it in the morning, with the anticipation of moving in soon.

Dropping by the rental agency after work the next day, Gloria finds Pam beaming. Her head, full of red permed curls, bounces as she rounds the corner of the counter to the waiting area.

"I saw you coming," she says to Gloria, her green eyes sparkling. "I hope you're ready to move in because your application has been approved.

Pam hands Gloria a rental contract and says, "Just take these home, look them over and fill them out, and we'll be ready to go."

"Thank you," Gloria says, grinning from ear to ear, taking the proffered documents. She has a smile on her face until she slides into her car and her phone begins to ring. She picks it up. "What's up, Charles?" She is determined not to let him spoil her good mood.

"Gloria, if you aren't coming home, you're going to have to bring back my car," he says, bluntly.

Gloria's heart drops. "Your car? It's half mine."

"Well then you can start making the payments," he says.

"Fine, how much are they?"

"Four ninety-five a month." He almost sounds triumphant, knowing she could never afford such a high car payment.

"That's ridiculous. Why are the payments so high on an Oldsmobile?"

"I had to pay a high interest rate on it." He doesn't even seem bothered by this fact.

Gloria is dumbfounded. The only reasonable explanation for paying such a high interest rate she can think of is bad credit. It makes sense. With all those past-due bills she saw coming in the mail, his credit must be in the toilet. That doesn't help her situation, though. There is no way she can afford such a high car payment. She has no choice; she will have to return the car and save up the money to buy a used car.

"Okay, Charles," she says, dejected. "I'll return it."

"If you don't return it soon, I'll come to get it," he warns her.

"I'll get it back to you by next week." She feels defeated and hangs up on him before he can make any more threats.

Now that she has qualified for the house, she is not sure how she will be able to make the payments and save for a car, too. It will take forever to save up a down payment, on top of a house payment. As she drives home, she tries to turn the problem over in her brain, but by the time she reaches the driveway, she doesn't have it figured out.

She sits in the car as she continues to think. She can't do without a car while she's saving up a down payment. The only thing she can think of, is letting the house go and using the money she has saved for the deposit to buy a car. By the time she walks in the door, her spirits have plummeted. She knows Charles is trying to force her to move back home, but she will not take the bait.

After the little ones are in bed, Gloria settles on the couch in the den with Dena and Jack. Her mom and dad are settled in, watching a *Mash* rerun on TV.

"Hey," Gloria says, leaning forward.

"What's up?" Dena looks away from the TV. Jack, on the other hand, hasn't even noticed she has come into the room.

"I have something to tell you." Gloria can feel the frown tugging at the corners of her mouth.

"What's happened now?" Dena looks heavenward and rolls her eyes.

Gloria knows her mom is just exasperated with all of Charles's shenanigans and is thankfully not upset with her. "I have to give the car back to Charles," she says. "I guess I should have seen it coming, but with everything going on, I just didn't think about it. There's no way I can afford to keep it and make the payments. You wouldn't believe what he's paying for it. Apparently, he purchased it at a very high interest rate. It's $495 a month. It's no wonder we could never make ends meet." She throws up her hands in exasperation.

"That's outrageous," Dena says.

"What's outrageous?" Jack turns; a look of surprise on his face.

Dena turns to him and says incredulously, "The payments on their car are $495 a month."

"That's crazy." Jack screws up his face. "You could get a Mercedes for that."

"I know." Gloria nods in agreement. "I think Charles has been throwing away our money all this time. He always has to have the latest model car. Anyway, I think he's doing this to try and force me back to him, but I'm not taking the bait. I'm going to return the car and figure out a way to get another one."

She adds, "I was approved for that little house today, but I figured out while I was sitting in the driveway that I'm going to have to put the deposit toward a used car instead." She shrugs.

"That's all I can think to do. I'll have to wait and find another house later."

"Things have a way of working out," Dena says, with a supportive smile.

"I know, Mom, but it's hard to see how sometimes. I'm not going to let my backbone crumble, though. I'm just tired and can't think right now." Gloria heads toward the bedroom. "I think I'm going to go to bed early tonight."

Crawling into bed beside Chrissy, Gloria feels her energy drained, and is reeling from all the lies and deception she never even knew about in her marriage. Charles always hid financial information from her, and now she knows why.

In the morning, she finds Dena in the kitchen wearing lime green pajamas, along with a pink apron her grandmother had sewn, and her well-worn white terrycloth slippers. She turns from the scrambled eggs she is preparing, gives Gloria a hug and says, "Honey, your dad and I had a long talk last night, and we would like to help you out. We can discuss it tonight but don't worry too much today. Things have a way of working out." Looking Gloria up and down, she adds, "Gloria, you have to eat. You're looking very unhealthy."

"I know, Mom. It's just hard when there's so much stress. I don't have an appetite. Nothing seems to taste good." As she's explaining, she turns toward the breakfast bar to sit down.

"I'll just have a few eggs, Mom," she says, settling onto a stool.

Dena serves up some scrambled eggs and adds a couple of pieces of toast. Handing the plate to Gloria, she says, "Please try and eat as much as you can. You are going to make yourself sick. I'm going to send you with some lunch, too. What would you like?" she asks, still holding the frying pan and spatula as she looks at Gloria expectantly.

"Oh, I don't know, maybe a turkey sandwich." Gloria tries to force as much of her breakfast down as she can. She knows her mom is right. She is concerned about herself. She will do her best to put on some weight, if only for the sake of the girls.

"Thank you, Mom. I promise I will try my best. I'm determined not to be his victim. I won't let him make me sick."

Dena flashes a smile, seemingly satisfied with her efforts.

When she walks out the front door, the warm air hits her. It's going to be a hot day. It's only May and is already sweltering. Looking down at her black slacks, she knows they will soon be sticking to her legs.

I should have worn a dress, she thinks. All she can do is shake her head at the thought. It's too late to go back and change. This evening, when she comes home, it will still be warm, and it won't cool down much after dark. If she had one word to describe Bakersfield, it would be hot. *And, it's not going to cool down until October*, she mutters, as she turns the key in the ignition, before backing out of the driveway.

Gloria jumps into the shower as soon as she returns that evening to the blissfully air-conditioned house. She has been on pins and needles all day, thinking about what her parents might want to discuss with her.

After dinner, they all have a seat in the den; leaning forward, her dad begins. "Your mother and I have been talking, and we both agree, we want to help."

Gloria sits quietly on the sofa as he explains, "The Mazda is four years old now, and we had already decided to buy a new car, so we would like you to have it. We've put quite a bit of mileage on it, but it's still a good car. You can make small payments if it makes you feel better, but we're not expecting anything."

Gloria begins to tear up, thinking of the blue Mazda sitting in their driveway. She sits in thought for a moment, trying to come up with something to say. The only thing she can think to say is, "Thank you," but it doesn't seem enough.

"And," her dad laughs. "We get our house back."

Through her tears, Gloria laughs, glad that he has lightened the mood in the room. "I absolutely want to make some kind of payments on the car," she says.

"Let's not worry about the car now. We can draw up some kind of contract on it later, if it would make you feel better." Jack waves a dismissive hand. "We just want to see you get on your feet."

"Thank you both," Gloria says again, still feeling it doesn't nearly enough convey how she feels.

Over the next couple of weekends, Gloria decided to visit some yard sales. She was thrilled to find a cream-colored imitation leather sofa, in excellent condition, the first weekend. Since then, she has found a dinette with a glass top and a black metal base and four metal chairs with upholstered seats. She is looking forward to recovering the seats with new fabric to complement her kitchen. She also found a TV, and she scored some great home décor. Thankfully, when it was all added up, it didn't cut too much into her budget.

On moving day, with her dad's help, they have made three trips with the pickup to move her belongings. Having left the girls sleeping at their grandparent's house, Gloria pulls into her driveway that evening, with the last of her stuff. She decides to leave it all in the car until the morning.

Opening the car door, she looks through her keys to make sure she has the house key in hand and can get into the house easily. The key is a little sticky in the lock, but it only takes a couple of seconds for her to get the door open. She reaches for the light switch as she closes the door behind her. When the lights illuminate the room, she gasps.

Charles is sitting slouched on her couch, his socked feet on the coffee table, and a glass of white wine in his hand.

Gloria puts a hand to her heart as she tries to catch her breath. She breathes, "Charles, how did you get in?"

"You really should get better locks, Gloria. All it took was a little jiggle of the back door, and voila, I was in." He swirls the wine in his glass and takes a sip.

Leaning her back against the front door, with her hand on the knob, she asks, "Where did you get the wine?"

"I brought it. I thought we could celebrate this new abode of yours. Now go to the refrigerator, get yourself a glass of wine, and come join me." He pats the seat beside him.

"I think I'll just go back to my parents' house," she counters, defiantly.

"I don't think you'll want to do that when you see what I've brought." He reaches to the side of the couch and holds up a picnic basket. "Don't you want to see what's inside?"

"No, Charles. I really don't."

He turns the metal latch on the basket, lifting the lid, he reaches in and pulls out a tiny gray tabby kitten. "Looks just like Sassy, don't you think? Now, if you don't join me, you can't have your present. And, if you don't want your present...well then, I just might have to put it down, if you know what I mean."

"No! Charles! I'll join you. We can visit for a while." Gloria, wide-eyed, begins to move slowly toward the kitchen. "I'm going to get some wine," she says. "Please don't hurt the kitten."

"I won't, but you be sure to come right back." He leans back into the couch.

Gloria opens the refrigerator door and pulls out one of two bottles - the one that has only a glass left in it. She doesn't know anything about wine, but she knows he probably spent a fortune on it. She reaches for a wine glass in the cabinet to the right of the sink and pours the remainder of the wine from the bottle into the glass. She sets the empty bottle on the counter and slowly shuffles back into the living room. She sets the wine glass down on the dainty vintage coffee table she found at a flea market. She places it as far away from his feet as she can, then reaches over to him.

"May I have the kitten," she asks. The kitten is beginning to squirm in his hand trying to get away, but he's holding on tight, and Gloria is afraid he will squeeze the life out of the poor little thing.

He sets his glass down on the coffee table and pats the seat beside him on the couch. "You come sit here, and I'll give you the kitten."

Gloria cringes, but she does as he says, reaching her hands out for the poor creature. Charles gently places the kitten in her hands, and she immediately hugs it close and pets it softly. "It's okay," she soothes.

"Now that's more like it." Charles picks up his glass and takes a big gulp. "I knew you would like it."

Gloria tries not to think of him sitting so close as she rocks the kitten and coos, "it's alright. You're alright, kitty."

"Looks just like Sassy, doesn't she." Charles grins, obviously proud of himself.

Gloria knows he picked this kitten for that very reason. He knew how much she loved her Sassy Cat. He did it to stab her right in the heart, and he succeeded. If she had any say, he would never touch this cat again. The only way to be sure of that would be to find it a good home. Although she would love to keep the kitten, it would never be safe as long as it was with her. She just has to get through tonight somehow, and she will make sure it's safe.

With a drink in his left hand, Charles places his right arm around Gloria's shoulders. Gloria tries not to flinch, but she's jumpy and doesn't quite manage it. The kitten has settled down, as she cuddles it protectively to her chest.

"Why so jumpy?" Charles asks. "It's only me. Remember me, Gloria—your husband."

"Sorry, Charles. I'm just nervous."

"There's no need to be nervous, Gloria. We're just sitting here having some quality time together. I see you like your present. It's just like old times. Now drink your wine before it loses its chill."

Gloria can't seem to remember the old times he is talking about, but she obeys, cupping the kitten in one hand while picking up the wine glass from the coffee table with the other. She takes a small sip. She knows she will have a migraine in the morning if she drinks much of it, but she tries not to think about it.

"Now that's better. See, isn't this nice?" He smiles a satisfied smile.

"Yes," Gloria lies, as she takes another sip of the wine before placing it back on the table. "I think the kitten is asleep. I should place her back in her basket." She feels off balance holding the kitten—like she can't adequately defend herself if she needs to.

"Yes, yes. Go ahead." Charles takes the last sip of his wine. As he removes his arm from around her shoulder, he pushes himself up off the couch. "I'm going to get another glass of wine."

Gloria doesn't respond. She is too eager to make sure the kitten is comfortable. Still holding the kitten in one hand, she takes the opportunity with Charles in the kitchen to grab a towel from the bathroom. Returning to the living room, Charles is already back on the couch. She places the folded towel in the bottom of the basket and gently places the kitten on top. Thankfully, the little thing is still asleep.

Charles pats the seat again. "Come sit."

She complies, and his arm is around her shoulder once more. "Drink your wine," he says, before taking a sip of his.

She reaches forward, picking up her glass and takes a small sip. "Now, this is more like it." He leans back into the couch again, making himself comfortable. "A glass of wine and my girl by my side."

She is going to have to figure a way out of this situation. She can't just sit and hope he passes out drunk. That would probably take more than two bottles of wine. She must come up with another plan to get rid of him; otherwise, he will be expecting to go to bed with her, and she can't allow that to happen.

Thinking of the valium the doctor prescribed for her anxiety, Gloria remembers she has only taken a couple out of the bottle. *How much would it take to knock him out?* She wonders. After all he's done, she still doesn't want to kill him. *Maybe five or six,* she thinks.

"I need to go to the bathroom," she announces, sitting forward on the couch and looking back at Charles.

"Okay." He looks at her and takes another sip of wine. His glass is almost empty now. "But come right back."

"I will," she promises.

Once in the bathroom, she closes the door and hurries to the medicine cabinet. Opening it quietly, she sees the bottle of pills right in front on the bottom shelf. She twists the cap off and counts out eight blue pills one at a time. She grabs some toilet paper and wraps the pills. Then, she sticks them in the pocket of her jeans. She looks in the mirror above the sink, trying to compose herself. Smoothing her hair, she stands tall and then reaches over to flush the toilet, before running the water and opening the door.

"Can I get you some more wine? She asks when she returns.

"Sure." He lazily hands her the glass.

She tries not to hurry too fast to the kitchen. Once there, she quickly pulls the pills out of her pocket. Thankfully, a decorative mortar and pestle are sitting on the kitchen counter. She hurriedly dumps the pills into the bowl and begins to crush them until there is only a fine powder. Stepping over to the fridge, she reaches in to grab the bottle. She is shaking so badly, she almost drops it on the floor. She stops in her tracks, trying to catch her breath and slow her heart rate. She can't return to the living room looking all flustered.

"What's going on in there," Charles calls from the living room.

"Nothing," she says. "I was just looking for some cheese to go with the wine." She goes back to the refrigerator and pulls out a block of cheddar cheese. It's all she has. "I don't have anything fancy, and I don't know what goes with this wine, but I thought it would be nice."

"Sounds good," he calls back.

She quickly pours wine into his glass and adds all the powder, stirring it with her finger. She grabs a plate from the cupboard and places the cheese on it. She then pulls a knife from the butcher block and places it beside the cheese. She doesn't like taking a knife near Charles, but she doesn't have time to cut the cheese without raising his suspicion. She has already taken too long.

178

Placing the wine bottle back in the fridge, she turns back to the wine glass, stirring it one more time for good measure. She picks up the plate with the knife and cheese and the glass of wine, before returning to the living room.

"Finally, you're back," he says, lazily, as she hands him his wine. She can see flecks floating in the glass, and her heart almost stops, but he takes a sip without seeming to notice. She can tell he is drunk and she hopes this works in her favor. She won't be able to stop trembling until he has consumed the whole glass. She sets the plate of cheese down on the coffee table and returns to her seat beside him.

"You're shaking, Gloria," he says, reaching out for her.

She has to think quickly. "I just got a sudden chill. I guess someone walked over my grave." This is her feeble attempt at humor. She chuckles and smiles, nervously.

"Come here." He grabs her around the shoulders and pulls her to him. "I'll warm you up."

She tries not to stiffen. *Breathe Gloria*, she tells herself. It's no use she can't relax until that glass of wine is gone. She looks up as he takes a long drink. Thankfully, there is only a sip left, but the flakes are still there! "Now, isn't this nice?" he says.

"Yes. It's nice." She hopes she won't have to endure his embrace much longer. Thankfully, he downs the rest of the wine. There is still a residue at the bottom of the glass when he sets it down. All she can do is sit and hope he doesn't notice.

It takes thirty long minutes before Charles begins to slur. "We should go to bed."

"Oh, let's stay up a little longer," Gloria suggests. "Aren't we having a good time?"

"Yes. We are," he slurs.

Gloria sits in dread for another long ten minutes before his head lolls back on the couch. She waits a few minutes longer to make sure he's out, before extricating herself from under his arm. He doesn't budge. She sprints to the kitchen and rinses the mortar and pestle, placing them in the dishwasher, out of sight. Returning to the living room, she heads to the front door. There, underneath the light switch is where she dropped her purse. She pulls her cell phone out from the side pocket. Hurrying to the bedroom, she calls 911, reporting her estranged husband has broken into her house and fallen asleep on her couch in a drunken stupor.

She doesn't have to fake the fright in her voice when she talks to the operator. She suddenly begins to feel like passing out. She sits on the edge of the bed and puts her head between her knees. Then she remembers, there are two glasses on the coffee table. She can't have it looking like they were drinking together.

After hanging up, she jumps up, grabs the glasses from the table, runs to the kitchen, and rinses them out. Drying them, she places them back in the cupboard just in time to hear a knock on the door. Bakersfield PD, a voice calls from outside the door. She looks back at Charles. He is still out. She breathes a sigh of relief and opens the door.

Thankfully, once she convinces the two officers that Charles does not live there, they drag him to their patrol car and take him off to sober up in jail. He is so out of it when they drag him out the door, he just looks at her, eyes at half-mast as he goes by, an officer on each side holding him up. He doesn't utter a word.

"Thank you, Officers," she says, before closing the door. She will have to call a locksmith first thing in the morning and have deadbolts added to her doors.

She rushes from the front door to the basket beside the couch to check on the kitten. Seeing it sleeping soundly, she picks the basket up and carries it to her bedside. Slowly she shuffles back to the kitchen, pulls a small bowl from the cabinet and fills it half way with water. When she returns to the bedroom, she gently places it inside the basket beside the kitten.

Gloria thinks about what she will do about the kitten. She knows Samantha, at the office, is a big animal lover. She would probably foster the little thing, if not adopt it, when she tells her how she came to have it. She knows she needs to be honest with Samantha. She should have been more honest with her friends from the start.

As she begins to undress, she realizes she needs to file a restraining order. Knowing it will probably not do much good, she nevertheless decides to apply for one tomorrow. She vaguely remembers filing a restraining order in the future. Now she's questioning whether it was a dream, as that's the only explanation that makes sense.

After signing papers at the police station, she doesn't feel much better. It will be a bit of a relief to have him served. Hopefully, he won't know how ineffective restraining orders are and maybe adhere to it for a while.

If she could only remember about before. All the details of her future life are fading away. The only thing she can remember clearly now is her relationship with Rick. She has a sinking feeling this is her life now, and the future is gone. Will she even meet Rick in this life?

She had asked to have Charles served with the restraining order at work. She knows this will put him into a fury, but if he is served in front of his coworkers, it might make him think twice before violating it.

Unfortunately, Gloria's feeling of safety hasn't come to fruition. As she sits at the kitchen table a few days later, she looks incredulously at the summons in her hand. Charles is suing for custody of the girls. She knows he doesn't want the girls. He wants to hurt her, and this is definitely the best way to do it.

She knows no judge will give him full custody, but he or she will probably demand that Charles has visitation rights. He has never taken care of them. Would he neglect or, heaven forbid, hurt them? He might have just found a way to force her back.

Gloria loses herself in her work during the weeks to come. It's a needed diversion from her real life. All has been quiet with Charles. She thinks it's probably because he wouldn't want to violate the restraining order before they go to court over custody. At home during the evenings, she looks at the date on the summons. She can see that the court date is coming up, and Gloria's pro bono lawyer has not given her much hope of being able to retain full custody.

"Charles does not have a history of abusing his daughters, so the judge, most likely, will grant him partial custody," her lawyer had warned. Gloria cringes at the thought.

She is sitting at her desk in her office, head in her hands, contemplating her situation. Mickey has stepped out, so she decides to pick up the phone in front of her. She has decided she should call Charles at work. Doing so, she hopes, will force him to be civil.

After getting him on the line, she musters up the sweetest voice she can, and asks, "Is there a way we can work something out, without going to court, Charles?"

"You can always come back home," he says coolly.

"I'm not ready, Charles. I was hoping for another solution for now. Would you consider dropping this, if I drop the restraining order?" She knows it's the only thing she can do.

After a few seconds of silence, he says, "I'll have to think about it, but right now I have to get back to work. Since I can't call you, because of the restraining order you just had to file, you will have to call me this evening."

It makes Gloria physically ill to take orders from Charles once again, but all she can do is agree. She knows she is not supposed to be calling him, per the restraining order, but what else can she do? "Okay," she says, before promising to give him a call around 6:00.

"Okay, bye." He hangs up abruptly.

Needing this settled, Gloria finds herself sitting at the kitchen table drumming her fingers, as 6:00 quickly approaches, trying to drum up the nerve to call Charles. She checks her watch, filled with dread over the conversation she is about to have, but she can't put it off any longer. Picking up the phone, she slowly punches in the number.

"Hello Charles," she says, nervously picking up a pen and beginning to draw circles on a notepad. She is doing her best to calm down and hopefully sound as pleasant as possible. As she speaks, she finds herself pressing harder while continuing to draw doodles on her pad, until the tip of the pen perforates the paper. She lifts her trembling hand, dropping the pen as he replies.

"Well," he demands, "are you going to drop the restraining order, or aren't you?"

"I guess it depends on what we can figure out about the girls," she says, trying to gain some composure. She knows he has the upper hand, but she still has a little leverage, and she is going to try and use it, if she can only keep her wits about her.

"What did you have in mind?" he asks.

She looks up toward the ceiling, trying to gather her thoughts. "Well, I know you need to see the girls," she says. Actually, what she knows is he really wants to see her and not the girls, so she decides to use this to her advantage. But, in the end, she knows it could actually lead to her destruction.

Deciding to go ahead with it, she suggests, "What if we meet someplace neutral, and I can stay while you visit with the girls?"

"What do you mean by someplace neutral?"

"Like maybe a park or the bowling alley," she suggests. "We could go bowling together. Chrissy can play with us, and we can put Sarah in the nursery. You could visit with her afterward."

She picks up the pen again and finds herself biting on the end as she thinks back. They haven't been bowling in ages, and she knows it was always something he liked to do. Maybe, just maybe, he will go for it. She quickly adds, "At least for the first few times, then we can figure it out from there."

"And you will drop the restraining order?" he asks, with a note of triumph in his voice.

"Yes," she says, knowing she is probably being foolish to do so.

"When would we meet?"

Never, she thinks, but says, "How about Saturday? We could do weekends, but you have to stop pressuring me to come back," she adds, hoping she hasn't gone too far; but she's on a roll. "And, you have to drop the custody hearing."

There is a lengthy pause, as she anxiously waits for his answer. "Okay, you have a deal, for now, but remember, I can re-file at any time. And, you have to show up."

She lets out a sigh of relief. Knowing this is the best she is going to get, she reluctantly agrees. "I will drop the restraining order before Saturday."

"What time do you want to meet?" he asks.

"How about noon," she says.

"Eleven o'clock," he comes back, always having to have the final say.

"I will see you at eleven." She is back to giving in as usual.

Gloria steps into the bowling alley Saturday morning, pushing Sarah in her stroller with Chrissy by her side. Taking in the atmosphere, the smell of lane oil and the sound of crashing pins reminds her of good times in her childhood, when her father used to take her along on his bowling nights.

Her smile fades as she spots Charles, but she plasters it back on and waves as she heads over to the reception desk where he stands. She rents shoes for herself and Chrissy, and notices he seems to be in a particularly good mood. Before the girls were born, he used to enjoy it when they would bowl in their mixed-doubles leagues. They were good memories for Gloria, too. It had not all been bad times with Charles. Things with him had just seemed to get progressively worse over the years. It was hard for her to remember there were good times, too—times when she was able to keep him happy.

The meetings at the bowling alley gradually grow to include Sundays. Once again, he is able to push her boundaries, but he has actually been playing it cool. She finds herself eventually letting her guard down a bit. This is the first time they have ever done things as a family, and she thinks it's probably good for the girls. How long "Good Charles" might hold out, she doesn't know.

Having a glimpse of how life could be is difficult for Gloria, but she knows the minute she lets down her guard too much, things could come crashing down. She is always anxious about new demands that are sure to come.

Instead of demands, Gloria is surprised when Charles first asks to cancel a weekend of bowling. He won't explain why. She is just happy to take a weekend off, but she is curious, very curious. When he cancels the following weekend too, she is stunned.

Four weeks go by without a word from him, and she has decided to live in a state of blissful ignorance. She begins to take Chrissy bowling Saturday afternoons, without Charles, and they have both been enjoying some mother-daughter time. Chrissy doesn't seem to miss her daddy coming along.

Sitting at her desk, fanning herself with a large manila envelope folded in half, she thinks about how it has always been hot in the back room. She pulls one of two box fans closer to her chair and catches sight of Mickey typing away on her keyboard, her bright red nails moving like lightning. Gloria is not quite sure, but judging by the look on Mickey's face, she could swear she has something on her mind.

"I like your dress. I'm not used to seeing you wear dresses to work," Gloria says after having decided to get Mickey's attention. Something's up. She can feel it.

"Thanks." Mickey swivels her chair around and smiles.

"I thought I might start dressing up for work. What do you think?" She smiles as she tilts her head and runs a hand down the length of the red wrap dress she is wearing.

"Well," Gloria says, "nobody really sees us back here. I say wear whatever you feel best in. But it really looks nice."

"Yeah, you're right." She screws up her face. "I feel better in jeans."

"Is there something on your mind?" Gloria raises an eyebrow. "You're looking a bit like the Cheshire Cat this morning."

Mickey's eyes widen as she flashes a grin and quickly rolls her chair over to Gloria's desk. "I didn't know if I should be the one to tell you, but . . . did you know Charles has been dating?"

Gloria's jaw drops as she sits in stunned silence. Someone could have knocked her over with a feather, as Mickey's expression turns from smiling to cringing.

"I'm so sorry," Mickey says when she sees the look of shock on Gloria's face.

Shaking her head slowly, Gloria says, "No, no, it's all right, I'm just a little taken aback. Dating? Really? But who?"

"Rhonda," Mickey whispers.

Gloria sits and lets it sink in before speaking. "The only Rhonda I know is Rhonda Matthews, the bartender at the country club, but she's married."

"No," Mickey says, "she's been divorced for a few months now."

It takes a few seconds before Gloria speaks again. "You know, Mickey, I'm glad you told me. I've been wondering why he's been leaving me alone. I hope it lasts a while, and I can have some peace." She sighs. Thinking about it further, she says, "You know, they're both drinkers, so I'm sure that's a plus for him. No, really, thank you for telling me, Mickey."

Visibly relieved, Mickey says, "I've been going over and over whether to tell you or not. I'm glad it was the right thing to do, now that I've done it."

"I'm glad you did, Mickey, really," Gloria says.

"Rhonda Matthews!" Gloria gets a sheepish grin on her face, and they both start laughing.

When she gathers her wits, she releases a huge sigh of relief, thinking about what this means. Charles's attention is focused elsewhere. She can hardly believe her luck.

Chapter 15

February 2018

<u>Before</u>

After dropping Sarah off at Chrissy's apartment, Gloria waved goodbye as she strolled back to her car in the parking lot. She put the car in drive and headed out of the lot, on her way to Rick's Big Bear cabin. This made her trip longer than driving to Ontario, but when she finally arrived, she decided it was definitely worth the extra time.

She turned a corner and spotted his quaint little gambrel cabin nestled in the pines, its small lawn in the front surrounded by a split-rail fence and flower boxes hanging under the windows to each side of the front door. Snow had been shoveled to the sides of the walkway up to the door, but Rick had instructed her to enter through the back.

She parked on the side of the cabin, walked around back, and found a canoe hanging from the redwood deck, which she felt added to the ambiance of the darling little place. As she walked under the deck and through the back door into the kitchen, as she had been instructed to do, she found Rick washing breakfast dishes.

"Suzie homemaker, I see," Gloria teased, as she attempted to duck when he turned to flick soapy water in her face.

"Dad!" she heard from the doorway. "That's mean!"

They turned to see Megan standing behind them with her hands on her hips, and a stern look on her face; Rick introduced them.

"I'm so glad to meet you, Megan. Your dad talks about you all the time." Gloria offered her hand to shake.

"I know," she said, breaking into a big grin. "He always does that," Megan said, reaching out and giving Gloria's hand a firm shake.

"That means he's very proud of you, and I can see why," Gloria said, releasing Megan's hand.

"Can I show her the cabin?" Megan's enthusiasm was infectious.

"Sure." Rick laughed, as Megan grabbed Gloria's hand and pulled her out of the kitchen.

Gloria had hoped they would get along, but this seemed to be more than she could have dreamed of. Megan sure wasn't shy around new people, and her enthusiasm seemed to rub off on Gloria as she followed slightly behind.

"I can't wait," Gloria said, as they headed into the next room.

"This is our living room." Megan was doing her best impression of a tour guide.

Gloria took in the quaint little room with a mocha-colored leather loveseat against one wall, facing a large flat-screen TV on the opposite wall. The matching sofa was placed underneath a window to the front of the house, with pine-tree throw pillows at each end. A pine coffee table sat in front of the couch, a large green bowl filled with pinecones in the center.

"And over here," she gestured to the right of the TV, "we have a wood stove. It keeps the cabin really warm."

"I can see that," Gloria said, taking in the blazing fire in the pot-belly stove that sat on its granite base with firewood piled to

189

the side. "It's very toasty in here. In fact, I'm going to take my coat off before I cook."

Megan was quick to help Gloria off with her coat. She took it to the coat closet, saying, "Don't go anywhere. I'll be right back."

Tugging at Gloria's arm, after she hung her jacket, Megan was eager to get back to the tour. As they rounded the corner, Megan had to show off the bathroom. It was painted cream with mint green tile above the bathtub and on the countertop. It had been decorated in a moose theme, with a matching shower curtain, towels hanging on the rail, and coordinating bathmats.

"Very cute," Gloria had to admit.

Releasing Gloria's hand, Megan was already halfway up the stairs. "Come on, my room is up here, and Dad's too," she gushed.

Going into each room, Gloria could see they were small but was impressed with the log furnishings in each one. It really added to the cabin feel of the place.

"Did you help decorate?" Gloria asked.

"I picked out my bed and comforter, and curtains," Megan announced proudly.

"You did an excellent job. You must like bears." Gloria took in the bear-themed room.

"Yes," Megan said, "I have a lot of stuffed bears in the closet, too."

"You're one lucky girl," Gloria mused aloud. Megan had so much, but she still seemed to be the sweetest little thing.

"Are you two lost up there?" Rick yelled from the bottom of the stairs.

"No, we're coming," Megan called down the stairs.

As Gloria followed Megan back into the living room, she marveled at all the father-daughter pictures that seemed to adorn every wall. They had obviously enjoyed many adventures together.

She was impressed with all the décor as well. She would never have guessed that Rick had it in him to decorate this way.

They both came downstairs to find Rick seated on the couch. Gloria and Megan each took a side, as he put his arms around them both and pulled them in. Gloria could tell he was a happy man, seeing them getting along so well.

Unfortunately, when the time came for Sarah to meet Rick; saying she didn't warm to him right away was an understatement. She eyed him suspiciously on the Saturday of their first meeting, a week after Gloria's visit to the cabin. After introductions, they had all taken a seat in Gloria's living room. Rick and Gloria sat on the couch while Sarah took the loveseat. Sarah sat there with arms crossed over her chest as they talked, suspicion emanating from her squinting blue eyes.

Sarah sat coolly as she stated, "You know, my mom is crazy," her eyes still squinting and lips pursed.

Gloria was taken aback to see her looking Rick straight in the eye. She never blinked. For a split second, she tried to think of what to do. She was mortified. Rick, on the other hand, just laughed, thankfully breaking the tension.

Without skipping a beat, he said, "That's okay. It takes someone crazy to be with me," and flashed a big smile, much to Gloria's relief.

Trying to break the ice, he invited Sarah to come to the cabin with Gloria sometime, enticing her with snowboarding lessons. Although Sarah had to play it cool and suggested she needed some time to think about it, Gloria could tell he had piqued her interest.

The next day, Sarah casually strolled into the living room with an announcement. "Mom," she said, taking Gloria's attention away from the TV. "I think I want to go to the cabin."

"Great," Gloria said, trying not to sound too enthusiastic.

191

"When were you thinking about going?"

"This weekend?" Sarah raised her eyebrows questioningly.

"Sounds like a plan." Gloria sat there casually, covered in her fuzzy white blanket, careful not to show her excitement. She could tell Sarah was trying to play it cool and didn't want her to know she was excited about going.

To celebrate Sarah's momentous decision, Gloria arranged to take Friday off work, and Sarah the day off school. They left bright and early Friday morning. As they began their ascent to the cabin, everything began to be covered in a dusting of snow. Sarah couldn't seem to take it all in. "It's so beautiful, Mom."

Rick met them at the back door. "Well, Sarah, how do you like it here?"

"It's gorgeous." She beamed. "It's the first time I've ever been in snow. It looks even better in person."

"Would you two ladies like to go shopping?" he asked before they could get inside the door.

"Shopping?" Gloria stopped in her tracks. "For what?"

"You two are going to need some snow gear." He pulled his debit card out of his wallet and flashed a grin. "I'm going to send you to find what you need."

"No," Gloria tried to protest. "We can just make do."

He took one look at the two Bakersfield girls, gestured, scanned them up and down with one palm flat toward the sky, and insisted, "Believe me, you need the right clothing. You'll need ski pants, or your jeans are going to be soaked, and you'll be miserable. And, don't get me started on your jackets. You'll freeze up there on the mountaintop. You need parkas. You will also need beanies and gloves at the very least."

Listening in bewilderment, Gloria knew this was going to cost a small fortune. "Maybe we should just do sightseeing this trip." She waved away the debit card.

"I'm not hearing of it." He continued to hold the card out stubbornly toward her. "This is Sarah's first time to the mountains, and she needs the full experience." He was grinning at Sarah, who Gloria was pleased to see, was grinning back.

"Please, Mom." Sarah turned with her hands clasped together underneath her chin.

"I guess it's two against one." Gloria reluctantly reached over and took the card from Rick.

"Off you go, you two." He waved them off, after hugging Sarah and giving Gloria a kiss.

"Thank you, Rick. I don't know what to say," Gloria said, looking into his eyes.

"Don't say anything. Get out of here, women." He chuckled. "By the way, the pin number is 4893."

Gloria and Sarah were lucky to find a parking spot in the middle of town. They picked a shop and began trying to find the most economical items on their list. As it turned out, shopping economically in Big Bear was not going to be possible. After they got sticker shock out of their system, they started to have fun trying things on.

They spent most of the day looking around the quaint shops, and Gloria thought they might have broken Rick's debit card. She was sure a salesperson was going to confiscate it, every time she used it. She did enjoy looking at all the mountain shops with her daughter, though. There were bears, moose, deer, antlers, and pine trees on just about everything they could think of.

"It would be so fun, decorating a cabin," Sarah commented, in one of the dressing rooms, as they tried on ski pants.

"You haven't even seen inside Rick's cabin yet," Gloria said. "Just wait. He's got it all fixed up."

That evening, Gloria returned Rick's debit card, and they sheepishly hauled in all their bags. They quickly headed upstairs to put them away, trying to sneak past Rick, who was sitting on the couch, reading a rock-crawling magazine, a raised Jeep with massive tires on the front cover.

"Just a minute, you two. Aren't you going to model your new stuff?" Rick looked up as they scurried by.

Sarah rushed straight up the stairs to put everything on, while Gloria turned back with her bags to sit on the couch with Rick. A short time later, Sarah came back down the stairs and did a couple of turns in front of them. "You look like a real mountain girl," he said.

"Thanks, Rick, for everything." She turned and ran back up the stairs.

"You're welcome," he called up to her. "Now, how about you?" He looked sheepishly at Gloria.

"You'll just have to wait until tomorrow. It'll be a surprise," she said and gave him a peck on the cheek.

He pulled her closer and demanded a proper kiss before Sarah came back downstairs.

They all sat that evening after dinner and put in a DVD of an old classic, *Young Frankenstein*. Sitting there laughing at the movie, Sarah and Rick agreed that Gloria looked a lot like Teri Garr, who was playing a dingy blonde with a German accent in the film. A popcorn fight and laughter eventually ensued between Rick and Sarah, with Rick, the instigator.

"Behave, you two," Gloria chided, laughing. "I'm not going to be the one to clean that up." They both just looked at her innocently.

Saturday, bright and early, Sarah was eager to try snowboarding for the first time. She was down on the snow more than she was up, but she took it with good humor. While Sarah was taking snowboarding lessons, Rick rented skis and boots for Gloria. After taking her to the bunny slopes, he was a patient and very loveable instructor.

Sarah was mesmerized by the snow and determined to build a snowman before leaving for home. Arriving back at the cabin, she seemed to regain some of her pep as she took to her task right away.

Oh, to be young and energetic again, Gloria thought, as she headed inside to change.

Rick helped Sarah with her endeavors. They laughed and threw snowballs at each other in between their combined efforts to construct Mr. Snowman.

"Sarah, why don't you go look for some limbs to use as arms," Rick said, as he rolled the third ball of snow around, making it bigger and bigger, to use as the head.

"Sure." Sarah immediately ran off to collect some branches.

Once Rick had the head in place, he disappeared into the house, bringing out items from the pantry and a couple of pieces of charcoal. "Here," he said, piling everything in front of the faceless snowman. "Pick out some things to make a face."

"I saw some marbles in Megan's room. I think they would make great eyes." Sarah was off again to gather the marbles.

Rick and Gloria settled on a couple of the patio chairs on the back patio and waited for Sarah to return. "I think she's having fun," Rick said, seemingly pleased with himself.

"She sure is." Gloria sighed with a feeling of contentment.

Sarah was back out the door quickly and back at her task. She placed the branches she'd collected in the sides of the snowman.

Then moved to his face, putting the marble eyes on first, then using a piece of coal as a nose. She rummaged around in the items Rick had brought out and came up with some dried beans for a mouth. She took off her green scarf and put it around his neck before placing the matching beanie on top.

Standing back to look, it appeared she was not entirely satisfied with her work. She began digging through the snow and gathering brown blades of grass from underneath. She quickly fashioned eyebrows and a mustache. Standing back again to look, she nodded, before turning around to smile. "Perfect."

"Yes," Gloria and Rick said in unison.

Afterward, as the sun set, they all sat in patio chairs underneath the deck drinking hot chocolate and admiring Sarah's somewhat lopsided snowman.

"I think it's perfect." Sarah smiled with bright red cheeks, her only complaint the lack of sunlight for pictures.

Sarah needn't have worried. Mr. Snowman hadn't melted overnight, and Gloria snapped a dozen pictures of red-cheeked Sarah with her masterpiece before leaving for home Sunday afternoon. Sarah had been animated on the way home, relaying her snowboarding experience in full. Apparently, she had an instructor who was "really cool."

Surprised, Gloria remarked, "I thought boys were a waste of time."

To which Sarah informed her, "Most of them are, but Mom, he's different," fluttering her eyelashes as her cheeks began to turn a bright shade of pink.

And that's how it starts. Gloria shook her head in dismay.

Hoping this would not be a turning point in her daughter's assessment of boys, Gloria continued to drive and listen. *How in the world do teenage girls have so much to say*, she wondered. By

196

the time they had driven into the driveway, Sarah had actually admitted she'd had an awesome time. Gloria wished she could have recorded that comment.

Monday evening, Sarah was standing beside Gloria at the sink, helping to dry the dinner dishes. As Gloria scrubbed, she was surprised to hear her daughter comment, "Mom, you actually have laugh lines!"

"Thanks a lot," Gloria said sarcastically, flicking water at Sarah. "Are you saying I'm old?"

"Older than dirt, Mom." Sarah laughed, ducking, and wiping at her face. "I guess that means you must really be happy."

Gloria paused for a moment, smiling and taking in how good it felt. She had evidently been smiling a lot more since Rick came into her life. All in all it had been a great weekend with Sarah and it seemed their relationship had received a much needed shot of optimism.

Chrissy finally met Rick over dinner in Bakersfield, the last weekend in February. They ordered in pizza, and thankfully both hit it off right away. They joked back and forth, at Gloria's expense, and took great pleasure in making her flush beet red. She couldn't help but laugh along with them, just happy they had warmed up to each other so easily. At one point, Rick had Chrissy spewing soda out her nose, which brought on a roar of laughter from Rick.

Gloria knew there were going to be conspiracies between the two of them in the future. She shuddered, thinking about what they might come up with. She would be no match for their quick banter. Thank goodness Sarah was staying with Cindy for the night. Gloria knew for sure she would have been mortified by their behavior. She was thankful, too that Alex had to work. Knowing him, it would have been three against one.

197

Gloria was beyond happy to have both her girls onboard. They had been so good to help keep her secret from Charles. She knew it was only a matter of time before he found out. But for now, she would bask in his ignorance.

Chapter 16

July 2003

<u>After</u>

Gloria looks at the calendar on the wall by her vanity. It has been a whole month since she has heard a word from Charles, and she begins to believe she might be able to build a life for herself and her sweet little girls. She only hopes Charles and Rhonda don't break up too soon. Maybe Charles won't show his true colors for a while. Or, *per*haps, she thinks, *Rhonda might be able to handle him.* She can only hope.

Since all has been quiet at nights, she has turned to thinking about Rick. She can almost feel her heart breaking. *Does he even exist in this life,* she wonders?

It's another sleepless night, with Gloria staring at the ceiling. Thoughts of Rick have been keeping her up. Slowly, over the sleepless nights, an idea has mushroomed. *What if I try to find him?* And then, she thinks, *What would I say to him? How would I introduce myself?* She tries to push the thoughts away, but she has become obsessed with the "what ifs."

Her other life, the future, has faded away until the life she is now living has become her reality. The only part of her future that seems to have stayed clear is her life with Rick. The memories drive her forward with a magnetic pull she can't resist.

But it's not only her memories of Rick that drive her now; it's the dreams, the nightmare of the future. They fill her with a sense of dread that is beginning to form in the pit of her stomach. She is almost sure she does not want to wake up. If she's going to stay here, she must find Rick. The clarity of their life together seems to pull her toward him.

She tries to remember what he had told her about his past. From what she can remember, he should be living with his wife, Veronica. At that thought, her hopes plummet. But then she remembers they would not yet be married. At this thought, her eyes grow wide.

He had told her about Veronica's hair-trigger temper, and how he would be forced to hold her back by the wrists as she would try to pummel him during their many heated arguments. It's hard for Gloria to picture Rick in a heated argument. One of the many things she admires about him is that he is such an even-tempered man.

Gloria never considered herself capable of being a home-wrecker, but when it comes to Rick, she seems willing to do just that. Not that she would get past first base, without him thinking her a nut case. The nagging temptation to find him, though, soon proves too much for her to resist.

On Wednesday evening, she finds herself lounging on the couch in her little lavender living room, staring at her sparkling fireplace in deep thought. Abruptly, she sits up straight. She scoots toward the end of the couch and grabs up the phone, and without thinking it through further, dials directory assistance. Before she knows it, she is asking for Richard Gaines' phone number in Ontario, California. To her surprise, the operator quickly reads off a number, and just like that she has taken the first step.

After sinking back into the couch in amazement that she is actually doing this, she begins to ponder how she might approach him? *My name is Gloria, and we know each other from the future* is not going to work, obviously. She needs a good reason to call him. She certainly doesn't want Veronica to answer the phone. A female voice asking for Rick would certainly throw her into a tizzy. With several scenarios vying for attention, she settles on one. She decides to drive to Ontario on a weekday and try to catch him at work.

On second thought, *it might be a good idea to call and set up lunch, before driving all the way there.* She admonishes herself to slow down and not to get ahead of things.

But her thoughts continue. She is going to need his work number. Luckily for her, she remembers where he used to work. She makes up her mind to find the number for South Western Communications and call him there. She realizes she must stop this madness and go to bed, but she needs to do one thing first, call directory assistance once more. Finally heading off to bed, she has both phone numbers in hand. Taking her purse from the bedside table, she folds the slip of paper and slides it into a side pocket before crawling into bed and turning out the light.

Almost dozing in front of her computer terminal after another sleepless night, trying to concentrate enough to do her job, she finds herself thinking of that little slip of paper in her purse. She reaches for her purse, takes it out, and begins staring at the phone numbers she has written down when she hears, "Is anyone home in there?"

She swivels around in her chair, dropping the paper to the floor. It's Mickey, and she had been standing only three feet behind her.

Gloria sputters, "I'm so sorry, Mickey. I didn't hear you." Well, she's awake now.

"Obviously. I've been trying to get your attention. Where have you been?" Mickey smirks.

"Nowhere, just daydreaming I guess." Gloria's voice is slightly tinged with guilt. She knows she has not been convincing, but thankfully, Mickey drops it.

"I was asking if the invoices are ready to mail. I'm going by the post office, and I can drop them off if they're ready." Mickey looks down at the paper on the floor.

Gloria inhales sharply as Mickey reaches down to scoop it up. "I think you dropped something," she says, looking down at the numbers. "Who's Richard Gaines?" Her eyes narrow with suspicion.

"Oh, nobody," Gloria says, flustered as she reaches for the paper.

"I don't believe you." Mickey waits a beat before handing it over.

"It's just someone I kind of know," Gloria says, dismissively.

"You aren't going to get off that easy, you know. By the looks of you right now, I think this is a significant someone you kind of know."

"I don't know," Gloria stammers. "We haven't really met yet." She is not quite able to meet Mickey's gaze. "I promise I will let you know if anything comes of it."

"You better. You've been keeping things from me lately, and I thought we were best friends." Mickey adds, "Do you have those invoices?"

"Oh, yes." Gloria is trying unsuccessfully to regain her composure. She turns back to her desk, reaches to her outbox, and hands the envelopes over to Mickey.

As Mickey turns, Gloria thanks her, but Mickey is shaking her head and chuckling as she leaves.

She looks at the paper in her hand and quickly folds and sticks it back into her purse. She admonishes herself and dives into work, but it isn't long before the little paper in her purse beckons to her again. Pulling it out once more, she realizes staring at it is useless, and finally works up the courage to call. With Mickey gone, the back office is empty except for her, and she knows there will never be a better time to do it.

"South Western Communications," a male voice answers after two rings.

"Yes, um, I'm looking for Richard Gaines." She lays her head down on her desk, unable to believe what she is doing.

"Hold on, I'll transfer you," he says. "Would you like to write down the number, in case we're disconnected?"

Sitting up in her chair, she quickly says, "Yes. Thank you," and hurriedly grabs up her pen to write down the number he gives.

In a couple of seconds, the phone is connected. "South Western Communications, this is Rick," he says, in an official-sounding voice.

Gloria pauses a moment too long, seemingly frozen, her mouth open, unable to speak.

"Hello," he tries again.

Finding her voice, she clears her throat and says, "I'm sorry, it's been quite a day," trying to explain away her awkwardness.

Gathering courage, she tries to put on her professional voice. "Yes, my name is Gloria Davis," and she quickly adds, "I promise I'm not a salesperson, but I do have some very important personal information for you. I was wondering if we might be able to meet for lunch to discuss it." She realizes she has rushed through all of this a bit too fast. She couldn't help herself; it all just poured out once she began to speak.

"Can't you just tell me over the phone?" He sounds annoyed.

"Well, it's something that's going to take quite some time to explain, and I feel it would be better to tell you in person." She

203

crosses her fingers. "I'm free any day next week if you would be willing to meet."

"Um," he says and pauses.

She uses the pause to say, "I know this is out of the blue, but I do have some information I think you will be very interested in." At the last second, she adds, "And, lunch is on me."

"I guess we could meet," he says slowly. "Monday is the only day I have free. I must say, now you've piqued my curiosity."

"I'm sorry. I don't mean to worry you, but I promise it will make more sense when we meet on Monday. Is there a restaurant where you would like to meet, and a time that's good for you?" She places a hand over the mouthpiece and takes a deep breath, then exhales.

"Does Spring House work for you?" he asks. "I usually take lunch at noon."

She takes her hand off the mouthpiece. "That works." She gives a silent sigh of relief.

Saying their goodbyes, she hangs up, while taking some deep breaths to try and slow her heart. She can't believe she has actually talked to him. She hadn't quite recognized his voice. It isn't quite as deep as she remembers. She supposes it might be because he's younger, or has she forgotten that too?

The rest of the afternoon, Gloria is unable to keep her mind on work, going over and over what she had said, and how she said it. Hopefully, she didn't come off as too looney. When 5:00 rolls around, she is startled to see she has not accomplished a thing since the phone call. She jumps up as Mickey is saying bye, and quickly asks if she might have Monday off. It had completely slipped her mind to ask earlier.

"That shouldn't be a problem, but I'll check the calendar tomorrow," Mickey says.

"Thank you. I have to go out of town, and I completely forgot. I'm sorry I waited until Thursday." Gloria hurriedly begins to shut down her computer.

Mickey gives her a suspicious look, but says, "Don't worry. It shouldn't be a problem. Until recently, you've never asked for personal days. I'm sure you have plenty saved up."

"Thank you," Gloria says again, as Mickey strolls out the door.

Chapter 17

April 2018

<u>Before</u>

April 12, 2018, Gloria received the phone call she had been dreading, as she sat in the living room of her parents' old house - her house now. Somehow Mickey seemed to be the grapevine, knowing things before Gloria ever did.

"Gloria, I'm not sure if you've heard, but Charles was released from jail yesterday."

"No, I hadn't heard. I've been dreading this. Thanks for letting me know, Mickey."

"Are you going to be okay?" Gloria could hear the concern in Mickey's voice.

"Yeah, I guess I have to be, don't I? Gloria began to nervously fiddle with the tie on her robe.

"If you need to come over, I'll be home all weekend," Mickey said.

"Thanks, Mickey. I'm hoping the restraining order will keep him at bay. Since he's been in rehab and now he's been in jail, I'm sure he can't afford to go to jail again over something stupid like violating the restraining order. I might just have him over a barrel."

"I sure hope so," Mickey said.

Gloria thanked Mickey once more before hanging up. Mickey was such a good friend. She had never quite realized how good of a friend she was until she left Charles. She had been wrapped up in Charles's world and hadn't even noticed

The previous night, Chrissy and Alex had been over for dinner. Before leaving, Chrissy stopped at the door. "You know, Mom, I would be happy to keep Sarah any time you would like to go to Ontario and visit Rick."

Gloria looked around to Sarah, who was standing behind her. "Would that be okay with you?" she asked.

"Yeah. Chrissy already asked me about it." Sarah shrugged like it was no big deal.

Smiling, Gloria turned back around to Chrissy. "Okay, then. I guess it's settled."

Gloria knew she was going to have to have a serious talk with Rick soon. He had been asking when she might be filing for divorce. She had been vague with her answers, and he had dropped it. Since the relationship seemed to be progressing, she knew she would have to open up to him, sooner rather than later. She decided to do said opening up during their next phone call.

Lying back on her bed, she clutched her pillow tightly with one arm, as she held the phone in her other hand. "I have something to talk to you about," she said, not knowing if this would be the end of things between them.

"That doesn't sound good." Rick sounded concerned.

"I'm sorry we haven't talked about this earlier, but honestly, I've been afraid to," she said, gathering her courage. "I need to explain the reason I haven't filed for divorce."

"Okay..." She could tell his okay came with a question mark.

Gloria sighed. "It's just that Charles is very volatile and reactive. I've been putting off filing for divorce so I could try to keep him at bay. I know I need to do it, but I've been trying to wait for the right time." She squeezed the pillow tighter as she waited for his response

"You know there will probably never be a right time, Gloria."

Unable to read Rick's mood over the phone, Gloria said, "I know. I never filed before, because I didn't think of meeting anyone. Then after I met you, I didn't want him finding out. I think he might try to ruin our relationship." Almost in tears, she continued, "Anyway, I've just been putting it off, but I know it's not fair for you to be dating someone who isn't divorced yet."

"I'm not going to lie. Your situation was becoming a concern. I was hoping we would talk about it eventually. I know you've been afraid of him, but what can he do? He's not going to try and kill you, is he?"

"I honestly don't know. He still thinks of me as his property," she began, trying to fight back the tears.

"That's ridiculous. He knows you aren't coming back by now, doesn't he?" Rick sounded incredulous.

"I think he is sure I will come back since I haven't filed. I didn't want to lead him on, but I just let things go too far by not standing my ground." Then she added, "I have to tell you the real reason it's gone so far, and I'm afraid you're not going to want to keep seeing me."

"I doubt there is anything you can tell me that will scare me away," he reassured her.

Gloria cleared her throat, mustered her courage, and just came out with it. "I think he tried to kill me." She held her breath as she listened to his startled reply.

"What? You think? What does that mean?" Rick was unable to cover the shock in his voice.

Gathering her courage once more, she began to speak slowly. "Sarah and I were watching TV when someone fired a bullet through our living room window." There, she had done it. She sat, waiting for her house of cards to come crashing down.

Finally, he spoke, "Okay, that is scary. I'm glad you two are safe, but . . . you're sure it was him?"

"Pretty sure," she said, before describing the incident in detail.

"Was this before or after we met?"

"Before." Gloria bit into her pillow.

"Well, that's good. I don't mean it's good, but if this happened after you'd met me, and you hid it, I would say we have a problem. I can see why, under the circumstances, you would wait. And you actually think it was him?" he seemed unable to believe the kind of man Gloria had been married to.

Letting go of the pillow, she said, "I almost know it. The police questioned him, and he lied, saying he had been home all evening. The deputy knew he was lying about it because the hood of his car was warm. After Charles was confronted with that, he changed his story. He said he had just gone out for some beer. He doesn't even drink beer, but they couldn't do anything, because there was no evidence. Deputy Wells said he could smell alcohol on Charles." She continued, trying not to cry: "I just know he was drunk and angry, and he fired a shot at us. Thankfully, the drapes were closed, and he missed."

"Why would he shoot into your living room, knowing Sarah might be there?" Rick asked in disbelief.

"Honestly, he resents the girls. He always has. I know in my gut, it was him," she insisted.

"This is a lot to take in," he said, letting out a breath, leading her to believe he was exasperated with the whole situation. "Actually," he explained, "I was thinking of Megan, and how much I love her. How could any man not have feelings for his own daughter?"

Deciding to break the long silence that had formed between them, Gloria said, "I understand if this is too much for you, and you don't want to have anything to do with it."

"No, just give me a minute. I'm trying to make sense of this. A large part of me wants to be your knight in shining armor, but I must admit, I am concerned. I can't encourage you to file for divorce if it would be unsafe for you or Sarah. Obviously, I understand your fear." After a moment, he said, "Honestly, I'm beginning to have strong feelings for you. Where do we go from here?"

"I'm not sure," Gloria admitted.

"I don't want to end things, but we will have to figure something out if we move forward," he said.

She let out a long breath she hadn't realized she was holding and was relieved he had not given up on her just yet. Where they would go from here, she knew was still a question mark. "I have to say, that's more than I could have hoped for."

An uncomfortable silence followed, and Gloria didn't know what to say. Putting them both out of their misery, she ended the call early.

Climbing under the covers, she could feel her face drawn down with worry. Rick had said they would figure something out, but he had been so quiet. Her heart sank at the memory of his reaction. Knowing she would be worrying all night, she padded to the bathroom and grabbed a bottle of sleep aid. Flipping off the cap, she poured two pills out into her hand, adding a valium for good measure. Throwing them into her mouth, she filled her cupped hand with water from the tap, sipped, and swallowed, before heading back to bed. It was difficult, but she decided she would not be the one to make the next move. She wouldn't bother him while he soaked it all in.

The next evening, Gloria was on pins and needles, hoping the phone would ring. She couldn't help but look at the clock every fifteen minutes after 9:00. She tried to read a book as she lay on the couch but kept having to reread the same paragraph, over and over again. She was beginning to feel nervous nausea, sitting and hoping he would call. She looked at the clock on the wall by the TV one last time; it read 10:10. Just as she turned out the lamp on the side table, she was startled as the phone began to ring.

Sitting there in the dark, she felt simultaneous sensations. She feared it might be bad news, but she also had butterflies. It was a very odd sensation. She picked up the phone after two rings, hoping for the best.

"Hello," Gloria said hopefully.

"Hi, why didn't you call tonight?" came his abrupt reply.

"I'm sorry, I thought you might need some space, so I was waiting for you to make the first call," she said, a little startled by his tone.

"Don't be silly." He seemed to calm a little. "I told you we would figure something out."

"I know, but I'm sure it was a lot to take in, and I didn't want to put pressure on you," she apologized as if she were the one who brought all of this upon herself.

"I'm here for the long haul," he said. "Don't forget that, no matter what."

Relief flooded through her veins as she began to tear up. Trying to keep the evidence from her voice, all she could say was, "Thank you!"

"I'm not going to push you on this any further. You'll figure out what you need to do. In the meantime, let's concentrate on us. I'm worried that you might be in danger, and I've been thinking." He took a slight pause before he asked, "Would you and Sarah consider moving in with me?" Then he paused again before saying, "For your protection?"

She had a hard time taking in what he was saying. He hadn't wanted to run; he wanted to move forward with her. His feelings for her must be deeper than she knew.

"Are you still there?"

"Yes, yes, I'm just overwhelmed," she said, a little breathless.

"I'm sorry, I didn't mean to rush things. I just thought it would give you some physical space from him, and someone to back you up."

"No, it's not that. I just thought you would want to stop seeing me after what I told you last night."

She thought for a moment about what Rick had proposed and knew her answer.

"I'm sure you need time to think on it. I'm just putting it out there," he said.

"I appreciate the offer, I really do, but I don't think I should pull Sarah out of school. I think it might be too much on her right now. She seems to be in a good space." She stood up from the couch and shuffled toward her bedroom, feeling her way in the dark.

"I can understand that," Rick said. Gloria thought she heard relief in his voice. She couldn't blame him.

"I'm not saying I wouldn't consider it in the future, at some point. I just don't think it would be right for us now." She added, "I don't want to force our relationship. Moving in so soon would probably not be good for you, either."

"I understand your feelings, I'm just worried about your safety," he said. "I just want to help out if I can."

Hoping to alleviate his worry, she said, "Sarah and I have made it okay by ourselves for almost a year and a half now. I don't mean to worry you. I just thought I should come clean if we're going to move forward."

"Let's do that. Let's try to move forward, and I will trust your judgment," he suggested.

"Thank you, Rick." Gloria felt relieved, glad to move the conversation away from Charles. She knew this would be hanging over their relationship, always in the background. She would have to try, in earnest, to figure out a solution.

Chapter 18

August 2003

<u>After</u>

Monday has finally arrived after a very long weekend. She is going to meet young Rick. At least that's how she thinks of him. He is going to be so much younger than she ever knew him, and it's going to be strange. Gloria has been over her strategy for winning him over a hundred times. After making the long, familiar drive, she is sitting on a bench, just inside the entry door of Spring House Restaurant, in Ontario. She watches a model train trek its way through, on tracks near the ceiling.

She remembers how Megan loved to come here, and how the train kept her mesmerized as the three of them had leisurely lunches. The train would snake through tunnels, over bridges, and go winding through the entire restaurant, enchanting children and adults alike.

She listens to the clackity-clack and the intermittent whistle of the train over the din of customers as she waits. With time to spare, she feels her heart racing, and wrings her clammy hands, trying to steady her frazzled nerves. An argument is raging in her brain:

It's only Rick, she reasons with herself, trying to slow her pulse.

But he doesn't know you. If you don't do this the right way, you'll scare him off for sure, her ugly, negative voice pipes up.

Back and forth, it goes:

You're here now. Just do it the way you practiced, and you will be fine, Gloria.

Yeah, but you're so nervous you'll get it all wrong, Ugly says.

I just have to calm down and think positive, she tries to reassure herself.

Negativity tries to poke its ugly head up again when she sees Rick walk in.

She can't help but stare like a moron as the door closes behind him. Trying to take in how young he looks—his hair so much fuller, his salt-and-pepper beard dark brown, and a boyishness to his face - Gloria tries to keep the surprise on her face from showing. Bringing herself out of her trance, she gathers her courage, puts on a big, hopefully friendly smile, and stands to introduce herself. Reaching out her damp hand, she is mortified but feels she must offer it to greet him. Hopefully, he won't notice. *But he will,* Ugly says, and she cringes.

"Rick, I'm Gloria." She covers a little cough, and says, "I'm sorry about my hands, I'm a bit nervous." She looks down, blushing, but quickly catches herself and forces herself to make eye contact again.

"Hello," he says, with a surprisingly friendly smile. Maybe she wasn't coming across as some kind of weirdo after all.

"Shall we tell the hostess we're ready to be seated?" she asks.

"Sure," he says, as they both approach the counter, where the hostess is already waiting with two menus in hand.

"This way," she says, as they follow her to a booth next to a window.

Laying the menus on the table, she announces, "Mindy will be right with you, to take your drink orders."

"Thank you," Rick says politely.

215

Seating themselves on opposite sides of the table, Gloria begins to make small talk. "How has your morning been?" she asks, to break the ice. She can feel the flush fading from her cheeks, thankfully. She picks up the dark emerald green napkin in front of her and discreetly wipes her hands, before unfolding it onto her lap.

"It's been good, how about yours?" he fires back, as he adjusts in his seat.

"Well, truthfully, I've made quite a drive to be here. I live in Bakersfield." Gloria looks up and flashes a nervous smile.

A surprised look widens his eyes. "Wow, this must be important for you to drive all that way to meet me."

"I feel it's important," she says, "I'm hoping you will, too." The words are coming more easily to her now.

The conversation begins to flow, interrupted only twice when Mindy comes to take their drink and food orders. He orders iced tea, and Gloria orders her usual Diet Coke. They both order turkey and avocado sandwiches. Gloria sits, amused at the fact that they have ordered the same sandwich. At least she didn't copy him since he had gestured for her to order first.

"Well," he says, as he pours a packet of sweetener into his tea. Beginning to stir, he looks up and continues, "Can you give me a clue as to why you wanted to meet today? Not that I mind meeting a beautiful girl who offers to pay for lunch, but you have piqued my curiosity." He flashes a genuine smile before taking a sip. Without thinking, Gloria picks up her glass as well and takes a sip from the straw.

Setting her glass down, she leans forward as she nervously fidgets with her napkin under the table. "This is all going to sound very strange, but I feel I have to tell you something. First of all, I don't believe I'm crazy, and I categorically have never believed in

216

this stuff, but now please don't run off when I say this . . . I have actually met you before." She tries not to cringe as she lets it sink in, while he sits back with a quizzical expression.

Brows furrowed, he says slowly, "I'm . . . pretty sure I would remember if we had met."

"Well, the thing is," she pauses and cringes, before continuing, leaning closer, and lowering her voice: "I actually met you in a dream. Now, I know that sounds crazy," she adds before he can get a word in, "but it hasn't been just one dream. I dream the same thing night after night, and in my dreams we're together." Under the table, her napkin is wound tightly in her hands, and she is holding onto it for dear life, as if it were her security blanket about to sprout legs, jump out of her grasp and make a break for the door.

Trying to get everything out on the table before he can protest, she rattles on: "The thing is, I knew where you worked from my dream, and when I called, you answered the phone. And, in my dreams, you've told me all about your life, so I know things." Ask me a question about your life," she adds, straightening her posture, "I bet I will know the answer."

Rick's astonished look suggests *he* would like to make a break for the door like her napkin, probably thinking Gloria is batshit crazy. She winces. But, to her surprise, he leans in, the startled look in his eyes, turning somewhat serious.

"It actually does sound crazy, but I'll bite. Tell me what sport I played in high school?" He raises his eyebrows.

As he reaches for his glass of tea, Gloria says, "That's easy. You played water polo."

Surprised, a bit of his tea sloshes out as he tries to place the glass back on the table. "Okay," he says skeptically, wiping at his hand with his napkin. "What was my sister's dog's name when we were growing up?"

"Snowball," Gloria says, adding, "She was a poodle who used to lay, what you called landmines, in the hall at night. Your dad would step in them and cuss up a storm, threatening to kill the dog every time." With a look of triumph, Gloria takes a sip of her drink.

"Wait, do you know my sister? Did she put you up to this?" He throws up his hands and grins.

Gloria lowers her voice again and leans in. "Honestly, no, I've never met your sister. You actually told me these things, like I said, in dreams. Ask me as many questions as you like. I bet I will be able to answer most of them." She is beginning to feel confident, encouraged by her ability to nail the answers to his first questions.

"This is crazy. I can't believe I'm even participating in this, but you have me curious now. I wonder how many questions you would actually be able to answer." He leans farther forward himself. He looks as if he's ready for a standoff. They are both locked, loaded, and ready to fire.

After a couple of seconds, she backs down a bit under his intense gaze. "I'm not saying I will know *all* the answers, but I'm sure I'll know most of them. Don't write me off as nuts just yet."

"It's going to take a lot to convince me. I really don't buy this kind of stuff," he says, twirling a fry on his plate, before taking a bite.

Gloria has an idea, and her eyes grow wide as she decides to try a different tactic. "I know you believe in God," she says. "Well, do you believe God can do anything?"

His forehead creases as he contemplates the question for a moment. "Well, yes," he finally says.

"Then, do you think God could have given me these dreams?" She cocks her head questioningly to one side.

"I guess, but why would he?" Rick screws up his face.

"Maybe, because he wants us to meet," Gloria says, half-questioningly. "Just ask me anything you can think of, and if you don't buy it, you never have to see me after today. I promise."

She has been talking and forgot about the food sitting in front of her. Deciding to take a bite of her sandwich, she chews nervously while waiting for his reply. She can tell he is highly skeptical, but she must have done some convincing since he is still sitting here.

"Okay, what's my favorite band?" he asks, now staring her down.

After she finishes swallowing, she says, "Intimidation won't work," and, with a chuckle, "That's an easy question, Little Texas."

Now she can tell he is determined to stump her, as he stares up at the ceiling and tries to concentrate on his next question. "What's my favorite song?"

"It's not by Little Texas," she says, and goes on to name, "What a Wonderful World, by Louis Armstrong. It's sentimental to you because it reminds you of a friend who passed away recently. I'm really sorry." She gives him a sad smile.

He is wide-eyed once more. She can tell he thought he would throw her off with that question. "Okay, who do you know? Is it one of my friends or my family? Who put you up to this?" He chuckles, looking around the restaurant, seeming to expect to find someone familiar laughing at him.

"I'm telling you the truth. You told me these things. If I were you, I wouldn't believe it either. I barely believe it myself. I've been fighting the feeling I need to meet you for a long time. The dreams are so real, and the feeling won't go away. So, I decided I would meet you once and let you decide if we should meet again, or go our separate ways." She pauses for a moment to catch her breath, before continuing: "I have all day, but I'm sure you will probably have to head back to work."

"Honestly, I do a lot of outside work, so they never know when to expect me back in the office." He checks his watch.

"Maybe we should at least eat these sandwiches," Gloria suggests, as she picks hers up to take another bite. His has been sitting there, untouched.

"Yeah, we probably should," he agrees, picking his up.

In between bites, Gloria says, "I'm on your schedule."

After finishing their lunch, Rick wipes his hands on the napkin in his lap and says, "I know your name and that you live in Bakersfield, but nothing else. I would like to know a little more about you."

Pushing her plate away, with half her sandwich untouched, Gloria says, "What would you like to know?"

"Are you married?"

He says it out of the blue, and it catches Gloria off guard for a moment. *He must be somewhat interested, if he wants to know my marital status*, she thinks. She really doesn't know how to answer him. Finally, she says, "I'm actually separated."

"I'm just curious, were you having these dreams before you were separated?" His tone is more relaxed than before.

"Yes," she said, "Quite a long time before, but the dreams have nothing to do with the reason we broke up. They became more frequent afterward, though. Truthfully, my husband is an abusive man."

"Oh, I'm sorry." He looks at her regretfully.

"I'm actually just a normal girl. I'm not into psychic stuff or anything. I was raised Baptist in Texas. My parents moved to Bakersfield when I was fifteen," she explains, tucking her hair behind one ear and sitting back as a calmness settles between them.

"When you aren't talking about dreams, you appear to be quite normal," he says.

"Thanks, I think?" She is not quite sure if this is a compliment. She explains, "I grew up in a normal family, on a farm in Texas, riding horses and dirt bikes."

"I would have never guessed that." Surprise lights up his eyes once more. "You look so girly. I'm sorry, I don't mean to be offensive, but I just would have never guessed."

"It's all right, I get that all the time. I am quite a country girl, though," Gloria admits.

Rick looks down at his watch, and casually mentions, "It's 2:30, and you have a long drive back to Bakersfield, don't you?"

"Yes," she shrugs, "but I can head back any time."

"I probably should head back to work. I just have one last question I'm going to throw at you before we go. I don't think I've ever told anyone this," he says, almost to himself. "Can you tell me what I told my drill sergeant the first time he yelled in my face?"

"Yeah, you told me that one." She laughs as she remembers. "You said, yeah, Sergeant, you're nothing compared to my mom. He was pissed. He turned beet red, and you had a hard time not laughing in his face. From what I hear, you were doing push-ups on a regular basis after that."

"I can't believe you know that." Rick says, in awe, before starting to crack up himself at the memory.

Gloria begins to think, *good, that will give him something to think about after I leave.* She was afraid he was getting cold feet when he brought up the time. Maybe this would give her a reprieve.

On the drive home, she couldn't help but go over everything they had talked about, mulling it over in her mind. She had given him her number before they parted, saying she would not contact him again. She didn't want to come across as pushy or intrusive, leaving it to him to make next contact. She hoped she would hear from him, but she was far from certain. *This is definitely going to be a waiting game.*

Chapter 19

July 2018

<u>Before</u>

Seeming to have put Charles and the ugliness of their conversation about the shooting in the background, by the end of the month Gloria was breathing a sigh of relief. It seemed Rick still wanted to move ahead with their relationship.

Since Sarah seemed to be comfortable at Chrissy's apartment, Gloria took Rick up on his offer to spend a week at the Big Bear cabin. They found themselves lying there, cuddling on his bed. Rick admitted to Gloria that he had never been with someone so sexually timid before, but assured her she could take her time in that regard. He could understand her reasons, and besides, he said, she would be worth the wait.

It wasn't that Gloria hadn't felt the same desires he obviously had. She found herself having the same problem of keeping her hands off his body. She knew he had already been more than patient with her, so she decided to toss her caution out the window. Surprising them both after a passionate kiss, Gloria declared she would sleep in Rick's bed that night, instead of in Megan's room.

She excused herself to retrieve her overnight bag from Megan's room. While there, she pulled out a sexy white silk teddy with black lace trim. Formfitting, and not leaving much to the imagination, Gloria slipped it on. The look on Rick's face when she walked back into the room, well, she would never be able to describe it.

"Wow," he exclaimed in bewilderment, as she crawled into bed beside him. As she did, she let out a sigh, and with it, she let go of all her inhibitions. Bodies wrapped tightly, they kissed the most passionate kiss of Gloria's life. From there, all bets were off.

Afterward, as they were lying there, all he could say was, "Wow, Wow, Wow," as she snuggled beside him, looking into his eyes.

"Where did you come from?" he asked.

"Texas." She chuckled.

He laughed groggily. "Really?"

Yawning, he reached over to turn off the bedside lamp, and she quickly fell asleep in his arms.

Waking the next morning, they repeated the dance of the night before. Afterward, they lay confiding their hopes and dreams, until they both agreed they must get up. It was midmorning, after all. They decided to shower together to save water, and once again be environmentally conscious, of course. When the water finally ran cold, they hopped out as the frigid water hit their skin, quickly dried off, and pulled on their robes.

"I like what you were wearing last night better," he teased.

"Yeah, well, I guess you will have to keep me if you want to see it again," Gloria said, as she smacked him on the butt, and ran out of the room. It wasn't long until he caught up with her and tickled her sides until she couldn't catch her breath. He wrapped his arms around her waist from behind and picked her up off the floor as she laughed.

"Are you hungry?" she said when she could breathe again.

"Famished," he said, finally releasing her from his grasp.

"Well then, you better start cooking breakfast." She sat at the table dramatically, to wait for her breakfast.

Picking her up, chair and all, he plunked her down in front of the fridge, and said, "I'll have bacon, eggs, and pancakes, please."

"Well," she said, standing up, pushing the chair aside, and opening the fridge, "I guess you win."

After the week was over, Gloria thought she was juggling things well, but the boom was bound to fall eventually. *Maybe there's nothing to worry about at all*, she told herself. For all Charles knew, she could have been off with a girlfriend. Thinking about that made her laugh a little. The way it sounds might have given him a different idea about her.

Chapter 20

August 2003

<u>After</u>

It's Friday evening before young Rick finally calls. That's the only way Gloria can think of him. She keeps picturing how young he looked. She doesn't really think of her Rick as old Rick when she thinks about the future. She just thinks of him as Rick. It's all becoming so confusing, keeping things straight in her head.

She was beginning to think she might never hear from him after their meeting at Spring House. Picking up the phone all week, she had prayed each time it might be him. By now, she feels foolish for still hoping.

As the phone begins to ring, Gloria rushes to the couch, with pictures of young Rick in her mind. She picks the phone up off the coffee table quickly and flips it open.

A little breathless, she answers, "Hello."

"Is this Gloria?" Rick asks.

Her heart leaps as she flops on the couch, "Yes, hello Rick. It's nice to hear your voice." She is sure her grin must stretch from ear to ear. "I thought I scared you off."

"I've been pretty busy this week, but I can honestly say I haven't forgotten you. In fact, to tell the truth, you have been occupying my thoughts more than I would like to admit," he says, sounding a little sheepish.

She covers the phone, so he can't hear her giggling like a little girl. When she recovers her composure, she takes a deep breath. "I'm happy you called."

He dives right in, "I've been wondering exactly what kind of relationship you see coming from this?"

Surprised at his bluntness, she pauses. "I'm not sure what kind of relationship I'm expecting, but in my dreams, we're a couple. Please know, I'm not pushing for anything. I would like for you to make up your own mind, where this might, or might not, go."

"You know, I have a girlfriend. We live together," he says.

"I know. Her name is Veronica. I hope I'm not being too bold, but you told me your relationship is kind of volatile." She is thinking she may have just stepped over the line.

After a pause, he says, "I don't like to admit it, but you're right. Even so, I think at this point, we should keep things on a friends only basis. By the way, it's still kind of freaky that you know so much about me."

"I'm sorry about that. It's quite weird on my end as well. I'm surprised you would even consider continuing to talk to me. I have to say, I am pleased though," she admits. "Maybe we can get to know each other. I'm not the best conversationalist sometimes, but I'm a great listener."

"I guess I'll just jump right in if we're getting to know each other. Do you have children?" He's cutting right to the chase.

"Yes. I should have told you before. I have two girls, Chrissy and Sarah, four years old, and one year old."

"I actually wouldn't have guessed that. I'm sure they're great. I've always wanted kids. Veronica has a daughter and doesn't want any more children. She doesn't even have custody of the one she has."

She flips onto her side and stares at her sparkling fireplace as she thinks. She doesn't want to tell him about his daughter in the future. Telling him something about his future might not be a good idea, she reasons. If what she knows is really the future at all. She's beginning to believe this dream story. It's starting to make more sense to her than a future that seems to be fading more and more into the background.

"Yeah, you would be a great dad," she says. Catching herself, she adds, "Not that I would know. You just seem to be that kind of guy."

She begins to question his friend idea when he asks his next question. "Do you want more kids?"

A little surprised, she pauses a bit. "I would be happy to have more, with the right man. Don't get me wrong, I love my girls, but I shouldn't have brought them into such a volatile relationship. I guess I always had the hope that things would change between us."

Clearing her throat, she continues, "I know he hasn't been happy being a dad, but I always had dreams he could change. I just wanted the girls to have a loving father. I know now, I shouldn't expect to change someone. What you see is usually what you get in a relationship."

"I guess that's what I'm trying to do in my relationship, come to think of it. I keep hoping she will change. Maybe you're right. Maybe we shouldn't go into a relationship with the hope of changing someone into what we need." He sounds deep in thought.

Gloria can't believe how deep the conversation is going. "Yeah," she says, "I actually discovered that in counseling recently. Charles, that's my soon-to-be ex, doesn't believe in counseling. He doesn't believe in sharing our problems with someone else. I just felt like I was going to crack under the pressure if I didn't see someone. It's actually been beneficial."

"Did the counselor tell you to leave him?" he asks.

Gloria pushes herself up off the couch, switching off the light, before ambling to the bedroom. "No. He left that up to me. He never guided me in one direction or the other. He just let me talk, and it became clear to me that the marriage was doomed. It's not good for the girls' health or mine." She shakes her head, switching the phone to her left hand as her right hand begins to go numb.

"I've asked Veronica to go to counseling with me several times, and she always refuses. She says I'm the one with the problems," he admits, sounding down.

"I know how it is. How many times have I heard that?" She pulls the covers down and slides into bed.

"Veronica is at the bar right now. That's why I was able to call. She would be furious if she knew I was talking to a woman." He gives a sad chuckle.

"I was kind of wondering if she was there," Gloria admits.

"She usually goes out on Friday nights, to drink with her buddies, mostly guys, but heaven forbid I should talk to a woman," he says. "I'm not much into the bar scene, so I usually pass."

"How long does she stay out?" Gloria hopes they have more time to talk.

"Late," he replies, "usually, really late."

They continue their conversation, talking comfortably until late into the night. They both agree it has been cathartic, and they should talk again soon. Regretfully, the time comes when they agree they should hang up, and they finally do. Surprisingly, that night, she is able to rest peacefully after their call.

Rick found a few minutes alone to call Gloria on Sunday. "I wanted you to know I really enjoyed our talk Friday night," he says. "I have to admit, I've never felt so at ease talking to a woman before."

Gloria feels the urge to give herself a high five, which is quickly followed by a feeling of guilt, for wanting to do so. She straightens up. "I enjoyed our visit as well."

"Well, I can't really talk. Veronica will be back soon. I hope we can talk on Friday evening again." He sounds hopeful.

"Definitely. It's a date. Well, you know what I mean," she corrects herself, shaking her head vigorously.

"I know what you meant." He chuckles.

That evening, Gloria finds herself standing on her parents' front porch, with the girls, as she knocks on their door. Jack opens up, dressed in his golf clothes and glowing bright red. "Wow, Dad, your sunburn is almost as loud as your pants." She has to laugh at his plaid golf pants. "Have you ever heard of sunblock?"

He waves a hand dismissively. "Aw, that stuff is for sissies."

"Sissies and blond people like us," Gloria teases.

"Come on in." He waves them in behind him. "Your mom and I have just finished dinner. Well, I've finished. Mom is still sitting at the table, finishing up."

After closing the door, they follow behind him to the dining room where Dena is sitting at the table. She turns to welcome them. Jack picks up his dish from the table and takes it to the kitchen sink to rinse before returning. Seeing Dena has finished too, he grabs her plate and heads back to the kitchen. Gloria takes a seat beside her mother and hands Sarah over for a hug. Chrissy has already jumped up in her grandma's lap and given her a hug before running off to play behind the bar.

"What's up?" Dena asks as Jack comes back to sit across the table. "Have ya'll had dinner?

"Yeah," Gloria says, before beginning to fill them in on the news about Charles's new girlfriend. Glancing at her dad, she can see he is deep in thought.

"Gloria," he says, "are you sure you're going to leave Charles for good?"

"Yes." She straightens her posture. "Definitely."

"Well." He leans forward. "I was just thinking, this might be the best time for you to file for divorce."

Out of the blue, she remembers something from the future. She sees Rick down on one knee with a blue velvet box, saying, "You can wear this ring when you are divorced."

At least, she thinks it's a real memory. He proposed to her in the snow, with a beautiful diamond ring nestled in a deep blue velvet box. She can almost feel the tears of happiness on her cheeks as she tries to bring more detail to the front of her mind, but it's no use; as fast as the memory came, it seems to fade away.

"Gloria, are you all right?" Jack looks concerned.

"Yes, I'm sure," she says. "I have actually talked to a lawyer, who represents women on limited income, about custody rights, but I've been too afraid to actually file for divorce."

"No, no." Jack waves a hand. "You need to find a good lawyer. I was just thinking, instead of making payments to us for the car, why don't you make small payments to us toward legal bills?"

"I hate to take any more help from you and mom. You've already done so much." Gloria shakes her head, frowning.

Jack insists, "It's important for the girls that you have a good lawyer. You need someone who will help you obtain sole custody, if possible."

Pausing for a moment, Gloria says, "I think you're right, Dad." She looks down in deep thought before looking up again. "I just feel so bad about taking more help."

"Look at it this way," her mother pipes up, "This is for Sarah and Chrissy. If you wait until you save up enough money for a lawyer, the situation could very well change, and he might put up more of a battle. That wouldn't be good for them."

Considering her parents' logic, Gloria has to admit it's probably the right thing to do. She sits and thinks for a while before deciding to take them up on their offer. She would have to start searching for a divorce lawyer as soon as possible.

"You're right. Thank you both again, and I will pay you back," she insists.

"We'll get this all sorted out, and you'll be doing fine on your own soon," Jack says, smiling at Gloria.

"I hope so. It would sure help my confidence to be doing things on my own. I hope to be able to take some college courses eventually. I would like to advance at the Agency and make a comfortable living for the girls and myself."

"It sounds like you're beginning to look toward the future. That's a good sign," Dena says, glancing over at Jack. Gloria catches a quick wink from her dad, as he looks appreciatively at Dena.

Monday morning, Gloria is sitting at her desk, on the hunt for a good divorce attorney. She finds herself flipping through the yellow pages since she dare not do personal business online at work. She has a few names listed.

Continuing her search, she asks everyone in the office if they might know of a good attorney, and thankfully comes away with two lawyers' names. Sitting back down in front of her computer terminal, she decides she will have to get back to work, but she promises herself she will call them on her lunch break.

Friday, at 10:00 a.m., she pulls open the heavy glass door, entering the office of Janice Fuller, LLC. Gloria had spoken to the attorney by phone Monday, during her lunch hour, and she has a good feeling about being here this morning.

Ms. Fuller's assistant, with friendly hazel eyes, looks up from the reception desk. Her red hair is teased and flipped up at her shoulders, reminding Gloria of Reba McEntire. She greets Gloria as she walks through the door. "You must be Ms. Davis," she says, cheerily. "I'm Myrna, Ms. Fuller's assistant."

"Yes. I'm Gloria Davis." She smiles nervously.

"Can I get you a cup of coffee?" Myrna stands up from behind her desk. She is dressed in a sleek black pencil skirt, crisp white cotton blouse, and cherry-red, open-toed pumps.

"That would be wonderful," Gloria says, thinking it will give her something to hold in her hands while she waits.

"Cream and sugar?" Myrna asks over her shoulder as she heads to the coffee pot.

"Yes. Both thank you." Gloria nods and takes a seat in one of two low-back, black leather chairs that sit around a round glass coffee table, with magazines fanned out neatly on top.

When Myrna hands Gloria her cup of coffee, she realizes her knee is bouncing. Myrna must have noticed before Gloria wills her knee to stop. She gives Gloria a comforting smile. "Don't worry, Janice is great."

"Thanks, I'm trying not to. I just don't know what to expect," Gloria admits, as she tries to keep her knee still.

"It'll all work out. You'll see." Myrna turns neatly on one foot before returning to her desk.

Gloria only notices she is bouncing her knee again when a hot splatter of coffee lands on her leg. She immediately stops but finds herself fighting to sit still. Wiping at her leg and tugging at her skirt to cover the red mark, she admonishes herself and is determined to wait patiently.

The phone on Myrna's desk beeps, and she reaches over to pick it up. "I will send her right in," she says, before placing the handset back in the cradle. She turns to Gloria. "Ms. Fuller will see you now." She pushes back her chair and gestures for Gloria to follow. She opens a large oak door and steps aside for Gloria to enter. She pauses in the doorway and turns to Myrna.

"Should I leave my coffee?" Gloria holds the cup out, not quite sure what to do with it.

"Goodness, no." Myrna waves a hand. "We're casual here. Make yourself at home. You're going to love her," she whispers conspiratorially.

"Thank you," Gloria says, as she walks through the door; Myrna closes it behind her.

Standing up from her burgundy leather executive chair behind her desk, Ms. Fuller greets Gloria as she crosses the expansive space between the door and the desk. She is tall and slender with jet-black hair pulled up in a tight bun. Gloria is welcomed with kind brown eyes. Her full lips break into a broad smile as she steps forward and reaches out a hand to introduce herself.

"I'm Janice. It's nice to meet you in person, Gloria."

Reaching over her massive gleaming walnut desk, Gloria takes her hand and shakes it firmly. "I'm glad to meet you, Ms. Fuller."

"Please just call me Janice," she says, cordially, taking a seat behind her desk. "Please have a seat. I'll be just a minute gathering some paperwork here, and I'll be right with you."

Gloria takes a seat in one of the two oversized burgundy leather tufted armchairs behind her, grasping her coffee as she looks around the office. Behind Janice is a large window, overlooking a beautiful green belt with large pine trees, grass, and flowering shrubs. Beside the window is a large fichus tree in a terracotta pot, its branches almost reaching the tall ceiling. Built-in bookshelves in dark walnut, matching her desk, cover the entire wall to Gloria's left. They are entirely filled with beautifully bound books.

Janice looks up while straightening papers in front of her and smiles. Then, setting the documents to the side, she folds her hands in front of her on the desk, leans forward with a reassuring smile, and begins to speak. "I know this is a difficult time for you. I would like to make the process as easy as possible. Remember, I'm on your side. We are going to get through this together if you decide to retain me as your attorney."

She continues explaining the process of filing papers, serving notices, attending court dates, and negotiating on her clients' behalf. And how she might help Gloria navigate through these legal proceedings.

When she is finished, she says, "To retain me as your attorney, I will need a retainer fee of $2,500. That will get you started. The total amount will depend on how easy or difficult, your husband makes it for us."

A bit overwhelmed by all the information she has tried to absorb in the past hour, Gloria reaches into her purse and pulls out her checkbook. The check for $2,500 from her parents is still tucked inside her wallet. She must deposit it right away, she thinks. Standing to retrieve one of the pens from a coffee cup full of pens, she sets her coffee on the gleaming glass top covering Janice's desk. She returns to her chair, opens her checkbook, perches it on her knee, and begins to write. When she's finished, she rips out the check and stands to approach the desk and hand it to Janice.

"That's great," Janice says, standing and reaching over the desk to take the check, before placing it in front of her. "I'm happy you chose me to represent you. I promise I will do my utmost to help bring an amicable conclusion to your case. What I need for you to do, before I see you again, is complete some paperwork with your information, assets, and children's information.

"I will need an idea of how you would like to split the assets, and custody of the children. Then we can discuss the best way to proceed. We can discuss all of this at our next meeting," she says, picking up the stack of documents on her desk and placing them in a folder. She steps around and hands them to Gloria before walking her out.

As Gloria leaves the building, she can feel a flush rising in her cheeks when she realizes she left her coffee cup on Janice's desk. *Not such a good first impression*, she thinks. She pauses and shakes her head before heading to her car.

Picking up the girls that evening, she pauses inside the front door and turns to her mom. She fills her in on how the appointment went with the lawyer, and how comfortable she had made her feel. "I really think I found the right one. I'm just afraid of how Charles is going to react when they serve him." She shivers at the thought.

Chapter 21

July 2018

Before

Returning from her week in Big Bear with Rick, Gloria finally found a cell phone signal after winding through the Tehachapi Mountains. She pulled over to the side of the road once she reached the flatlands and reached over to the passenger seat to grab her iPhone from her purse.

"Hi, Mom." It was Chrissy, and, from the sound of her voice, she had terrible news.

Her gut began to churn, and she grimaced before asking, "What's wrong, Chrissy?"

"I don't want to tell you this, but Sarah is at Dad's," Chrissy said in almost a whisper as if that would make the blow less painful.

"What do you mean at Dad's?" Gloria said in a measured tone, trying not to implode.

"Mom, Dad has been trying to get ahold of you, and when he couldn't, well, he came over. We tried to tell him you were at Grandma and Grandpa's, but he called them. When he found out you weren't there, he came back and took Sarah."

"He took her?" Gloria was working hard to keep panic from taking over.

"Well, I shouldn't have said it that way. He insisted that she go, and she didn't want to, but she went anyway. She didn't want to make a scene. You know how she is. It was just a couple of days ago," Chrissy said regretfully. "I tried to stop him, but Sarah begged me just to let her go. I'm really sorry, Mom."

"It's not your fault. He's doing this so we will have to meet up when I come home. I'm sure he won't hurt her." At least, she was pretty sure. She couldn't help the anxiety flooding in, anxiety that wouldn't let up until Sarah was home, safe.

"It's okay, Chrissy. Don't worry. You did what you had to do. I'll take care of it from here." Gloria was trying to remain calm for Chrissy.

"Sorry, Mom. I love you." Chrissy's voice began to crack.

"I love you too, honey. Thank you for keeping her." Gloria said, doing her best to be supportive of her daughter.

"Sure, I just wish I could have done a better job." Chrissy sniffled.

"No worries, I'll let you know when I have her home," Gloria tried to soothe. "Please don't worry, honey."

After hanging up with Chrissy, she hated to think about the phone call she was about to make.

"Hello Charles," she said coolly when he answered. "I know you have Sarah."

Knowing there was no escape, she agreed to meet. Charles was holding the only card that mattered, and she would make sure he played it safely. After thinking about it, Gloria said, "I'll just come to pick her up."

"You do that," he said before hanging up abruptly.

Pulling back onto the road, the drive seemed interminable until she finally made it to the tri-level house she used to share with Charles. When Gloria arrived, she had to swallow a lump that seemed lodged in her throat. After climbing the steps to the front porch, she used the brushed-metal knocker to knock on the door.

238

He quickly answered. Sarah ran down the stairs from the living room, past him, and hugged her. "I'm glad you're back," she said, nervously fidgeting after leaving Gloria's embrace.

"Sarah, go get your stuff and take it to the car," Charles ordered.

As Sarah ran downstairs to gather her things, Gloria stood looking at the ground, while Charles stared at her. "I know you're seeing someone," he whispered.

The hushed tone sent a shiver through her body. What could she say? It didn't matter what she said - she knew all too well he wouldn't like it. "We shouldn't be talking with Sarah here," she said, imploring him to be quiet.

"Sarah, hurry up," he yelled over his shoulder.

Sarah ran back, her auburn hair flying and her arms full. "I have more at Chrissy's," she said frantically.

"Go to the car, now," Charles demanded.

"Here, Sarah." Gloria held out the car keys. "You'll need these to turn on the air conditioning."

Balancing her load, Sarah reached for the keys and hurried toward the car. Charles started in right away. "Who are you seeing, and where have you been for a whole week?"

"It doesn't matter, Charles, you know it's over between us," Gloria said, unable to keep a note of desperation from her voice.

"Maybe you know that, but I don't. You kept saying you needed more time. Well, I've given you time, and you step out on me." She looked up to see his face twisted in rage.

"It's been a year and a half. You had to know I wasn't coming back, Charles. All I can say is it's over." There, she had finally said it out loud, and she couldn't help it - it felt good, before the fear set in.

"So I guess this means it's serious," Charles said, fists clenched by his side.

Gathering her wits, she said, "No, that's not what it means. It just means we're not getting back together." The finality in her voice was new to both of them.

"You might want to think things over. You wouldn't want to end up like Sassy," he hissed.

She didn't have time to take in what he was saying to her as he suddenly lunged forward, reaching out to grab her. She jumped back, just out of his reach, immediately turning and running as fast as she could down the steps and to the car, not daring to look behind her. Yanking the door open, she jumped into the driver seat. With shaking hands she put the car in gear, thankful Sarah had already started it. The tires squealed as she sped off.

"What the heck, Mom?" Sarah threw up her hands and stared at her.

"I'm sorry, I thought he was chasing me." She had to tell the truth; what other explanation could there be?

"Mom, he wouldn't do that. He's not crazy. I mean, I know he's out there, but he's only weird when he's drunk, and he's not drunk. That was such an overreaction, Mom. Are you losing your mind?"

Gloria knew it must have looked like she was losing it. She began to question if that was exactly what was happening to her, but she had heard those words come out of his mouth. "You wouldn't want to end up like Sassy." That could only mean one thing - she might disappear. What had he done all those years ago? She knew Sarah would never understand or believe what had just transpired. She also knew she would never tell her. Tears sprang to her eyes as she drove—tears of fear and tears of grief all over again for Sassy.

"What's wrong, Mom?" Sarah said. "I'm sorry I yelled at you. I didn't mean to make you cry."

"It's not you, honey." Gloria sniffed, wiping at her tears with the back of her hand. "I guess I'm just a little overwhelmed right now."

"It's going to be okay, Mom." Sarah rubbed Gloria's arm.

"I know. I'm sorry," Gloria said, trying to regain her composure.

Gloria couldn't help it. She found herself with an aching heart at the loss of Sassy all over again, as Charles's words kept repeating themselves in her mind over the next week. She constantly checked the door locks and slept fitfully, stirring every time she heard a noise during the night. She couldn't share her fears with the girls or with Rick. Sarah already thought she was losing her mind. Chrissy would probably believe her, but Gloria didn't want to burden her with more of her problems. And, with Rick, well, she didn't want to bring any more of Charles into their relationship.

A week later, Gloria received a call. It was Chrissy, and she sounded excited. "Mom, I think I got Dad off your back for a while."

"What do you mean?" Gloria was confused. Charles had just threatened her life, and now Chrissy was saying she'd gotten him off her back?

"Well, he came over to visit, and all he wanted to do was talk about you. I told him, I thought this thing with Rick . . . I didn't actually mention his name, but . . . I said I think it's going to fizzle out soon. I basically lied. I think he actually bought it. I told him if he just waited, you were probably going to break up, so he needed to just act cool. I convinced him, if he leaves you alone and doesn't upset you, you might come back to him," Chrissy said, breathless after getting it all out.

"Did he say anything about the day I came over to pick up Sarah?" Gloria asked.

"No. Dad never said anything about it. What happened?"

"Oh, nothing," Gloria said, dismissively. "He was pretty upset, though. I'm just surprised at his change of heart. I guess I owe you big time if this is true."

Chrissy chuckled. "I'll let you know how you can pay me back."

"Thank you, honey. Thank you so much. I'm exhausted. I can sure use a break." Gloria sighed heavily.

She waited for the other shoe to drop for the next few months. She heard Charles and Chrissy were talking regularly. Chrissy relayed that he always asked about her and how she was doing as if he genuinely cared. Gloria hoped he wasn't reeling Chrissy in, just to break her heart.

By the time another month went by, Gloria had begun to relax a bit. Mid-November, she asked Chrissy to meet her between classes at Burger King near the Cal State campus. Something had been weighing on her mind, and she felt they needed to talk.

She looked around the restaurant and saw Chrissy was already sitting at a table with a textbook open, reading, and munching on fries. Gloria decided to skip the food counter and head on over. "Hello," she said as she reached the table and took a seat.

Looking up from her book, Chrissy smiled. "Hi, Mom. So what's this important thing we need to talk about?" She closed her book and slipped it into her backpack, which was lying on the bench beside her. Looking up again, she said, "I'm all ears."

Deciding to delve right in, Gloria said, "Chrissy, I appreciate you dealing with your dad, but I've been thinking. It's been unfair of me to allow you to shoulder your dad's problems like you've been doing."

Taking a sip of her Coke, Chrissy shook her head. "I don't mind, Mom. I know it's helping you out."

"Can I have a sip of your Coke?" Gloria reached across the table, her mouth suddenly dry.

"Sure," Chrissy said, handing it over.

Handing the cup back after taking a long drink, Gloria continued, "It hasn't been fair of me to put this all on you. It can't be healthy for you, Chrissy."

"I'm stronger than you give me credit for, Mom, and I know things haven't really changed with him. I take a call now and then, and I listen. That's all. I don't let it get to me, and I don't expect a fuzzy father-daughter relationship to ever come of it." Chrissy gave Gloria a tight-lipped smile.

"How does Alex feel about you talking to your dad?" Gloria asked.

"Don't worry. He's okay with it." Chrissy waved a fry before popping it into her mouth.

Gloria looked at Chrissy questioningly. "So, you're really okay."

"Yes, Mom. Really, don't worry. If it gets to be too much, I promise I will cut off contact. You need to relax." Chrissy stared her dead in the eye.

"Okay, if you're sure," Gloria said, holding her daughter's gaze while trying to see the truth in her eyes. All she could see was determination. She knew better than to argue with Chrissy. Once she made up her mind about something, Chrissy could really dig in her heels.

After talking to Chrissy, Gloria began to think of filing for divorce, but she was afraid to wake the sleeping dragon. The threat

Charles had made was constantly in the back of her mind. Every time she thought about it, she could feel the ache of grief for Sassy all over again.

On Thanksgiving, Rick and Gloria were enjoying a beautiful day of skiing. Gloria was becoming quite proficient but still wasn't able to keep up with him. Thankfully, he was content to stay away from the advanced slopes and spend the day with her. When they were finished, they sat at a picnic table at the lodge, enjoying hot chocolate.

Rick stood, and, before she knew it, he was down on one knee in the snow beside her. She gaped at him when he pulled a blue velvet box out of his pocket. He held it out and asked, "Will you be my wife?" while opening the box to reveal a beautiful diamond ring.

"Yes," Gloria said excitedly, her wide eyes sparkling.

"There's one condition," he said, his tone becoming quite serious. "You have to file for divorce. We can't be engaged while you're still married."

"I know. I'm sorry. I've been unfair to you, trying to keep the peace at home. I promise I will file right away," she said beaming.

"I'm going to give this to you. When you're divorced, you can put it on your finger. As far as I'm concerned, we're engaged." His eyes still conveyed seriousness as he handed her the box.

"Thank you for being so understanding and patient. I don't feel I deserve you," she said, as she tried on the ring, watching it dazzle in the sunlight. She moved her hand this way and that, gazing at the sparkles as the sun gleamed off the ring's facets. It was beautiful even through the tears brimming in her eyes.

"Nonsense, you're a wonderful woman, and I want to spend the rest of my life with you." He reached up and brushed a tear from under her eye. Finally, getting up off his knee, he sat beside her on the bench and pulled her into a hug. "Everything is going to be all right. You'll see."

After Thanksgiving, Gloria was true to her word and met with an attorney. She laid out her wishes, and finally signed papers.

She sat cross-legged on her bed the day she returned the papers to the attorney's office and called Rick.

"Rick," she said as soon as he picked up.

"What," he exclaimed teasingly.

"I filed for divorce. Well, actually he's not going to be served until after the first of the year, but I did it," she said triumphantly.

"That's great, Gloria. Congratulations. I know how hard it must have been for you."

"Yeah, I just didn't want to ruin the girls' holidays, with all the fighting and everything. That's why I'm having him served after the first."

"Don't worry about it, Gloria. At least you filed. That's great news." He sounded quite relieved.

"Thanks for understanding, I think things are going to be okay until the first, but after that, I'm afraid to think of what might happen. I'm really scared, Rick."

Chapter 22

August 2003

<u>After</u>

Friday, August 27th, Gloria decides to put all thoughts of future Rick behind her, firmly plant her feet into the now, and deal with this reality. Thinking about him is just making her heart ache, and she is determined to be present for the girls. They deserve that from her. Young Rick might not know her well in this reality, but she is determined to change that. One other thing she is determined to do is deal with the nightmares that continue to plague her. She is sure, if she can find out what they mean, she can move on and leave them behind for good.

With the little ones in bed for the night, Gloria, not so patiently, waits for Rick's Friday-night call. He said he would probably call around 8:00, and that's precisely when the phone begins to ring. *How prompt*, she thinks with a smile, as she lounges on the couch, her head resting on a throw pillow. She turns on her side and reaches over to the end table and picks up her phone after the first ring.

Rick immediately begins to explain, "Veronica is driving me crazy. I probably shouldn't be talking to you about this, but honestly, I haven't had anyone to confide in before."

Gloria thinks she probably should dissuade him from this topic, but can't help but listen supportively as he continues: "She's always accused me of cheating when I have been one-hundred percent faithful. I'm a monogamous guy. I feel a little guilty talking to you now, but sometimes I feel like, you know, if she is going to accuse me of doing something, I might as well be doing it. No," he says, "I know that's not right, but hell, what am I supposed to do? We had a big fight before she left, and I reminded her that she's the one going out to the bar while I'm staying home. Sometimes I think she picks a fight on Friday nights, just to have a good reason to leave." He lets out an exasperated sigh.

"I'm sorry." Gloria doesn't know what else to say. "It sounds like you're living in a pressure cooker."

"Exactly! That's exactly it," he says. "What am I supposed to do? I grew up with shouting and hitting. I don't know why I still put up with it." After a pause, he seems to calm down a bit and adds, "I guess it's what I'm used to. Maybe that's it."

"Is that what you think you deserve?" she asks. "Sometimes we don't think we deserve any better. At least that has been my experience. It sounds like we've been through a lot of the same experiences in our relationships."

"Yeah, you're probably the smart one for leaving," he says. "I honestly think she might have me killed if I ever leave her."

"Really?" Gloria says. She knew Veronica was more than a little crazy, but she never knew Rick thought she would contemplate killing him.

"No, really," he replies. "How has your husband reacted since you left him?"

"He was pretty threatening for a while, but get this: He has a girlfriend. Now I haven't heard a peep from him in weeks."

"Maybe that's what I have to do." He laughs. "Hook her up with one of my friends from work. Wait, no, I wouldn't wish her on any of my friends."

Gloria can almost hear the wheels turning in his head. "I've found that we each need to do what's best for ourselves. It's been a long time since I've even thought of what I want out of life. Don't get me wrong, I think if a marriage is salvageable, you should try to save it, but some relationships are doomed from the start." She finds herself feeling introspective for a moment.

"I've never really thought of it that way," he says, before becoming silent.

Giving him a chance to think, Gloria waits a minute before continuing. "Well, that's just the way I see things. Everyone, I'm sure, looks at it differently."

"Yeah, well, it's something to think about," he says.

Gloria glances at the clock and notices how late it's getting. She thinks she should probably mention the time. "We had probably better be hanging up about now, hadn't we? Won't Veronica be coming home soon?"

"You never know with her," he says. "She could be out until 10:00 or till 1:00 in the morning. I never know. I just try to be asleep before she comes in, so I don't have to deal with her, especially when she's drunk."

"I know how that goes, for sure!" Gloria agrees, and they both chuckle, before saying their reluctant goodbyes.

Every time Gloria finds herself thinking about her future during the week, she admonishes herself. She must live her present, as it is now. She has promised herself to plant her feet firmly into this reality, and that's precisely what she is determined to do.

Thankfully, Rick is able to sneak in a short call to her in the middle of the week. He has apparently come up with an idea for meeting again. "Do you have any vacation days?" he asks.

"I sure do." She smiles widely as she tucks Chrissy into bed. She steps over to Chrissy's bookshelf, picking out a few books.

"Can you hold on a second, Rick?"

"Sure," he says.

She holds out the books to Chrissy. "Here. Pick one for us to read."

Chrissy takes the books and begins to look at each one carefully, before laying it to the side and looking at the next, concentration furrowing her brow.

"Go ahead, Rick. I'm sorry about that. I'm just trying to get Chrissy to bed."

"I'll be quick," he says. I don't want to keep you. The thing is, I thought about telling Veronica I have to go out of town for work; instead, I would come to Bakersfield for a couple of days. Could you take off as soon as next week?

"Yes, I can take off next week." She says smiling as she sits on Chrissy's bed and tucks a strand of hair behind her little ear.

"Great. I was thinking about Wednesday and Thursday," he says expectantly.

Gloria is encouraged by his eagerness to see her. "That will work for me, but we'll talk about it Friday. I think Chrissy is ready for her bedtime story."

"Sounds good. We'll talk then," he says, before saying goodbye.

Having finally selected a book, Chrissy holds it out to Gloria. She smiles down at her daughter, before settling in to read. "Do you want to read tonight, or do you want me to read it to you?" Gloria asks.

Chrissy yawns. "You read, mommy. I'm tired."

Gloria takes the book, cuddles up to her daughter, opens it to the first page, and begins. Chrissy only makes it to the third page before her eyes are shut tight. Gloria closes the book, picks up the others lying beside her on the bed and gives Chrissy a kiss on the cheek. She places the books back on the shelf, turning out the light before heading for her own bed.

She thinks of the phone call she just had with Rick and the thought hits her. How would this look to her parents or Dr. Dyson. She shouldn't be talking to someone already, let alone someone who is living with someone else. And, there is the fact that she is just beginning her own divorce, which makes it look even worse.

She has a lot to think about. She's going to have to keep their plans to herself. If she tells anyone the truth about having met Rick in the future, or in a dream, they will think she's lost her marbles. She hopes she can navigate these murky waters without going under.

Chapter 23

August 2003

<u>After</u>

When their meeting day arrives, Gloria takes the girls to her parents' house, making the excuse of not feeling well, and asks them if they might babysit. She's not sure her parents buy it, but what else could she do? It's going to be another scorching day, so whatever they do, it should probably be indoors.

Gloria stands in front of the mirror, trying on one outfit, and then another, throwing each one onto her bed before finally settling on a floral print sundress. She has been lying out in the backyard on weekends, trying to get a tan on her pale limbs. She has had some success and now has a light sun-kissed glow. Her hair has grown quite a bit past her shoulders and has become a lighter blond from the summer sun. She decides to wear it sleek and straight.

When she arrives early at Marie Calendars, where they decided to meet, she seats herself in the bar. She chooses a booth next to the window, so she can see Rick arrive. She didn't even ask what kind of car he has, so she tries to guess. He was driving a company truck when they met at Spring House, so she has no idea.

She sits, trying to guess the make, model, and color of his car. *Let's see, it would be black, probably four-wheel drive, and maybe a Jeep.* As she's thinking, she doesn't even see him pull in. Before she knows it, he's walking by the window wearing jeans, his tan arms standing out in sharp contrast to his white polo shirt. She jumps up and greets him around the corner, signaling for him to come sit in the bar.

As they sit, she says, "I didn't see you drive in. What kind of car do you have?"

"A Honda Civic," he says while sliding into the booth.

"I really got that wrong. What color is it?" she asks, leaning in.

"What do you mean you got that wrong?" he asks, before saying, "It's white."

"Well, wrong on all counts." She laughs. "I tried to guess what you would drive. I guessed a black four-wheel drive. I got that really wrong."

He laughs and says, "Although I would love to have the vehicle you describe, I drive the Civic because it's great on gas."

She nods. "Ah, yes, that makes sense," Thinking of all the things she knows about him, she doesn't know what car he has in 2003.

"I thought you knew everything about me," he points out, a little sarcastically.

"Well, as I told you before, not absolutely everything—" she smirks "—unfortunately."

"And just when I was starting to believe in this dream business." He chuckles. Leaning forward, he rests his chin on his folded hands.

"What can I say? You've found out my secret. I'm not perfect." She smiles, sheepishly.

Ordering nonalcoholic drinks all afternoon, they talk the hours away. Finally, they decide they should order dinner. The waitress brings a couple of menus, and they both peruse them hungrily.

"Everything looks good," Gloria says. "I haven't eaten all day. It's probably nerves, but I'm famished now."

"Nerves," he teases. "It's just me."

"I know, I can't help it, so don't laugh." She swipes at him with the menu.

"Okay, but you're taking the fun out of it," he says, leaning back, as he looks back down at his own menu.

Gloria giggles. "Stop it; what do you want to eat?"

By the time they're finished with dinner, he suggests he check into his motel. "And," he says, "Maybe we can sit in the pool to cool off and talk a bit more."

It doesn't take Gloria long to make up her mind. "I will have to run home and get my swimsuit."

"Okay, you do that, and I'll check in to the motel around the corner."

They wave as they pass each other, driving, through the parking lot. Out the open window, Gloria yells, "You're going the wrong way. There's no exit that way," she laughs.

In her rear-view mirror, she sees him pull into a parking spot and turn around to come up behind her. She shakes her head, laughing. She knows he can see her shaking her head, and she will probably hear about it when they meet up.

Rick calls from the motel, as she is grabbing her suit. He tells her to come to room 109 and meet him. He suggests she change there. Flipping the phone closed, she heads out the door. She feels like a schoolgirl; the teenager she was before she moved to Bakersfield. She hadn't realized it, but Rick has brought her back to life.

Knocking on the door to his room, Gloria waits nervously for a few seconds, pondering why she is still so nervous. *It's a good sort of nervous, though*, she is thinking when she hears the deadbolt sliding out. Then there he is, in black swim trunks.

He wipes the back of his hand across his forehead. "Doesn't it ever cool down here?"

"Sorry, not much," Gloria says, as she heads through the door and into the bathroom to change. She pulls on her lime green one-piece and throws on the matching cover-up, which looks like a very short dress. She considers wrapping a towel around her waist to hide a bit more leg, but in the end, thinks that might look a little silly. When she comes out holding a towel in front of her, his eyes widen, and Gloria is sure she is turning ten shades of purple.

They lounge in the shallow end of the pool, cooling off while they talk. As the sun sinks in the sky, there aren't many swimmers left. They are both turning into prunes, but neither of them seems to care. The swimmers who are left slowly head off to their rooms, and Rick and Gloria eventually have the pool to themselves. There is a sign on the fence that displays a 10:00 p.m. closing time, so they only have a short time left. When the hour in question does roll around, Rick turns to Gloria and smiles expectantly. "What would you like to do after this?"

"I'd like to borrow your shower to rinse off. Hopefully, I'm not being too forward, but I was wondering if we might watch a movie?" She looks at him with a gleam in her eye.

"You mean in my room?"

"Yes," she says. "Don't worry, I won't molest you."

"How forward of you, madam." He chuckles and splashes water in her face.

"Well then, I guess I will just have to go home." She wipes at her face, trying to look serious.

"Hang on, I was just joking."

"So was I." Gloria laughs.

As they settle in, Rick turns on the TV. Gloria sits properly on the edge of the bed while Rick takes the remote and sits in the only chair in the room. As he flips channels, they finally decide on a movie to watch. After half an hour, she declares, "This is silly and uncomfortable. We've been sitting all day, why don't we both prop up some pillows and lounge on the bed? On top of the covers, of course," she adds.

With a look of relief, Rick is on the bed without much hesitation. Before the end of the movie, they are cuddled up to each other, fast asleep, still fully clothed.

Rick wakes Thursday morning to the TV playing and Gloria snuggled up next to him, still fast asleep. He tries to extricate his arm from underneath her without waking her up. He has almost made it when she opens her eyes. Abruptly, she sits upright. "Oh no, I guess I fell asleep. I'm sorry. I didn't mean to spend the night." She begins to frantically scurry off the bed.

"It's okay, I fell asleep too. I just woke up," he says, before adding, "Nothing happened. We're both fully dressed."

She knows they are slipping into dangerous waters when it comes to his relationship. She certainly doesn't want to cause him more distress. She can't help but feel a bit guilty, but if she's honest with herself, she would like this to go a lot further.

"Would you mind if I go home and freshen up a bit?" She stands beside the bed, nervous and wide-eyed.

"Not at all," he says. "After that, do you think we should go for breakfast?"

"That would be great. I can meet you in about an hour." She sits back down on the edge of the bed and pulls on her sandals. Reaching for the brush in her purse, she sprints to the mirror and blushes as she looks up. She has dark smudges of mascara under her eyes, and her hair has a mind of its own, sticking up in all directions. At first, she feels mortified, but then she doubles over laughing.

"What's so funny?" Rick gives her a quizzical look.

All she can do is point at her head, she is laughing so much. And, she can see he is trying to suppress a laugh himself.

"It's okay. You can laugh. It's funny," she says, as she catches a breath, and he bursts out laughing too.

Through his laughter, he says, "It's okay, you're even cute when you're ugly," which makes her laugh even harder.

Finally straightening up, and putting herself somewhat together, she heads to the door. They're both still chuckling as she leaves.

Sitting in the booth at breakfast, they bat ideas around about where they should go. It eventually comes down to the bowling alley or the movies. They decide to spend the rest of their day at the bowling alley, in air-conditioned comfort. He is decidedly better than her at bowling, but she knew that. She was trying to have a healthy competition, though. In the end, she gives up and resigns herself to being the loser of every game. He didn't even let her win one, and she lets him know that he isn't being a gentleman.

"When did I ever say I was a gentleman?" he asks, raising an eyebrow.

As they sit talking over lunch at the snack bar, Rick looks at his watch. "It's already 3:00," he says. "I probably should be heading back." Gloria nods her head in agreement.

"I've had such a great time." Gloria reluctantly stands as he does.

With a sad smile, he looks into her eyes. "Me too."

After walking her to her car, Rick gives her a hug, which, to her surprise, turns into a kiss. A long kiss. Looking into her eyes afterward, he says, "I think I'm falling for you, Gloria."

"I'm afraid I've already fallen for you," she says. *Mission accomplished*, she thinks.

Giving her one more hug, he says, "I'll call you as soon as I can."

"I'll be waiting." She slides into her car, and he shuts the door.

Tears well up in her eyes, as she watches him walk toward his car and finally drive away. He's not even out of sight yet, and she already misses him.

Gloria had called to check in with her parents a couple of times during the last two days. They told her everything was going just fine, and not to worry. Her heart had been playing this strange tug-of-war between enjoying being in Rick's company and feeling guilty for pawning off her girls; not to mention lying about not feeling well. She wonders what kind of mother she really is and why her life has to be so complicated.

Chapter 24

September 2003

<u>After</u>

Sitting with the usual pillow clutched to her chest, in front of Dr. Dyson, Gloria begins, "the dreams I've been having are getting worse and more disconnected. I've been keeping my dream journal, but it doesn't seem to be helping. I feel I must find out what they mean. I know in my bones, it's something that has happened to me," she says, as she begins to describe her latest dream. "This one is new."

She leans back into the chair and tucks her chin into the pillow. "Do you mind if I kick my shoes off?"

"Go right ahead. Make yourself comfortable," he says, crossing his legs and leaning back, looking like he is getting comfortable himself.

After she slips off her shoes, she sets the pillow to the side and draws her knees up to her chin, wrapping her arms around jean-clad legs, she places her socked feet on the chair. This subject is becoming uncomfortable, and she has the feeling she wants to hide. "Dr. Dyson," she says, "I think it's time for me to meet the Other Gloria."

"Well." He taps his pencil on his chin then stops, uncrossing his legs, and scooting forward in his chair. "How do you feel about hypnotherapy? It could help clarify what you're experiencing in your dreams. And, we may be able to recover memories the Other Gloria is holding onto."

"Can you do that?" Her head pops up from her knees. She would have never considered this before, but now she feels desperate.

"Yes, I can," he says.

"I'm ready to do it. I have to find out what's going on in there," she insists, poking a finger at her temple.

"We can start next session when we have more time." He leans back and crosses his legs again. "Would you like to explore your dreams further now, or is there anything else you would like to talk about?"

I would like to tell you all about Rick, she thinks. *I would like to talk about him all session and have you tell me how right we are together.* But, she knows that's not what he would say. He would say she hasn't been out of her relationship with Charles long enough to start a new one. He would tell her she's rebounding.

What she does as she lifts her chin from her knees, is say: "I served my husband with divorce papers."

"Oh, and how did that go?" he asks calmly, pausing to take notes.

He is always so calm, she thinks. It seems like his default mode is calm. It's soothing and at the same time, unnerving.

"Not well, as you might expect," she says, still clutching her legs.

"How so?" He looks up from his notepad.

"Basically, he blew up on me, and I hung up on him. And, I think he could actually kill me," she says matter-of-factly.

"You really think he might kill you?" He is now looking steadily into her eyes.

"I'm not sure. I mean, I don't know. If he's backed into a corner, I think he might," she explains.

"On a scale from 1 to 10, how would you rate your fear of him harming you?" he asks, jotting it down as she speaks.

Pausing to think for a moment, she says, "Probably about a 7."

"That's pretty high. You should probably trust your gut instincts here." He looks at her with concern.

"I'll try," she promises, not knowing how exactly to keep that promise.

"Is there anyone who can stay with you for a while?" He stands and walks over to the bookcase behind his desk. He reaches up and pulls out three pamphlets, carrying them over to hand to her.

"No. The only thing I can think of is to going back to my parents' house until it's all over." She releases her legs and places her feet on the floor before taking the pamphlets from him.

"These are some resources you might find helpful," he says, taking a seat again. "And there's a hotline number you can call for help any time."

Grabbing his notepad from his desk, he jots something down and says, "You might want to think about staying with your parents for a while, from what I'm hearing."

"I think I might do that." Pulling her shoes back on, she stands to leave, knowing her hour is up. She is always aware of the time with Dr. Dyson. She makes sure she notices when it's ten minutes before the hour. When he does it, she feels like she's being kicked out the door. It puts a negative spin on the whole process. *Well, your time is up, I must throw you out like a piece of trash, so I can get on to more important clients*, she always thinks in those moments. It makes her resent the whole process sometimes.

Gloria returns to work that afternoon, sitting with her elbows on her desk and her head in her hands. She is going to have to call her parents and see if she and the girls can move back in for a while. She wishes she had Mickey to confide in right now, but she is off for a couple of days, and it wouldn't be fair to interrupt her free time, so Gloria grabs the phone and begins to dial.

"Hello," Dena answers.

"Hi Mom," Gloria says. She knows she sounds glum.

"What's he done now?" Dena sounds suspicious.

"I think I'm going to have to move back in for a while. I'm so sorry," Gloria says, feeling like a failure.

"That's okay, honey, what's going on?" Gloria can hear the worry in her mom's voice, and it only serves to make her feel worse.

"My counselor thinks I might be in danger from Charles. I actually think he might be right."

"Tell me what's going on," Dena says.

"Nothing really that I can put my finger on. I'm just not feeling safe lately."

Dena doesn't hesitate. "Go ahead and pack up and come on over."

"Thanks, Mom," Gloria says, before ending the call.

As she packs her things that evening, she tries to think about Rick. At least he is something positive in her life, and of course her two beautiful girls. She has so much to be thankful for, and she finds herself cheering up as she thinks about it. Charles might try to throw a wrench into her life, but she doesn't have to dwell on it. She needs to let it go until the next encounter. At least if she is with her parents, he might be civil. She is sure her parents' house is the safest place for her now.

Chrissy doesn't question all the moves they've been making. She seems to be happy wherever she is. She likes their new house, with her playhouse in the backyard. Gloria tells her they will be back soon, and she can play at Grandma's and Grandpa's until then; after all, she has a little playhouse there too, behind the bar. It doesn't take much to satisfy Chrissy, thankfully. Before Gloria knows it, she has everything packed, and they have moved in once again with her parents.

She hopes Charles won't do any damage to her house while she's away. She has grown quite fond of their little cottage. Unlike before, she has met most of her neighbors and waves and talks to them regularly. The freedom she has felt there is indescribable. She is going to miss her little place, but she will keep up the payments, and there will be a time when they can return.

She called Rick at work before she left, and let him know where she would be staying. She had also given him her parents' phone number. She wonders how in the world she is going to explain Rick's phone calls to her parents when they start coming in late at night.

Chapter 25

September 2003

<u>After</u>

    Gloria is bouncing her knee again, this time waiting in Dr. Dyson's lobby. *Why do I arrive so early? It's just nerve-wracking,* she thinks, as she tries to concentrate on a *Cosmopolitan* magazine, open and currently bouncing in her lap. Flipping through the pages, not really seeing what is on them, she keeps glancing back at her watch every couple of minutes.

    Finally, a burly, broad-shouldered guy steps out of the doctor's office. His wavy blond hair seems to stand out in contrast to his tan skin and brown eyes. She tries not to stare at his biceps that strain at the fabric of his button-down shirt. Forcing herself to look down, she catches a glimpse of his wedding ring.

    She wonders if his wife might have forced him to come. Charles's ego would never have allowed him to be caught dead in this office. Looking like a solid oak tree, she couldn't imagine how this man could be budged in any direction he didn't want to go. Could he have actually made the decision on his own? She blushes at the thought of him admitting he needed help. It suddenly makes him more attractive than she already found him.

    As the man heads toward the exit, Dr. Dyson informs Gloria he will be just a moment, before disappearing back into his office. He always spends the extra ten minutes in his office doing something, until the top of the hour. She guesses he is either making notes from the last client or reviewing her file.

Gloria looks at her watch as Dr. Dyson motions her in. *Yep, ten minutes on the dot*, she thinks.

"You were interested in hypnotherapy, were you not?" he says as Gloria heads to her usual chair. "If so, you would probably be more comfortable on the couch." He points to the couch to the right of the door she has just entered.

Turning back, she takes a seat in the middle of the deep brown leather sofa. She reaches over to grab a pillow from one end as he turns his chair to face her. He reaches over to his desk to pick up his notepad and moves around to take a seat. He smiles as he crosses his long Levi-clad legs and rests the notepad in his lap.

"It's important that you are as comfortable as possible for this, so arrange yourself in the most comfortable position on the couch you can find," he says.

Gloria leans back uncomfortably, then scoots to the side to lean into the corner. Seeing her unease, Dr. Dyson says, "Don't be afraid to lie down. You're safe here. You're going to have to trust me and completely relax for this to work."

"I'll try, but I don't know if I even know how," Gloria admits.

"I can help you with that. It may take you a few sessions to completely relax, but we can do work in whatever state you allow yourself to fall into," he says, as he relaxes back into his chair. "This isn't like hypnosis you see on TV. Just think of it as a deep relaxation, where your worries and thoughts get out of the way, and you are able to concentrate on what you need to work on. I won't ask you to do anything you aren't comfortable with."

He seems to be talking in slow motion, drawing his words out. She can't help herself; she's already beginning to relax.

Finally, giving herself permission to make herself comfortable, she kicks off her shoes before grabbing another pillow at the end of the couch. She allows herself to lie down on her back, placing one pillow under her head and gripping the other tightly to her chest. "Okay," she says timidly.

"Are you ready?" he asks in a slow, smooth voice.

Gloria nods her head. Her nod seems to match the pace of his voice.

"Now, what is the most important thing you would like to work on?" he asks.

After a pause, Gloria says, "I guess, maybe, my dreams, and maybe the Other Gloria, but I'm afraid. Sometimes I feel like I can't wake up from my dreams."

"Don't worry, I will make sure you don't go further than you can handle. If you meet the Other Gloria, you are in charge of your interaction with her. In fact, we can make a signal for when you want to stop. All you have to do is raise your right hand, and we will stop. I promise," he says, slowly and rhythmically.

Gloria slowly nods her head, closing her eyes as he draws out his next words.

"Now," he says, "I want you to think of a place where you've been and where you were comfortable. A place where you feel calm and safe. Let me know when you are there. Visualize it. Try to feel it."

She lies motionless, trying to think of that comforting place. She soon finds herself thinking of a beautiful beach in Florida she visited with her mother and father. They were staying in a condo there, right on the beach. She had never seen sand so white or water so blue. No, not blue; it was more aqua. She remembers lying on a lounge chair underneath an umbrella, as the cool breeze gently blew across her skin on a gorgeous spring day. She remembers how she listened to the gentle waves roll in as she lounged, staring off into the invisible horizon, where water met sky.

"Are you there?" he asks softly, after a few moments.

Gloria slowly nods her head.

"I want you to begin to relax every part of your body, one part at a time. We will start from your toes, and move all the way to the top of your head. Are you ready?"

Gloria nods her head slowly.

"Are you ready to meet the Other Gloria?" His voice is calming.

"Yes," she whispers.

"Tell me what is happening now," he says.

"It's really quiet. I can't see anything. Wait. I hear a woman's voice. She's telling me everything is okay. She sounds authoritative. Very confident.

After Gloria goes silent, Dr. Dyson asks, "What is she saying?"

Gloria says, "She is telling me not to be afraid. She needs me to know something. She says I'm not ready to know yet, but I will be soon. It's enough that we have met today. She is saying not to worry, she will talk to me again soon."

The next thing she knows, she is in the dream and then before she knows it, she is awake and alert. All she can remember afterward is relaxing every part of her body. She is shaking when she comes around but calms down almost immediately.

"We're done." Dr. Dyson leans forward in his chair, smiling.

"What happened?" Gloria sits up, blinking her eyes.

"You will probably start remembering things slowly. We have a lot of work still to do, but you did well. I'm surprised you were able to relax as well as you did," he says, smiling broadly.

"Did I raise my hand?" She looks around, trying to get her bearings.

"You sure did," he says.

Walking out of the office, Gloria feels relaxed, but also very tired. She's not sure how she could have delved into her dream and come out on the other end relaxed. Completely the opposite feeling she has when she wakes during the night from a dream—the feeling of panic. She senses the Other Gloria didn't show up. She is sure she would know if they had met. Part of her feels disappointed, but a large part of her is relieved.

That night, she falls asleep quickly, with none of the usual difficulty. As the dream begins, she feels unnaturally calm. She is standing in a meadow of green grass and wildflowers. Looking up, she sees a lone cloud. A woman is standing in the midst of the cloud, her blond hair blowing in the slight breeze. She wears battle armor—the sun glinting off its shiny silver surface. Standing with fists on hips and feet shoulder-width apart, she instills in Gloria a sudden feeling of safety. As the haze around her clears, Gloria can see the woman has her face. She has a proud look—a fierce look, even. She has an immediate understanding of who this is: The Other Gloria.

Gloria wishes for the cloud to come down so she can communicate. It becomes clear that she has just found the other part of herself. The brave part that has been there all along. Then, as quickly as she appeared, the cloud rolls away, and the Other Gloria is gone. Gloria reaches out to her as she goes, pleading with her to come back. She feels as if a part of her has been wrenched away and she is left feeling broken.

Waking from the dream in the middle of the night, Gloria feels frozen in place. She reaches for her dream journal, but it's not on her nightstand. Groggily, she tries to remember where she put it.

It's no use; her mind doesn't seem to function, and soon she is once again asleep.

Friday morning comes and she wakes with no memory of her dream. Had she dreamed? Her day goes by quickly. She is productive and full of energy. She can't remember the last time she felt like this, if ever. She hasn't been worrying about the divorce, the dream, or Charles. It's so unlike her. She thinks Dr. Dyson might have performed magic.

Rick hadn't called during the week, and thankfully, she didn't have to explain anything to her parents. Knowing he will call tonight, she corners her mom when she is alone in the kitchen that evening.

"Mom, I'm expecting a call, from an out-of-town friend. It might be late, so I'll get the phone when it rings." She can't seem to help the sheepish look on her face.

Dena eyes her suspiciously. "A friend?"

She never could pull one over on her mother. Her father is another story, but her mother will want to know every detail.

"Okay, okay, Mom. It's a guy I know. We're just talking. Please don't tell Dad. It feels good to have someone to talk to." She bows her head, unable to look her mother in the eye, as she continues, "If you know what I mean."

Dena snickers. "Don't worry, I won't tell Dad."

Looking up to see the expression on her mom's face, Gloria finds her smiling warmly. "I just want you to be happy. Well, I want you to be careful and happy," she says, quickly correcting herself.

With a huge sigh of relief, Gloria can check that chore off her list.

Chapter 26

October 2003

<u>After</u>

Gloria doesn't catch herself thinking about the future as often as she used to. Since her relationship with young Rick seems to be progressing, she finds it easier not to think about the Rick of her future quite as much. She is glad that Rick finally moved out of the house he shared with Veronica. He laughed when he told Gloria, Veronica moved a guy into the house only two days after he left.

It also helps that her sessions with Dr. Dyson have been going so well. Things aren't making much sense yet. It's all disjointed and nonsensical, but she is sure there is meaning in what they are uncovering.

Back in her little cottage, after unpacking her things, she stands at the kitchen door as Chrissy helps her sister down the path to her playhouse. Gloria follows slowly behind to keep an eye on them, her phone in hand, waiting for Ricks call. He has visited her house over a couple of weekends, and the girls have fallen in love with him right away.

When the girls return to the house, Gloria tries to corner Chrissy to brush the tangles out of her long hair. She always has a hard time pinning Chrissy down for too long, and she was only able to get her hair half-way brushed earlier that morning.

Chrissy never asks about Charles, but she does have a question about Rick. "Why doesn't Rick yell, Mommy?"

"Not all men yell, Sweetheart." Gloria tries to explain.

"Just some?" Chrissy asks, spinning around and pursing her lips, her little blond head cocked to one side.

"Yes, honey, just some." Gloria spins her back around, so she can finish brushing her hair.

Chrissy looks thoughtfully at her in the mirror. "I don't like yelling."

"I don't, either." Gloria laughs at her daughter, who can't sit still.

"I like Rick," Chrissy says, grinning into the mirror.

"I'm glad. Me too." Gloria smiles back, whimsically at her fidgety daughter.

At that, Chrissy is off the stool, her hair mostly brushed. Not skipping a beat, she is out the back door and heading to her playhouse again. With Sarah on one hip, Gloria follows behind to the kitchen, where she takes a seat at the table and watches out the window, waiting for Rick to show up for the weekend.

Chapter 27

October 2003

<u>After</u>

Monday afternoon, once again, Gloria finds herself melting into Dr. Dyson's couch. He has blocked out a two-hour session for her today. They discussed it, and Gloria feels ready to delve deeper into her nightmares.

He explains, "We probably won't need the full two hours today, but I don't want to disturb you until you're ready."

"Where are you?" he asks, once Gloria is completely relaxed.

"I'm knocking on Charles's door," she says quietly.

"Tell me what it looks like. What do you see?" he says rhythmically.

"The door is metal, green. It has panels and a brushed-metal knocker," she says slowly.

"Do you know why you are there?"

"I'm picking up Sarah. He was served with divorce papers on Friday. I think he's getting back at me. He took Sarah again." Her breathing is coming faster.

"What do you mean again?"

"He went to Chrissy's again to pick her up. He did that once before," she says.

"Are your daughters older now?" he asks confusion in his voice at this turn.

"Yes. Chrissy is married, and Sarah is fifteen. Chrissy is watching her sister for the weekend."

"What do you see?"

"He's opening the door . . . I'm looking for Sarah. I don't want to go in, but she's not coming to the door. I'm calling for her, but she's not coming . . . I don't want to, but I'm going in to look for her. After I walk by him, he tells me she's not here. He says she went back to Chrissy's. I'm turning around . . . He's holding something," she says, breathing heavier. She becomes silent except for her heavy breathing. She seems frozen in place.

"What is he holding?" he asks methodically.

"She's letting me see through her eyes now—the Other Gloria. She is floating above me. I see myself. I see him."

"What else is she seeing?" he asks.

"It's a bat, a baseball bat," she says frantically. "He's swinging it." She gasps. "He hit me in the back. I'm on the floor. He's above me, swinging again." She becomes quiet and still.

"What's happening, Gloria? What do you see?" he says calmly.

"I don't know," she says, confused. "Wait . . . Now I'm in the trunk. I'm seeing from her eyes again. I can see myself in the trunk . . . I'm afraid and flailing about." She pauses. "My bindings are gone. I was able to calm down enough to squeeze my hands free and untie my ankles. There's a box behind me . . . I found something. I think it's a screwdriver . . . The trunk is still moving. I don't know where we're going . . . I'm afraid."

"You are perfectly safe, Gloria," he soothes.

"I hear tires on gravel. We're slowing down . . . Now we're turning around." Then she becomes silent.

"What's happening now, Gloria?"

272

"I hear gravel again . . . We're stopping. I think we're pulling over."

She pauses for a few seconds, and he encourages her to go on.

"I hear the car door open and footsteps. Oh no . . . I hear a key in the lock." Her breathing increases. Her chest is heaving.

"What's happening now, Gloria?" he asks. "Remember, you are safe. You can always go to your safe place," he says in a slow, measured pace.

Her breathing slows and then rises again. "Light! It's blinding me . . . He's bending over . . . He's grabbing me!"

Her breathing is frantic as she says, "I'm stabbing at him with a screwdriver . . . I keep stabbing and stabbing . . . He's trying to grab my arms, but his hands slip . . . I'm stabbing and stabbing. I feel it go in . . ."

She pauses. "I feel something . . . It's warm, and it's pouring on me."

Her breathing slows a bit.

"Can you tell me what you see, Gloria?" he asks gently.

"He's grabbing his neck. He's holding himself up with the other hand on the car. He's just standing there slumped over me.

Now he's stumbling backwards . . ."

Her chest is still heaving, but she becomes quiet except for her breath, before saying, "I think he's gone."

"I have to get out of here while he's gone. My legs are shaky, and my left foot is asleep, but I'm dragging myself out . . . I'm holding onto the car . . . I'm dizzy. I will need the keys. Where are they?" she says frantically, moving her head about.

"What do you see, Gloria?"

"Oh . . . I see them hanging out of the trunk lid. I'm slamming it down and grabbing the keys."

She holds her breath.

273

"What do you see now, Gloria?" he asks patiently, waiting for her to continue.

Letting out a breath, she says, "I don't know where he is, but I'm looking down over the edge. I have the feeling it's so far down. I'm frozen, looking into the blackness . . . I can see the edge, where it drops off. Was he going to throw me over the edge?" she says, gasping. "I have to move. I have to go. I'm looking back. I don't see him . . . I have to hurry . . . I can't stop to think." Breathing rapidly again, she says, "I have to get in the car, now!"

She pauses. "I'm in the car. I'm feeling around for the door locks. I can't find them. I'm trying to put the key in the ignition, but I'm shaking. It's the wrong key. I'm trying another one. I'm trying . . ." Her breathing is still rapid. Her breathing begins to slow once more. "I started the car. I'm speeding away. I'm going very fast," she says. She no longer has the sense that Dr. Dyson is there. She feels as if she is on her own. Things are beginning to fade away in her mind. Everything is just gone.

Chapter 28

<u>After</u>

It's happening again. There's a missing memory. This time, Gloria realizes with frightening certainty, it's a serious lapse. She comes to full consciousness, finding herself behind the wheel of a car, speeding down a dark highway. She must remember what happened to bring her here. Something about the road seems familiar, but there is only a vague recognition. She has no idea where she is driving from - or for that matter, driving to.

There are few passing cars to light up the night. The blackness seems to swallow her whole, sending her careening into the dark and utterly blind as to what lies ahead. Only able to see where her headlights direct, she has no idea of her destination.

Finally, she spots a road sign. As it quickly comes into focus, she can see she is heading down Highway 58. And then another sign, indicating she is 21 miles from Bakersfield. It makes sense that she would be driving to Bakersfield - after all, she lives there. But Highway 58? This means she has driven through the Tehachapi Mountains. She has absolutely no memory of it.

A car begins to pass as she looks slightly downward. The quick flash of lights reveals what looks like a massive amount of blood on her hands, which are currently perched at ten and two on the steering wheel. Her eyes widen as she flinches, jerking the wheel.

She almost sideswipes the rear of the passing car. Her car crosses farther into the left lane and then farther, almost hitting the concrete barrier as she tries frantically to correct. Fighting hard for control, she is finally going in a straight line once more. The red taillights of the car that has just passed are nearly out of sight, and the leaden darkness envelops her once more.

There is a trembling that seems to originate in the pit of her stomach and emanates out through her hands. A nagging voice from deep inside pushes her forward, but, try as she might, she can't remember a thing up until a few minutes ago.

She glances at the speedometer and realizes she is slowing. Somehow she musters the courage to bring her full attention to the task at hand. Her hands still shaking violently, she fights to keep control as she continues to slow. Pulling onto the shoulder, she pushes the shift lever to park.

With her head now on the steering wheel between her hands and her breathing coming in long hard gasps, she waits a moment to try the impossible: Compose herself. *There's a simple explanation for all of this*, she thinks. At least, she is trying to think. She is mostly reacting at this point. With her hands trembling on either side of her aching head and her chest heaving, she attempts to bring her breath under control.

For a moment, she focuses on her aching head. It's beginning to feel like a bass drum resounding in rhythmic beats off every inch of her skull. She doesn't know how long she will be able to keep on like this, but something urges her forward.

Remembering her hands, she is unable to comprehend the blood she has just seen. She can't understand, with all that blood, why she hasn't passed out by now. Another car is coming up behind her, and she lifts her head, praying what she saw was just an illusion, a trick of the lights, or her out-of-control imagination. Her eyes widen in shock as the car passes, and she realizes what she has seen is real.

She fumbles around the dashboard, frantically turning every switch and knob until she finds the interior lights. She winces and closes her eyes tightly once she has switched them on. Slowly opening her eyes, she begins to inspect her hands. They are still shaking. There is a lot of blood, so much blood, but she can see no cuts of any significance. Still, she turns her hands over and over again.

Pull yourself together, she demands of her muddled brain. She's running on adrenaline now. *Slow down and think, Gloria*, she chides herself, as she looks out into the utter blackness beyond her headlights. It's no use. Her mind is spinning in a hundred different directions.

She turns her head slightly to look down at her right arm. What she sees makes her stomach churn. She thinks, for one terrible moment, she might throw up. Her entire sleeve is covered in blood, drenched in it. Looking further, she sees her white shirt is now almost completely stained red. Her mouth gapes in horror as her brain attempts to take it in. She can't comprehend this as reality.

Her mind finally takes in the gruesome fact - what used to be a white, long-sleeved shirt is now mostly red with blood, only a few white patches remaining. She attempts to calm her wildly beating heart. After a moment, she begins to unbutton her sleeve, gently pulling it up as high as it will go. Try as she might, she can find no cuts deep enough to cause such heavy bleeding. All the while, she is thinking she might pass out from her ever-growing headache.

As she reaches to pull down the visor and look into the mirror, she thinks the blood might be coming from her head. She gasps at her reflection. Blood smeared on her face and in her hair. Makeup smeared all over her face. She looks like a clown from a horror movie, dark tear stains of mascara running down to her chin. Her red lipstick, intermingled with blood, is gobbed in streaks around her mouth.

As she scrutinizes her own reflection, she finds a knot about the size of a golf ball forming on the left side of her scalp. It went nearly unnoticed under her matted hair. Pulling her blond hair aside to examine further, the lump is blue and ugly, but there's no blood to speak of.

She decides to examine the rest of her body. Every movement is painful. It's not only her head that aches; her entire body seems to be aching. Gently pulling up the sleeve of her left arm, she finds no cuts. Next, she unbuttons her shirt to inspect her stomach and chest. It's hard to tell with so much blood covering her, but the bleeding, wherever it's coming from, seems to have stopped.

Think! What happened tonight?

It's no use. She lowers her head to the steering wheel again, hoping to find some clarity. She feels she could sleep, but she knows, with a head injury, sleeping could be dangerous.

Snapping out of her mind and back into her gruesome reality, she raises her head to inspect the interior of the car. There are streaks of blood on the steering wheel, the shift lever, the dash, and the seat around her, but nowhere else that she can see. The interior is light gray. This reignites the confusion. She has never owned a car with a gray interior.

Suddenly a sickening dread comes over her. The feeling of someone watching. It's overpowering. *Is there someone in the car?* She can't bring herself to turn and look into the back seat. Then she feels it. She's had this feeling before . . . the feeling . . . of nothingness. She feels herself drifting away. She is going deep inside herself. She wants to let go and let it happen. She wants to let her brain fly away.

She is jolted to consciousness with a shouting in her head. "Get out of here. Wake up and keep moving."

How long has she been out? Minutes? Hours? It's still dark, it must not have been too long, but she feels an urgency now. The voice won't let up. "Put the car in gear and drive."

The feeling of someone watching her becomes overpowering. She forces herself to turn and look into the back seat. She lets out a long breath; she didn't know she was holding, when she sees the back seat is empty.

She's back now, finally pulling onto the road and driving into the night. She realizes city lights have come into view, and she races toward them. Looking down, she sees the needle on the speedometer, pointing to 95 miles per hour. Slow down. She must slow down, but the pull toward the lights makes that a difficult task.

She forces herself to ease up on the gas pedal until she eventually slows to 65 miles per hour. She frantically reads off-ramp signs as they go by, but nothing looks familiar. She feels panic rise in her chest; she is unable to figure out where she should exit until eventually the car bumps over two sets of rumble strips and the highway abruptly ends.

She sits at the red light at the end of the highway for a long moment. There are no cars in sight. The feeling of floating off into darkness is inviting, but the feeling of being watched is still overpowering and pushes her forward. She has made it to the city, but which way should she go? *Right or left*, she asks herself.

It must be very late at night, she thinks, finally looking down at the digital clock on the dash. It shows 1:05. *1:05? Is it one in the morning?* Confusion is rolling around in her head like a bowling ball. Her vision is becoming blurry, and she thinks she will soon be unable to function due to her aching head.

"You must keep driving," a persistent voice in her mind urges. Not knowing what to do, she makes the decision to turn right and then takes another right onto Stockdale Highway. As she drives under an overpass, she thinks things might begin to look familiar. Should she go to the hospital? Right now, she couldn't even find one if she wanted to.

She has an overpowering feeling she is going the wrong way and makes the decision to turn left on Oak Street. Nothing familiar, nothing, nothing, nothing! And after what seems like only a few seconds, Oak Street ends, too. Right or left, right or left? She asks her brain to do the seemingly impossible—make a decision. "Left," the voice in her head finally shouts. She follows the voice and turns left.

As she drives, things begin to seem familiar. *If I keep driving*, she tries to convince herself, *I will recognize something that will snap my brain out of this horrible fog.* She realizes she has seen very few cars this whole trip. However, she can't shake the feeling of being followed. She is afraid to look around, but she forces herself to do so. She has to know if someone is following her, but as she looks, all she sees is nothing - no one.

She decides to take the next side street to the right, in case there is someone following her. She begins to have the feeling of being near home. She finds herself passing neighborhoods, with their big block walls encircling them, but there's no recognition yet. Finally, she is heading into orchards, which line both sides of the road. Just as she thinks she should turn around, the car begins to sputter. Before she realizes what is happening, the car sputters again and then dies.

She looks at the gas gauge in disbelief, willing it to not be on empty. She thinks somehow, if she is in a dream, she can make it point to full. She quickly decides to coast in between a row of trees in a large orchard on the right side of the road. It isn't much cover this time of year, with no leaves on the trees, but at least it's something.

Sitting there, seemingly helpless, she decides she needs to lock the doors, but the car is still unfamiliar. Where is the lock button? Anyway, if she stays in the car, she's a sitting duck. Maybe she should run to civilization.

As she slowly opens the door, the crisp night air hits, along with the smell of damp earth, heightening her senses. As she swings her bare foot up out of the car and onto the ground, her ankle twists painfully. She winces as she tries to put weight on it, but it keeps giving way. Confusion and dread grip her as she swings her right foot out and tries to stand upright. To her relief, her right foot holds steady.

She stands up out of the car and takes a step forward, not bothering to close the car door. She realizes her left foot is not going to cooperate. It's numb! She is turning her ankle every time she tries to take a step. She takes one step with her right foot and wobbles on her left, causing her to take another quick step with her right.

After a few steps, her bare feet feeling the hard-clotted earth beneath her, she stops to look around. As she looks up, she sees the trees surrounding her against the backdrop of the lights from the city. The branches have the eerie look of skeletal fingers reaching out toward the inky blackness of the sky. They look like death, and Gloria is beginning to wonder if that's what is coming for her in the darkness, on her own out there in the orchard - *death*.

With her head pounding and her feet aching, she almost feels like giving into the darkness. Somehow, from somewhere deep inside, she musters the will to move. Finally, she gets into a rhythm, and her left foot begins to cooperate a bit, but she realizes running is not an option. Step, drag, step, drag. It seems to go on forever. The side of her left foot is becoming raw from the awkward way it scrapes the ground, but she finally makes it to the pavement of the road.

After what seems like an eternity, Gloria finds herself out of the orchards and in a neighborhood. She feels she is moving at a snail's pace. She isn't sure how she can keep pushing on. Maybe she should knock on someone's door and ask for help. But then, she has the feeling of being near home.

What now? Which way? she thinks as things start to spin. The street lights are spinning. The sidewalk is spinning. The parked cars are spinning. The next thing she knows, the sidewalk comes closer, she is shaking, her knees wobble, and then everything goes black.

Chapter 29

January 2019

Deputy Brian Steadman, a deputy for the Kern County Sheriff's Department, is nearing the end of his graveyard shift. At thirty-nine, the stocky deputy rubs the back of his neck and blinks his bloodshot eyes. He is a transplant from Los Angeles. He moved his family of three to Bakersfield four months prior, to take advantage of the good school system. The low housing costs were just a bonus. His daughter Kaitlyn is a freshman and has settled into Liberty High School quickly. He and his wife Linda are happy they made the move, and are settling into the Rosedale area quite nicely. *Yes*, he thinks, *we made the right move.*

Thankfully, it has been an uneventful night. Rosedale is usually a pretty quiet, upper-middle-class area, but this night has been especially quiet. He's gone on one domestic call and backed up Deputy McClarin on a suspicious subject at a nearby farm. He stopped a reckless driver, was called out for a shoplifting call at a convenience store, and he has backed up other deputies on minor incidents. That has been the total of his shift so far.

The Tule fog has rolled in this morning. It's a ground fog and quite common this time of year in Kern County. He can see over the hood of his cruiser, but his headlights are hiding beneath the mist. It gives everything an eerie feel. The fog is a nuisance, but not nearly as much as the socked-in conditions Bakersfield frequently experiences.

The radio crackles, bringing him to attention. It's 4:05 a.m.

"1 Paul 31, Control 1," Dispatch calls.

"1 Paul 31," Steadman answers.

"1 Paul 31, possible 901 occurred near Coffee and Hageman," the dispatcher says, letting him know there has been a hit-and-run. "No vehicle information. Victim, Caucasian female, mid-thirties, blond hair, wearing what is described as a bloody shirt and blue jeans. Victim is located on the southbound side of Coffee, south of Hageman. Ambulance and CHP en route."

"1 Paul 31 copy," he responds.

Steadman is on Rosedale Highway, three blocks from Coffee Road. He switches on his lights and heads in that direction. He turns on Coffee and approaches Hageman. As he nears the intersection, he sees a man standing over what looks like a body in the mist.

"1 Paul 31, 10-97," he announces to the dispatcher, letting her know he has arrived on the scene.

He steps out of his car and, as he approaches, observes a woman lying still, limbs splayed in all directions. She is wearing a tailored shirt that, as he gets closer, seems to be covered in blood. She is wearing jeans and no shoes. She is of medium build, with long blond hair.

The man standing over her looks to be in his late twenties, tall, his dark hair mostly hidden under a blue baseball cap with a Dodgers logo. He is the only witness and gives his name as James Turner. He states he was driving home from a late shift as a guard in the oilfields at Elk Hills. He almost missed seeing her lying on the sidewalk, underneath the fog. He didn't see the incident but thought it must be a hit-and-run, because of all the blood, and the odd position he found her in.

Steadman quickly kneels and puts a finger to the woman's neck, feeling for a pulse. He finds her pulse is steady. Not what he was expecting. This woman has obviously been through some serious trauma. He stands, turns to Mr. Turner, and says, "Could you hang around for a few minutes? I might need some further information from you."

"Is it okay if I sit in my truck?" Turner asks, rubbing his stubbled chin and pointing to a late-model silver Ford truck on the opposite side of the road.

"That will be fine, just don't go anywhere," Steadman says.

He kneels again and sees the woman's shirt sleeves have been pushed up and her arms and hands are covered in scrapes, bruises, and blood. Her wrists look as if she has been in restraints. The entire front of her shirt is bloody, and there are spatters on her neck and face, and in her hair.

He looks again at her face, and gently brushes her hair back, revealing a lump on the left side of her scalp. He doesn't want to move her from her awkward position until the ambulance arrives since she could possibly have a spinal injury. It's hard to tell what has happened. There are no tire marks in the street or on the sidewalk, leading him to believe this might not be a hit-and-run. All he can do is stay with her and wait for the ambulance.

He touches her shoulder and calls out, "Miss, miss, can you hear me?"

No response.

Again, he tries to wake her, speaking louder, "Can you hear me?" Her eyes flutter open. "I'm Deputy Steadman, can you hear me?"

She moans.

He can hear a siren approaching. Granger, a seasoned silver-haired officer with the CHP, pulls up and steps out of his car. He is a sturdy man, with just a little paunch and an air of authority. He approaches Steadman. "I hear we might have a hit-and-run."

"Maybe," Steadman replies, "but I don't think so. There are no signs of tire marks or any other evidence a vehicle was involved. The witness who made the call didn't see anything. He just spotted her on his way home from work. That's him, sitting over there." He nods in the direction of Mr. Turner's truck.

"How is she doing?" Granger asks.

"She has a strong pulse; other than that, I'm not sure. It sounds like she's starting to come around. Maybe she can tell us what happened."

Chapter 30

January 2019

As Gloria comes around, she can hear a siren. She realizes someone is speaking. It's a policeman. She is conscious but unable to utter anything more than a moan. She looks up and sees another officer in a different uniform standing over her. The ground is cold and damp, and there is so much fog. She's not quite sure if she is imagining the fog or if it's really there. The last thing she remembers is feeling dizzy.

She hears the officer who is kneeling beside her speaking, and she realizes he is asking her a question. Even if she could answer, she can't make out a word he's saying. It's like she is the tiniest person inside this body, looking out from a great distance.

At last, she finally hears clearly. "My name is Deputy Steadman. What's your name?"

"Gloria," she answers, choking a little. At least, she thinks it's her answering. Everything feels so weird, kind of fuzzy, and far away.

She realizes she is lying in an odd position. Her knees are bent, and her legs are spread apart. She is on her right side, with her right arm pinned underneath her. She tries to sit up, so she can free her arm. The police officer restrains her.

"You should stay still until medical help arrives," he says, calmly.

"Can I at least move my arm? It hurts this way." *What do you know*, she thinks, surprising herself at being able to get a sentence out, but it still sounds odd to her ears.

"I guess we could move it very gently." He carefully helps her free her arm from its pinned position.

"You're injured. Are you in pain?" he asks.

"Yes . . . my head and my back," the strange version of her replies. She is still deep inside, with a very unusual view of what is happening. She feels as if someone else is answering for her, but her rational mind tells her this is not the case.

"I have a terrible headache," she says, trying to reach for her head, before being restrained again.

"Don't worry, there's an ambulance on the way."

As he says this, she can hear the sound of a siren. It's almost upon them.

As an afterthought, she says, "My left foot doesn't work." She realizes immediately how dumb that sounds, and she wishes she hadn't said anything.

"What do you mean it doesn't work?"

"I don't know what I mean. I just can't make my toes move. They're numb."

"Oh," he says, in a sympathetic tone. "Can you lie still while I talk to Officer Granger?"

"Yes," she says, as he stands, lowering his voice as he takes a step toward the other officer.

She can still hear him speaking: "Her feet are bloody and scraped. I pushed up her pants leg, and she has what looks like restraint marks on her ankles."

"What has happened to this poor woman?" the other officer says.

"It looks like she's been walking a great distance barefoot, and at some point has been restrained. Wherever she came from is probably not close, by the looks of her feet," Deputy Steadman says.

He turns to look at her. They both exchange looks and shake their heads. Just then, Officer Granger turns to listen to an accident call on his radio. He informs Deputy Steadman he has to go, and jumps in his patrol car and speeds away, lights and siren blaring.

Deputy Steadman squats back down beside Gloria, putting a hand in comfort on her shoulder. "Were you hit by a car?" he asks, as two other deputies arrive on the scene. Gloria can't see them, but she can hear their voices.

Deputy Steadman stands up to fill the other officers in on what he knows, before squatting beside her again.

"Do you have an ID?" he asks, with a kind smile.

"I guess it would be in my purse." She tries to remember the last time she saw it, but her mind comes up short. She can't even remember what it looks like.

"Where is your purse?" he asks.

"I don't know." She tries to look around for it. Again, Steadman restrains her.

"You really shouldn't move. You can injure yourself further. If you have a back injury, you could be paralyzed, so I hope you understand how important it is to lie still. I know how difficult it is for you." He gives her a sympathetic smile.

It's hard to comply since she is so uncomfortable, but she does her best to try.

"Where did you come from?" he asks, seemingly hopeful she might be able to help at least a little.

"I don't know," she says, tears welling up in her eyes as she realizes she is unable to answer the simplest of questions.

289

"Where do you live?" He knits his brow.

"In Bakersfield," Gloria replies, feebly.

"Do you know your address?" He attempts to return the reassuring smile to his face; it doesn't quite meet his eyes.

"I can't seem to remember," she says, after frantically searching her brain. *This is crazy*, she thinks. *I know I have memory problems, but I should know where I live.* She's beginning to feel panic at the utter blankness in her head.

"Do you know where you are?" So many questions.

She thinks for a minute, but the only answer she can come up with is, "No."

"You're in Rosedale," he tells her. "Do you know where you've been this morning?"

This morning - is it morning? She digs deep into her foggy memory, and all she can say is, "I don't know. I'm really trying to think, but I just don't know." She is so tired. She would fall asleep if it weren't for being in pain and so uncomfortable on the damp sidewalk. Even so, she is beginning to feel that everything is going black. She snaps out of it when she realizes he is speaking again.

"Do you have family?" he asks, tapping her on the shoulder, causing her to open her eyes again.

"Two daughters." She thinks of Chrissy and Sarah. "I know that for sure. They must be so worried about me.

"Do they live with you?" he asks, as the EMTs arrive on scene with a gurney. The ambulance has arrived, and she hasn't even noticed.

She tells him, "yes," but she is really not sure.

"Do you have a phone number for them?" He begins backing away to let the EMTs do their work.

She thinks and again comes up with nothing. "No, I'm sorry. I just can't seem to think right now."

"Where do you feel pain?" the EMT leaning over her asks. He looks young, maybe in his twenties, with dark hair and kind hazel eyes. She gives the same answers she gave the deputy.

Steadman explains, "She was unconscious when I found her. She came around about ten minutes ago. She's talking, but her memory seems impaired."

There isn't much time to think about his last comment, as she feels the blood pressure cuff being strapped on and inflated. The EMT asks her to rate her pain from 1 to 10, 10 being the worst pain she's ever felt in her life.

She replies, "About an 8. My head hurts the most."

Another EMT brings out a plastic board, but as she moves her head to look, the one beside her tells her to lie still. After he inspects her body, his partner comes up behind her, and they gently roll her onto her side and press the board up against her back. They then roll her onto it. She is finally lying flat on her back. What a great relief.

They strap a large brace around her neck. Now at each end of the board, they lift her onto a gurney. They push the gurney into the back of the ambulance and tell Deputy Steadman which hospital they will be headed to.

It's blindingly bright in the ambulance. Gloria has to squint before her eyes can adjust. The EMT who stays in the back with her introduces himself as Jay. He is wearing a long-sleeved white shirt tucked into black cargo pants. He pulls a tiny flashlight out of the pocket of his shirt and flashes it into her eyes, one at a time, flicking it quickly back.

The other EMT hops into the driver's seat, and they take off. Through the back window, she can see the reflection of red lights flashing on the block fences as they pass by.

Jay inserts an IV needle into her hand and hooks it up to the tube hanging from an IV bag on a pole above her. He begins to inspect her wounds. The blood on her shirt is pretty dry now.

"I need to unbutton your shirt," he says, apologetically.

Her head is aching so that she doesn't have the presence of mind to be self-conscious.

After gently unbuttoning her top, he begins to inspect her chest and stomach for any wounds. "Do you have any idea what happened to you?" He looks solemn as he examines her body.

"No, I'm sorry. I have been trying to think, but it's all a blank."

"We want to keep you awake because of your head injury." He grins. "You'll just have to look at my ugly mug for the rest of the trip,"

She laughs, and then immediately cringes in pain, as he pulls the mic from above her head. He informs the hospital they are on their way, gives them her information, and returns the mic to its perch above her.

"Deputy Steadman said you were complaining of your foot being numb. Is that right?" He slides down the shiny metal bench he is sitting on to inspect her feet. He pulls a pen out of his pocket and rubs it on the bottom of each of her feet. It tickles, and she flinches. "Looks good," he says, sliding back up to face her again.

"I don't know how to explain it, but I can't move my toes," she tries to explain.

He slides back down again and places his hand on the top of her foot and asks her to push up toward him. She tries to do as he requests and is unable to comply. She can move her left foot down but is unable to pull it up.

"Hmm," he says, sliding back to face her and smiling. "We'll get it all figured out. Don't worry."

292

"I need to ask you a few questions because of the bump on your head. Do you know what day it is?"

Gloria tries, but no luck. "No. What day is it?"

"It's Sunday," he says. "How about the year? Do you know what year it is?"

"2019?" she replies, unsure if she is right.

"Yes, that's right." He gives her a big grin as if she has just passed the bar exam.

Gloria begins to feel panic rising in her throat. "I think I might throw up," she blurts out.

Quickly unbuckling her from the gurney, Jay rolls her, board and all, to the side, so she doesn't choke. Thankfully, there is nothing in her stomach to speak of. "Let me know when you're finished, I don't want to lay you down flat until you're done." His tone is reassuring.

"I'll be okay now," she assures him, before admitting just how embarrassed she is.

"Don't worry. This is my job. Believe me, I've seen much worse. Are you sure you're going to be all right now?" He rolls her onto her back.

"Yes. I feel better." She gives him a weak smile.

Before she has time to think about it further, they pull underneath the covered entrance at the hospital ER. The driver comes to help Jay take her in. Having rolled her into the hall, Jay stays with her as the driver steps away to inform the nurse they have arrived.

"Take her to room two, and we will be right there," Gloria hears her say. "We have prepared for your arrival. Dr. Massy is on this morning. I'll let him know you're here."

Gloria is becoming very uncomfortable, strapped to this board. She can't move at all. *Oh no, not right now of all times*, she thinks as the pressure from her bladder suddenly becomes uncomfortable. Things are starting to feel very real now. That far-off feeling has fled, and all she can think about is how much pain and discomfort she is in. The pain and discomfort seem to vie intermittently for her attention. The pressure on her bladder, her throbbing head, the all-over bruised feeling, and the inability to move a muscle are causing her to feel as if she might scream.

The driver finally returns, and they roll her into a room with a large glass door. There is a curtain with some kind of faded blue print, which they pull closed for privacy. A nurse enters the room wearing scrubs with cartoon character renditions of different dog breeds. Before she can introduce herself, Gloria informs her shyly that she, unfortunately, needs to use the restroom.

"I'm afraid we can't let you up until we take x-rays. I'm sorry, we have to make sure you don't have a spinal injury - I'm Vicky, by the way. I'll be your nurse while you're in the ER," says the thirty-something, slender woman with a long luxurious brunette braid running down the back of her scrub top.

"As soon as you're out of x-ray, we'll see about giving you a bedpan—oh, here's Dr. Massy," she says, as a jovial, white-haired doctor enters the room, his white lab coat open to reveal a tie with the Tasmanian Devil twirling around at the bottom. It seems the morning staff has a sense of humor.

"Yep," he says, pointing to his name badge. "That's what it says right here." He laughs. "Now, what do we have here?" His smile is infectious. "Looks like this beautiful young lady has had a tough morning."

Jay fills the doctor in on her symptoms, as Dr. Massy begins his examination. "She has a contusion on the left side of her skull. She can't remember what happened to her. She also has some cuts, bruises, and abrasions. She is complaining of a headache, her left foot being numb, and pain in her lower back. She was unconscious when the deputy found her but has been conscious and alert since we picked her up," Jay reports.

"Looks like you've had a rough time of it, little lady," Dr. Massy says, his kind eyes smiling behind wire-rimmed glasses.

"Okay, let's get her onto the bed here. Did you find the source of this blood?" he asks.

"No, it doesn't seem to be hers," Jay says, as they lift her, board and all, onto the bed.

As the EMTs exit, Dr. Massy checks her as thoroughly as he is able to and comes to the same conclusion. The blood is probably not hers.

Just then, a portly man with a crew cut, wearing green scrubs, comes through the curtains. "Is this the urgent x-ray?" he asks and walks over to the bed. "My name is Robert. I will be taking you to x-ray."

Everyone steps back as he releases the brakes on the bed, and wheels her out of the room. After they turn the corner and roll out of the ER, he pushes a button, which opens double doors to the next corridor. They take a right, and they are immediately in the x-ray room, a stark white room with blinding bright lights.

"I hope this doesn't hurt, but I need to move you carefully onto the table." Robert waves to a tech walking down the hall and says, "Can you give me a hand?"

"Sure," a lanky kid in gray scrubs says, shuffling into the room. Together, they gently move Gloria onto the table.

"Don't move. I will move the equipment around you. It's imperative that you do not move your neck. I know it's hard, but it's very important." He puts the emphasis on *very*.

It's not long until she is back in the ER, even though it seems like forever to her. Outside the curtain, she can hear a conversation between someone and the doctor. "I'm going to need all of her clothes as evidence. I'll need pictures of all her injuries. Also, we will need a rape kit."

After a moment, a portly man wearing a rumpled chocolate brown suit enters the room. "My name is Detective Bosley." He smiles. Gloria thinks the smile looks forced. His bloodshot eyes lead her to believe he has either been up all night or was woken from a deep sleep to be here this morning.

"You will probably be seeing a lot of me until we figure out what happened to you. Have you remembered anything new since you talked to Deputy Steadman?" He is unable to mask the weariness in his voice.

"No," she says slowly. "I've been put through the wringer here, and I haven't had a second to think. I'm sorry. I really am trying." After a moment, she says, "Am I in trouble?"

"No. Don't worry about that, just get some rest, and we'll talk again. If you begin to remember anything, be sure to tell the nurses; otherwise, I will let them get to work here, and I'll see you later," he says, forcing another smile before exiting the room.

All the hubbub finally slows down, and she is left alone with her thoughts. Looking around the room for the first time, it seems so sterile. There's only her bed, one chair, and a crash cart. By the sink are jars with cotton balls and tongue depressors. The curtains are a faded mix of beige and light blue.

It feels stark and lonely. She wishes Rick would come. As it is, though, she can't even think of his phone number, so how would she get in touch with him? She can't figure out how to get in touch with Chrissy or Sarah either. She is disturbed by her inability to remember the simplest of things. This is different than her usual memory lapses. She doesn't forget her own address and phone number. She doesn't forget how to get in touch with her daughters.

Vicky enters the room with a big grin on her face. "I have good news and good news. The Doctor has looked at your x-rays, and you can finally have a bedpan." She presents it from behind her back like Gloria has just won a prize. She continues, "Also, he is giving you something for the pain. It will probably put you to sleep. I'm sure you need it. You've been through quite an ordeal. I just want to warn you we will be waking you up quite a bit to do more testing, but try to relax." She places the bedpan beside Gloria before turning to leave, giving her some privacy.

Finally, Gloria thinks, and thanks the nurse profusely, as she quickly walks out of the room.

It seems she has just fallen asleep, finally somewhat comfortable, when Dr. Massy enters. She awakens with a start. "I'm sorry to wake you, but I have some good news. The x-rays didn't show anything serious. We still have some tests to run, and you've had a concussion, so we're going to admit you for a few days. You're on the schedule for an MRI this morning. Your symptoms seem to indicate you may still have a soft-tissue injury in your spine. The MRI will show it if that's the case." He continues: "After you're admitted, a neurologist will come to see you. Also, I would like you to see a counselor. I can have one come by."

"Wow, that's a lot to take in. Do you know how long I'll have to stay?" Gloria notices a little slur in her voice as she fights to stay awake.

"That will be determined by how the test results turn out. Just rest, and try not to worry." Dr. Massey pats her shoulder kindly.

"Thank you," Gloria says, as he turns to leave the room.

Vicky comes in next, saying, "Well, it looks like we're keeping you. An orderly will come and take you up to your room very soon."

Sheepishly, Gloria pulls the bedpan from under the covers that she has thankfully been able to use. As she hands it to Vicky, she apologizes for doing so.

"Don't be silly," Vicky says. "That's what it's for." That's the last thing Gloria hears before drifting back off to sleep.

Finally, she is settled in her room and finished with tests. She has at last been allowed to shower, under the watchful eye of Trish, the young nurse assigned to her, who is sporting a purple streak in her shoulder length-platinum hair. Gloria can't help but admire her perky personality, as she helps her through the rigors of cleansing her body. Although it's painful to stand on her scraped feet, and her left foot is still numb and not cooperating, thankfully she finally feels clean.

Everything seems to be aching as she returns to bed. "May I have more pain medication?" she asks Trish.

Trish checks her orders and shortly comes back into the room with a syringe. She injects the medication into the port of Gloria's IV, smiles, and says, "That should help. I hope you can rest."

Before drifting off, Gloria hopes she will be able to remember how to get in touch with her family and Rick by the time she wakes up.

Chapter 31

January 2019

Gloria wakes with a start, panting and drenched with sweat. Confusion clouds her brain, and she is unable to control her trembling body. Where is Dr. Dyson? She has finally remembered everything. She must tell him the horrible news. She killed Charles! She remembers driving to the orchard. She remembers being in the hospital. The Other Gloria had allowed her to see everything through her eyes. Maybe it was a horrible mistake to meet her. She must speak with Dr. Dyson.

As she looks around the room, she has the terrible realization she's not in Dr. Dyson's office. She's in the hospital. She looks to her right; her hand is raised. The signal to him that she is ready to come out of hypnosis. He's not waking her up. She's still in the hospital. The same hospital room she remembered from her dream.

She feels her heart race, the monitor above her beeping in time. She wants to wake up. She doesn't want to be here. She wants the do-over. She wants to go back. Why can't she wake up? Her mind can't accept this reality. The one where she killed Charles. *Will I go to prison*, she wonders, horrified at the thought.

I want the do-over. I was happy there. I was building a life, a happy life, with Rick. I want to wake up on Dr. Dyson's couch, she thinks, raising her right hand higher. Tears spring into her eyes as she frantically presses the button to call the nurse.

A woman in pink scrubs with a steel gray-bob and a well-worn face enters the room. Her features soften as a concerned smile forms. "I'm Sally, your nurse this afternoon. You're finally awake. Oh dear, are you all right?" she says, as she approaches Gloria's bed, looking up at the monitors.

"Where is Dr. Dyson?" Gloria asks, frantically.

"It's okay, you're in the hospital. Your daughters are on the way back to see you. They were just here," she says, patting Gloria's shoulder.

"How did they know I'm here?" Gloria asks, grabbing the nurse's hand for reassurance.

Sally leaves her hand for a moment on Gloria's shoulder as Gloria holds tight, desperation in her eyes. Sally's tone is soothing when she says, "From what I hear, the police found the car you were driving. They found your purse inside the trunk. It had the information they needed to contact your daughters."

Confusion clouds her brain as she tries to figure out what car Sally might be talking about. Would it be the car from her dream? "Is Dr. Dyson here?" Gloria asks, trying not to panic. She wants to grab onto Sally's arm with both hands and beg her to find him.

"No, honey. I'm sorry I don't know a Dr. Dyson. Is he your regular doctor?" Sally studies Gloria with concern.

"He's my counselor." Gloria is feeling breathless now.

"No. I'm sorry I don't know him. He hasn't been here, but we'll try to find him," she soothes. "I'll go right now and try to locate him."

As Gloria watches Sally leave the room, she lets out a heavy sigh of relief, praying she will find Dr. Dyson. She dozes off before hearing someone enter the room. Waking, startled, her hand flies to her mouth as she sees Detective Bosley.

"How are you feeling?" he asks, taking in her startled reaction.

"I'm very confused." Tears of panic spring to her eyes.

"Do you remember me?"

Gloria nods her head. Her heart sinks, realizing the year she's in is 2019.

"Have you remembered anything about your incident?" He smiles a bit more genuinely than he did the last time she saw him.

Still, she is startled. She's not ready to talk about it. She wants to make it all go away. What she does is lie. "No," she says, hoping he will believe her.

"I'm not feeling very well," she says, as her body starts to tremble and nausea rises again. "Could you get the nurse?"

As Bosley steps out of the room, Gloria holds her hand over her mouth. She wants to get up and go to the bathroom before she gets sick, but she's hooked up to monitors and an IV. When Sally comes in, all Gloria can say is, "I'm going to be sick." Thankfully, Sally reaches under the sink, pulls out a basin, and hands it to Gloria, just before she loses it. She has nothing but bile in her stomach.

Having come back into the room and seeing her distress, Detective Bosley says, "I'll just come back later when you are feeling better," before walking back out the door.

Gloria feels herself calm a bit once he is out of sight, but she doesn't have much time to think about it. After Sally helps her get cleaned up, Chrissy and Sarah come rushing into the room and, one and then the other, hurry over to give her a big hug, before standing beside her bed. "We were so worried," Sarah says, a look of bewilderment in her eyes. "What happened?"

An irrational part of her brain was expecting to see her little girls. *They're grown*, she thinks, fighting the confusing and conflicting emotions battling inside her.

"I don't exactly know," Gloria says shakily. But all the while, she's thinking, *I think I killed your dad.* She feels like she might be sick again, but after a moment, the feeling passes.

"You were supposed to pick up Sarah from my house last night. We didn't know if you were here or in Ontario. The police finally called us. You don't remember what happened?" Chrissy says, clinging onto her hand.

"Not really," Gloria shakes her head. She actually knows everything, but she is not going to tell anyone that. She's not sure what she will do, but she thinks, for now, she should stay quiet.

"Dad is coming in a little bit," Chrissy says, with a watery smile.

Gloria's eyes widen in horror, "What do you mean your dad is coming?"

"What's wrong, Mom?" Confusion is written all over Sarah's face. "You don't look good. You look like you've seen a ghost."

With a trembling voice, Gloria says slowly, "I don't want to see your dad," while thinking, *He's supposed to be dead.*

"Why not?" Sarah asks, utterly confused. "He and Megan are almost here from Ontario. He's been looking for you there and waiting at home for you to show up. We've been looking for you everywhere. He's worried."

"Yes he is," says Chrissy, wiping at her eyes. "He's very worried, and so is Megan."

It takes a moment for Gloria to register that Megan is coming with Sarah and Chrissy's dad. Her head begins to ache, trying to figure out why Charles would be with Megan. They've never even met. Her heart rate monitor begins to beep faster as she tries to figure out what's going on. Her brain can't process the information they are trying to impart.

Looking past her daughters to the door, she sees Rick walking in. Both girls immediately run into his arms, simultaneously saying, "Dad."

He hugs them quickly and rushes over to Gloria. "Are you okay? You don't look well." His brow is creased with worry. He grabs her hand, holding it in both of his. "I'm glad we found you. We've all been so worried. Megan stopped to pick up something special for you in the gift shop downstairs, but she'll be right up."

"Okay," is all Gloria can manage to get out. Her head is spinning. Everything is happening so fast, and it's not adding up.

She looks at him warily, and slowly asks, "Why...... did they just call you dad?"

"What's wrong, sweetheart? They told me you'd lost some memory. Don't you recognize me?" She thinks she sees tears beginning to brim in his eyes.

"I recognize you. You're Rick. My fiancé. But why did they call you dad?"

"They've always called me that," he says, worriedly. "I'm your husband, sweetheart."

"My husband?" she chokes out. In disbelief, she eventually sputters, "Then what do they call Charles?"

"They call him their father." He squeezes her hand, concern deepening in his eyes.

Gloria feels like she might pass out. The room seems to spin. "No, you're my fiancé. We aren't married." She can feel herself begin to hyperventilate as she shakes her head. "When did we get married?"

Concern still clouding his eyes, he holds her hand tightly and says, "In April 2007."

"This is a joke, right?" Gloria tries to force a smile.

"No, honey. It's not. I think I'd better get a nurse. You're looking pale, and your monitor is beeping pretty fast."

"Okay," is all she can think to say.

Just then, Megan walks into the room. Gloria knows it's Megan, but she looks very different. Her hair is brown, but it's lighter. Her facial features are different, too; they look a lot like Gloria's own features. Megan seems to be about eleven years old. "Mom, are you okay?" She runs over to give Gloria a big hug.

"Look, Mom. I got you a teddy bear." She stands up and presents a fuzzy pink bear with *Get Well* embroidered on its belly.

"I love it." Gloria takes the bear and reaches up to pull Megan to her again. Her maternal instinct has kicked in, and she knows in her heart that Megan is hers. Megan is her daughter.

"I'm so glad. You scared us, Mom," Megan says, tears beginning to fall.

As she stares into Megan's eyes, she notices they are blue, not brown. She thinks, *we married in 2007, and Megan is obviously my daughter; I can feel it in my bones.* This is a reality she never dreamed of. She opens her arms wide, trying to bring them all into a hug at once. She's not the only one crying. They all are.

"Do you know anything about what happened?" she asks Rick after they all untangle from each other.

"All I know is you were supposed to pick up Sarah from Charles's, and you disappeared. Sarah had actually gone to see Chrissy, but forgot to call to let you know." Ricks look is a mixture of concern and relief.

"You mean we live in Ontario, and I came to Bakersfield to pick up Sarah?" She's trying to put together the puzzle pieces.

"Yes," Rick says, smiling. "Exactly."

"She was visiting her father?" she asks, her mind still a spider web of confusion as she slowly untangles this strange mystery.

"Yes, he has visitation rights." Rick begins to sound more relieved with each revelation she makes.

After a moment, Gloria asks, "Could you girls go to the gift shop for a few minutes? I need to talk to Rick alone." Her body is still trembling from apparent shock. "I promise he won't let anything happen to me, while you're gone," she says in an unsteady voice. "I bet Rick . . . I mean, Dad, can give you some money to spend." She smiles, weakly up at Rick.

Rick pulls out his wallet and hands each girl a twenty. With that, the girls head out the door together. Once they leave, still trembling, Gloria pulls Rick down into a big hug, and whispers, "I have just one question."

"You're shaking, honey. Are you all right?"

"I don't know," she says, laughing nervously.

"What's your question?" He pulls himself up to look at her.

"I know this is a silly question, but . . . how did we meet?"

"Well," he says, "it was the funniest thing. I met this crazy woman who said she met me in a dream." He beams.

She reaches to him with trembling hands and pulls him into another hug, holding on tightly, hoping this really and truly is her reality - their reality.

Epilogue

September 2019

Rick and Gloria sit together on a wooden swing in their backyard near Fort Worth, Texas. They watch the sun come up over the placid lake just outside their back door on an unusually cool September morning. Rick has kept a promise he made after the incident and brought his wife back to her beloved Texas. They swing back and forth, sharing memories and feeding bread crumbs to the ducks, who have claimed their yard. Gloria loves taking care of all their little Texas critters.

There are memories Gloria has never recovered, but Rick has tried to fill in the gaps. To Gloria's delight, she finally remembers giving birth to Megan, and she is thankful for that. She also remembers their wedding on April 14, 2007. It was a casual affair in Bakersfield. Jack and Dena were there, of course. Mickey was her maid of honor, and all her friends from the Insurance Agency came as well. They were all sorry to see her move away to Ontario but were glad she found such a good guy.

Memory is a very strange and elusive thing for Gloria. She has been left with partial memories of two lifetimes. Her new therapist is hopeful that once she has truly met and accepted the Other Gloria into her consciousness, the secrets she holds will help merge her memories into one cohesive life. The memories she has been slowly recovering are providing hope that this will be the case. However, with dissociative disorder combined with a physical trauma to the brain, there is really no telling.

In any case, by reliving her past, Gloria has made it through a great journey of discovery. For her, it was a very real quest toward finding herself - her true self. She knows now that no man can dictate her self-worth, but there is one man who will stand beside her through her triumphs and even through her inevitable failures along the way. Rick will be there as she picks herself up, brushes herself off, and continues on this path called life, learning more about herself each and every day. She is thankful for the Other Gloria—that other part of herself. She knows now that she has been strong all along, and she never knew it.

Chrissy stayed behind in California, moving from Ontario to Bakersfield after she graduated high school in 2016. Her father bribed her, saying he would pay for her education if she attended Cal State Bakersfield. Gloria knows it was a ploy to get back at her for leaving him, but she allowed Chrissy to make the decision. While attending college there, she met Alex, and they soon became a couple. At this point, they are engaged and living together off campus. They have not set a wedding date as of yet, but they have made the decision to find employment in Dallas when they both graduate.

Sarah is still at home and attending high school in Ft Worth. Still, as spunky and independent as ever, she has no plans for a serious boyfriend in the near future. She wasn't too happy about moving and changing schools, and as usual, she let Rick and Gloria know about it. After moving, though, she soon fit right in.

Easygoing Megan was excited to move to a home on the water in Texas. She says she wants to be a police officer when she grows up. Rick is not too happy about that idea and hopes it will soon pass. He has turned out to be quite the protective father.

Gloria feels fortunate she will soon have all her children close, and especially loves the thought of becoming a grandma someday, even though Chrissy assures her, it will be well into the future. Still, she plans to spoil her grandchildren on a regular basis. She will let them eat sugar and stay up late, and will laugh when she returns them to their parents, all sugared up and exhausted. She does feel a little guilty when she thinks this way, but she also has an ornery side, Rick seems to have brought out in her, with a little help from Chrissy.

She is slowly recovering from the trauma of that night. After a long search, Charles's body was found near Tehachapi, at the bottom of a deep ravine. The blood on Gloria's clothes that night matched his blood. Even so, no charges were ever filed, since she had obviously been beaten and bound.

She hasn't quite been able to get the feeling of being watched completely out of her mind, but at least now she knows who the watcher is. It's not someone to be feared as she thought. Instead, it's her protector, the Other Gloria.

I hope you have enjoyed reading, *The Other Gloria*. I can't tell you how much an honest review on Amazon and/or Goodreads would mean. Thank you in advance.

CPSIA information can be obtained
at www.ICGtesting.com
Printed in the USA
FFHW010104151119
56042956-61999FF

9 780998 949673